HOW TO PLAY WINNING

BRIDGE

HISTORY, RULES, SKILLS & TACTICS

HOW TO PLAY WINNING
BRIDGE
HISTORY, RULES, SKILLS & TACTICS

DAVID BIRD

LORENZ BOOKS

This edition is published by Lorenz Books

Lorenz Books is an imprint of
Anness Publishing Ltd
Hermes House, 88-89 Blackfriars Road
London SE1 8HA
tel. 020 7401 2077; fax 020 7633 9499
www.lorenzbooks.com; info@anness.com

© Anness Publishing Ltd 2007

Anness Publishing has a new picture agency outlet for images for
publishing, promotions or advertising. Please visit our website
www.practicalpictures.com for more information.

ETHICAL TRADING POLICY
Because of our ongoing ecological investment programme,
you, as our customer, can have the pleasure and reassurance
of knowing that a tree is being cultivated on your behalf to
naturally replace the materials used to make the book you are
holding. For further information about this scheme, go to
www.annesspublishing.com/trees.

UK agent: The Manning Partnership Ltd
6 The Old Dairy, Melcombe Road
Bath BA2 3LR
tel. 01225 478 444; fax 01225 478 440
sales@manning-partnership.co.uk

UK distributor: Grantham Book Services Ltd
Isaac Newton Way, Alma Park
Industrial Estate
Grantham, Lincs NG31 9SD
tel. 01476 541080; fax 01476 541061
orders@gbs.tbs-ltd.co.uk

North American agent/distributor:
National Book Network
4501 Forbes Boulevard, Suite 200
Lanham, MD 20706
tel. 301 459 3366; fax 301 429 5746
www.nbnbooks.com

Australian agent/distributor: Pan Macmillan Australia
Level 18, St Martins Tower
31 Market St, Sydney, NSW 2000
tel. 1300 135 113; fax 1300 135 103
customer.service@macmillan.com.au

New Zealand agent/distributor: David Bateman Ltd
30 Tarndale Grove, Off Bush Road
Albany, Auckland
tel. (09) 415 7664; fax (09) 415 8892

A CIP catalogue record for this book is available from the
British Library.

Designed and produced for Anness Publishing by
THE BRIDGEWATER BOOK COMPANY LIMITED.

Publisher: Joanna Lorenz
Editorial Director: Helen Sudell
Project Editor: Sarah Doughty
Editor: Rosie Gordon
Photography: Paul Winch-Furness
Designers: Stuart Perry & Sylvia Tate
Art Director: Steve Knowlden
Editorial Reader: Molly Perham
Production Controller: Steve Lang

10 9 8 7 6 5 4 3 2 1

CONTENTS

INTRODUCTION

What is the world's greatest card game? Not everyone will give you the same answer but there are two clear frontrunners for the title – bridge and poker. Poker is as much about gambling as it is about tactical play. Bridge is quite different. It is sometimes played for money, yes, but it is also immensely stimulating intellectually. Although you can play and enjoy bridge after just a few hours of instruction, it is a game so deep that not even the greatest masters can claim to have learnt everything that the game has to offer.

A big attraction of the game is that it is played in partnership. You and your partner sit opposite each other at the card table, competing against two other players, also in partnership. However good you may be as a single player, you will not achieve very much without the cooperation of your partner. A long-term bridge partnership in many ways resembles a marriage. You must enjoy each other's company, maintain a pleasant relationship and refrain from criticism or argument, whatever bridge disasters you may experience.

Why do players in their millions take up this game and play it throughout their lives, scarcely able to imagine what "life without bridge" would be like? Firstly, it is a wonderful way to make friends. If you choose to play bridge in the environment of your

Above: Most players sort the cards in their hand so that all the cards in one suit are together, with the highest-ranking card on the left and the lowest-ranking on the right.

Above: Bridge tournament in progress. The player with her back to the camera is the declarer and the face-up cards, on the table opposite her, are those of the dummy.

home and your friends' homes, you will build a circle of close friends who meet perhaps once a week, play bridge and greatly enjoy each others' company. Perhaps instead you join the local bridge club. Immediately you will have a new group of acquaintances. There will never be a shortage of anything to talk about. Whenever bridge players meet, they can chat happily for hours, discussing exciting hands that they have played. It's the same if you visit an unknown country or town. You can present yourself at the local bridge club and receive an immediate welcome.

It may be that you are competitive. In that case bridge is just the right game to learn. You will begin by entering competitions at your local club and then advance to local championships. If you have some aptitude for the game and work hard, you may eventually play in national competitions. For the favoured few, there are European and world championships to be won.

What role can this book play in helping you to get started on the wonderful game of bridge? An early section will explain the basics, such as tricks and trumps, assuming that the reader knows nothing at all about the game. From then on, there are Basic, Intermediate and Advanced sections on all three aspects of the game – bidding, dummy play and defence.

A deal of bridge

In bridge, the deal consists of two parts. First the four players, each looking only at their own hand of 13 cards, conduct an auction of ever ascending "bids". This will be fully explained in the text of the book but, for example, a player might bid "one heart" to tell his partner that he holds an above average collection of high cards (aces, kings, queens and jacks) and that hearts is his longest suit and might therefore make a good trump suit. When a suit eventually becomes "trumps", it is more powerful than the other three suits; a low trump will defeat even an ace in one of the other three suits. When the bidding comes to an end, one or other partnership will have set themselves a target for the second part of the proceedings: the play. For example, they may have said they will attempt to make ten tricks with spades as trumps. The play begins and that partnership must then try to make the target of ten tricks. The two defenders will do their best to prevent it. If you are new to the game and find this hard to follow, do not worry. Everything will be clearly explained in the main text.

Using this book

Once you have absorbed the instruction in this book, you will already have become a better than average player. You may not find it an easy task, it is true, but if the game were a simple one it would not provide such endless fascination. You can be sure that something interesting will happen every time that you play.

Apart from instruction, the book contains a summary of the history of bridge and a brief look at some of the most famous players in the world, past and present, and the deals they have played. It is possible to play bridge on the Internet nowadays, perhaps with players from the other side of the world. This aspect, too, is fully described. By learning bridge you are taking the first step on what may prove to be an enjoyable and life-long journey. Good luck!

BRIDGE IN PRINT
♠ ♥ ♦ ♣

The four players in a bridge game are called North, East, South and West, according to the seat that they occupy. During a session each player is likely to become the declarer (the player who attempts to make the contract) several times. As you read this book, you may be puzzled why South is always shown as the declarer. This is a convention followed by all bridge books and newspaper columns. The South cards are "nearest" to the reader and so allow him or her to imagine being the declarer as the play is described.

THE HAND DIAGRAMS
♠ ♥ ♦ ♣

On the right you see a typical hand diagram. The bidding, which takes place before the play, is shown in the green table at the bottom. South makes the first bid of 1♥ (one heart) and the final bid of 4♥ becomes the contract. South will play the contract, trying to make ten tricks with hearts as trumps (which is what the bid of 4♥ means). South becomes the declarer and will play the cards both from the North hand, the dummy, which will be laid face-up on the table, and from his own hand. East and West will become the defenders and try to prevent the declarer from scoring ten tricks. If you are unfamiliar with basic terms such as "bid", "1♥", "tricks", "pass", "contract", "play the contract", "trumps", "defenders", "declarer", "dummy", do not worry. Everything is clearly explained in the section called *Starting Out (The Basics)*.

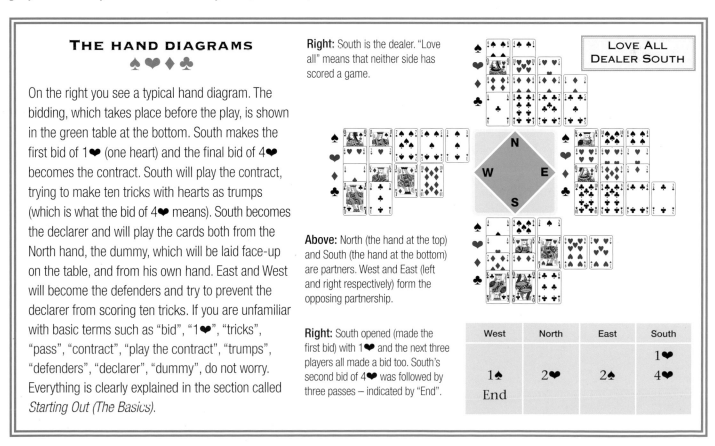

Right: South is the dealer. "Love all" means that neither side has scored a game.

LOVE ALL
DEALER SOUTH

Above: North (the hand at the top) and South (the hand at the bottom) are partners. West and East (left and right respectively) form the opposing partnership.

Right: South opened (made the first bid) with 1♥ and the next three players all made a bid too. South's second bid of 4♥ was followed by three passes – indicated by "End".

West	North	East	South
			1♥
1♠	2♥	2♠	4♥
End			

CHAPTER 1

STARTING OUT

This section assumes no knowledge of the game and will explain clearly all the basic concepts. You will learn the ranking of the various cards, how to deal and how to "sort out" your cards. Next you will see the meaning of the term "trick" and how the play of the cards progresses. On most deals one of the four suits is chosen as "trumps" and this, too, will be explained. Once you understand the importance of the trump suit and how tricks are scored in the play, the idea of "bidding" will be discussed. By making "'bids", the players decide whether a suit should be made trumps and what the target number of tricks should be for the partnership who bids highest.

Right: Declarer is about to play a contract of 4♠. Before playing a card from dummy he should make a plan.

THE BASICS

Four players take part in a game of bridge and are conventionally known in bridge literature as North, East, South and West. The players in the North and South seats form one partnership and sit opposite one another. They will compete against East and West, who form the other partnership.

For each deal, one of the players is the "dealer". (In a social game, the dealer for the first deal is chosen by a cut of the cards. Thereafter, the deal passes clockwise to the next player. In tournament bridge, the plastic or wooden board containing the cards indicates who is the dealer.) The dealer deals the pack of 52 cards in a clockwise direction, one card at a time. When the whole pack has been dealt, each player will hold a "hand" of 13 cards. It is customary to sort these into suits, with the cards in descending order within a particular suit. For example, you might sort out your hand like this:

♠A Q 9 5 4   ♥A 8 5 3   ♦K 9 4   ♣5

Above: West has five spades to the ace–queen, four hearts to the ace, three diamonds to the king and a singleton club.

You have sorted all the spades to be together. The rank (order of importance) of the cards is: ace (highest), king, queen, jack, 10, 9, 8, 7, 6, 5, 4, 3, 2 (lowest). As you see, the five cards in the spade suit are arranged in descending order of rank, with the ace on the left and the 4 on the right. If someone were to ask you afterwards what hand you held, you would reply

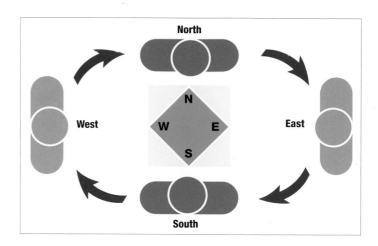

Above: For both the bidding and play, the action takes place in a clockwise direction. If South makes the first call in the auction, for example, West will make the second call. If West later leads to the first trick, the second card will be played by North.

"I had five spades to the ace–queen, four hearts to the ace, three diamonds to the king and a singleton club". A "singleton" is a holding of just one card in a suit; a "doubleton" would be a holding of two cards. When you describe a hand, you cannot be expected to remember the low cards (known as "spot cards") and would usually name only the "picture cards" (aces, kings, queens or jacks) that you held.

So, each of the four players holds a hand of 13 cards. These are held close to the chest, so that the other three players can see only the backs of the cards. The subsequent action consists of two parts: the "bidding" and then the "play" of the cards.

Although the bidding occurs before the play when you are actually engaged in a game of bridge, it is not possible to understand the bidding until you know how the play will go. For that reason the play will be described first here. So that you can understand the basics, if you are new to the game, the idea of tricks and trumps will be addressed first. Later the bidding will be described and a sample complete deal of bridge will give you a general idea of how the game is played.

Above: Bidding sequence. In tournament bridge each player creates a line of all his calls during the auction. Here, the player has made three bids.

What is a trick?

The play of the cards, at bridge, is very similar to that in the old game of whist. It consists of a sequence of "tricks". A trick consists of four cards, one played by each player. The highest card played will "win the trick".

This is a typical trick, with the cards played in a clockwise direction around the table:

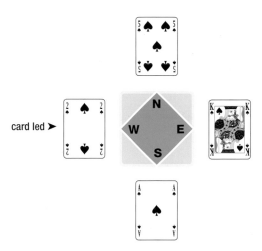

West plays first to the trick and chooses to play the ♠2. You might also say that "West leads the ♠2". (You will see later how it is decided who leads to the first trick and to each of the subsequent tricks.) West "leads" the ♠2, then, and North plays the ♠5. East plays the ♠K and South "wins the trick" with the ♠A. He wins the trick because his card is the highest one played in the suit that was led. Remember that the ranking of the cards is: ace (highest), king, queen, jack, 10, 9, 8, 7, 6, 5, 4, 3, 2 (lowest). Because South won the trick, he will lead to the next trick. It will be his choice whether to lead another spade or to play some different suit.

A ROUND OF TRUMPS
♠ ♥ ♦ ♣

The term "round" is similar in meaning to "trick". If declarer plays a "round of trumps", this means that he leads a trump and the other three hands play a card to the trick. If, for example, both defenders hold at least one trump, this round of trumps will draw two trumps from the defenders' hands. For that reason, you might also say "declarer draws a round of trumps". You might also say "declarer draws trumps in three rounds", meaning that he had to lead trumps three times, on three successive tricks, in order to remove all the defenders' trumps.

If you hold a card in the suit led, you must "follow suit". In other words, if a spade is led you must play a spade if you have one. When you cannot follow suit, you must play a card in a different suit. Unless you play a card from the suit chosen as the "trump suit", your card in a different suit cannot win the trick, however high it is. Suppose the trump suit is spades and South leads the ♣J here:

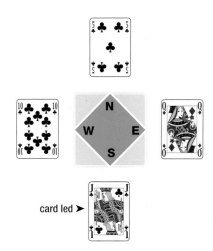

South, who won the previous trick, leads the ♣J. The next two players follow with lower cards in the same suit and East has no clubs left in his hand. He "discards" the ♦Q. South's ♣J wins the trick because it is the highest card in the suit that was led.

What are trumps?

During the bidding, which will be explained in a moment, a suit may be chosen as "trumps". This suit then becomes more powerful than the other three suits. A low trump, such as the two, will defeat even the ace of a different suit. When you have no cards left in the suit that has been led, you can play any card in the trump suit and win the trick with it. Let's assume that spades are trumps and this trick arises:

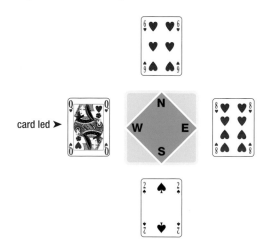

West, who won the previous trick, leads the ♥Q. The next two players follow with lower hearts. South, who has no hearts left, plays the two of trumps. Even though his trump is a lowly two, he wins the trick. Bridge players would say "South trumped with the two" or (more commonly) "South ruffed with the two".

Sometimes two players have no more cards in the suit that was led and both choose to play a trump. In that case the higher trump will win the trick:

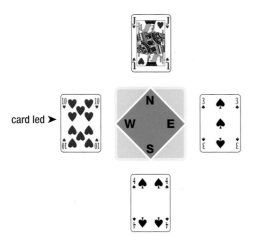

card led ▶

West leads the ♥10 and North beats this with the ♥J. East has no more hearts and attempts to win the trick by ruffing with the ♠3. South "overruffs" with the ♠4. He wins the trick because his card is the higher of the two trumps played.

You can see how useful trumps are. You can use them to prevent the other side from winning tricks with their high cards in other suits. You can also use them to score extra tricks of your own – by ruffing low cards of a non-trump suit, cards that would otherwise not win a trick.

NOTATION FOR CARDS IN BRIDGE
♠ ♥ ♦ ♣

When a suit symbol precedes a number, or a letter that denotes a picture card, this represents a card. It is the accepted shorthand for representing a card in print, perhaps in a bridge book or article or in a newspaper. So, ♠3 is short for the card known as the "three of spades". ♦K is the "king of diamonds".
♠A J 7 6 is the written form of a spade suit containing four cards: the ace, jack, seven and six.

The bidding

During the bidding each partnership tries to assess how many tricks they will be able to make during the play, also which trump suit they should choose. (The trump suit is the most powerful suit during the play of the cards, remember. Any trump, however low, will win against a card from any other suit). A further option is to play the hand in "no-trumps", in other words without a trump suit.

We will see in a moment how you make a bid. For the moment, let's suppose that the bidding ends with South announcing that he, in conjunction with his partner's hand opposite, can make ten tricks with spades as trumps. The cards are then played and South must attempt to score ten tricks out of the 13 that are available. The other two players, known as the defenders, will try to prevent him from achieving this target.

That is the purpose of the bidding, then. One side, usually the one with the most high cards (aces, kings and queens) between them, will set themselves a target of tricks and choose whether they want a particular suit to become trumps.

What is a bid?

During the "bidding", or "auction", each player may make a "bid" when it is his turn to speak. He may instead choose to "pass". (There are two other possible calls, "double" and "redouble", which will be explained later.)

The first actual bid, as opposed to a pass, is known as the "opening bid". To open the bidding, you need slightly better than an average hand. The strength of a hand consists of two main factors – the quantity of high cards (such as aces and kings) and the length of your suits. A hand with plenty of high cards will obviously offer a good prospect of scoring several tricks when the time comes for the play. So will a hand that contains one or more long suits – seven spades, for example. That is because you can make such a suit trumps and score several tricks with it.

To measure the high-card strength of a hand, a point-count system is used. An ace is worth 4 points, a king 3 points, a queen 2 points and a jack 1 point. As a rough guide, you can open the bidding when you hold at least 12 points. Suppose you are the dealer and therefore have the first chance to bid. Your hand is:

♠A J 9 4　♥K Q　♦A K Q 7 5　♣6 3

You have 19 points (5 in spades, 5 in hearts and 9 in diamonds) and this is easily enough to make an opening bid. You will bid 1♦ (one diamond), since diamonds is your longest suit and at this stage it is therefore your best guess as a satisfactory trump suit.

Above: Since you have a strong hand, you will open the bidding. Your longest suit is diamonds and you will open 1♦.

During the play there will be 13 tricks available. A bid at the one-level says that you think you can score seven tricks with your chosen suit as trumps. In other words, you will make seven tricks and the defenders will make six tricks; you will score more tricks than the other side, but only just. The first six tricks are known as "the book" and your bid says how many extra tricks, over the book, you think you can make in conjunction with your partner's hand opposite. Here your bid of 1♦ means that you think you can make seven tricks with diamonds as trumps. A bid of 2♥ would mean that you thought you could make eight tricks with hearts as trumps. Similarly, a bid of 3NT (three no-trumps) would mean that you thought you could make nine tricks in no-trumps, in other words with no suit as trumps.

Once someone has made an opening bid, the auction continues in a clockwise direction around the table. Each player, when it is his turn, has the chance to pass or bid. If he chooses to bid, he must make a higher bid than the last one that was made. This is why the bidding is also called the "auction". You can make a bid at the same level, here the one-level, provided your suit is ranked higher than the suit bid previously.

This is the ranking order of the five possible "denominations":

- NT no-trumps (highest)
- ♠ spades
- ♥ hearts
- ♦ diamonds
- ♣ clubs (lowest)

So, a bid of 1♥ (one heart) is a higher bid than 1♦ (one diamond) because hearts are ranked above diamonds. Spades and hearts are known as the "major suits"; diamonds and clubs are the "minor suits". If all the possible bids were stretched out from the lowest to the highest, this would be the order: 1♣, 1♦, 1♥, 1♠, 1NT, 2♣, 2♦, 2♥, 2♠, 2NT, etc... 7♣, 7♦, 7♥, 7♠, 7NT.

An opening bid of 1♣ is the lowest possible bid, meaning that you think you can score seven tricks with clubs as trumps. A bid of 7NT is the highest possible bid, meaning that you think you can score 13 tricks (seven plus the "book" of six) with no trump suit.

Look again at the line of bids. Suppose someone, either your partner or an opponent, has already bid 1♠ and you have a hand on which you want to make a bid in clubs. You cannot bid 1♣ because this bid is lower than 1♠. You would have to bid 2♣. (You might also choose to bid 3♣, or some higher bid in clubs, on certain types of hand.)

The auction continues until there are three consecutive passes. The last bid then determines what is known as the "contract". If the last bid was 4♠, for example, the partnership making that bid would then try to make ten tricks (four plus the book of six) with spades as trumps. So, the bidding sets a target number of tricks for one of the partnerships.

NOTATION FOR BIDS

When a suit symbol is placed after a number, this represents a bid (rather than a card). So, 2♥ is short for the bid of "two hearts". This would mean that the bidder thought his partnership could score eight tricks (the book of six, plus two) with hearts as trumps. Similarly, 3NT is short for "three no-trumps". If you read in a bridge article that "West led the ♦6 against 4♠", this would mean that West led the six of diamonds (a card) against four spades (the contract, determined by the final bid in the auction).

The play

It is an unusual aspect of bridge that one player becomes the "declarer" (the player trying to make the number of tricks specified in the contract). Suppose, as in the previous section, that the contract is 4♠. The player who first made a bid in spades becomes the declarer. The player to his left (one of the defenders) will lead the first card of the first trick. This play is known as the "opening lead".

Once the opening lead has been made, declarer's partner lays his entire hand face-up on the table. The hand, known as the "dummy", is arranged in four lines facing towards the declarer, with the trump suit (if any) on the left. Declarer's partner will take no further part in this deal. The declarer will play the cards from the dummy as well as from his own hand.

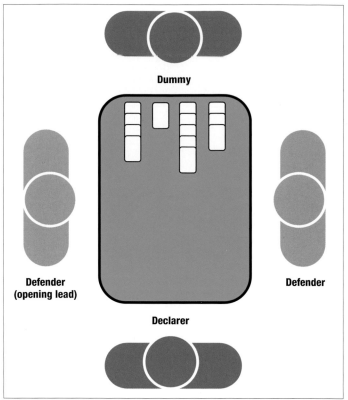

Above: The four players. The defender on declarer's left makes the opening lead and declarer's partner (the dummy) displays his hand face upwards on the table. Declarer plays a card from dummy, the other defender plays a card and declarer completes the trick with one of his cards.

Above: The dummy is arranged in four vertical lines, one for each suit, with the cards in descending order of rank (highest at the top).

For the rest of the play, the dummy (and its remaining cards) will be visible to declarer and to each of the defenders. Whichever of the four hands wins a particular trick, this will be the hand from which the first card is led to the next trick.

Bidding a game

Even in this basic summary of the game, it is necessary to mention something about the scoring. That is because it has a critical effect on the bidding. If you make the contract determined in the auction you score these points for each trick bid and made:

When ♦ or ♣ are trumps: 20 points for each trick
When ♠ or ♥ are trumps: 30 points for each trick
In no-trumps, 40 points for the first trick and 30 points for each subsequent trick

One of the main aims in bridge is to "make a game". To achieve this, you need to score at least 100 points. In no-trumps this can be done by bidding and making the nine-trick contract of 3NT, since 40+30+30 = 100. When the trump suit is spades or hearts (known as the "major suits", remember), you need to bid the ten-trick contract of 4♠ or 4♥, since 4 times 30 is 120. Most difficult is to make a game with diamonds or clubs (known as the "minor suits") as trumps. You would then need to bid 5♦ or 5♣, since 5 times 20 is 100. This will require you to make 11 of the available 13 tricks.

During the auction the partnership that holds the majority of the high cards will have two main decisions to make. They must decide which suit to make trumps, or perhaps to play in no-trumps. They must decide also whether their combined strength merits attempting a "game contract". In very rough terms, since suit lengths are also important, a partnership can make a game contract when they hold 25 of the available 40 high-card points between them. During the bidding they will attempt to discover if this is in fact the case.

A typical hand of bridge

The time has come, in this brief summary of the game, to see a complete hand of bridge (see below).

North, who was the dealer and holds the 19-point hand that we saw earlier, opens 1♦. East has a poor hand and passes. South holds 6 points. To "respond" to an opening bid at the one-level (in other words, to make a bid when your partner has already opened the bidding), you need 6 points or more. South has enough to respond and bids 1♠, suggesting spades as trumps. This is a higher bid than 1♦ because the spade suit is ranked higher than diamonds.

West has a strong club suit and decides to enter the bidding. He cannot bid 1♣, since this would be a lower bid than 1♠. He therefore overcalls 2♣. The word "overcall" means to make a bid after the opponents have already bid. North is pleased that his partner has bid spades because he also holds spade length. This means that spades will make a good trump suit. He plans to "agree spades as trumps" by making a further bid in spades himself. He will have to choose how high to bid in spades – the higher he bids, the stronger the hand he will show.

Since his own hand is very strong, North judges that the partnership can make a game in spades. (As a

---

FINDING A TRUMP FIT
♠ ♥ ♦ ♣

To make a satisfactory trump fit, you usually need at least eight of the available 13 cards in a particular suit. On this deal North holds four spades and knows, from his partner's 1♠ response, that South holds at least four spades too. The North–South partnership has therefore "found a trump fit". North confirms that spades will be trumps by "raising his partner's suit". Because his hand is so strong he raises it to 4♠, a game contract. If he held a minimum opening bid of around 12 points, he would instead raise to just 2♠.

---

rough guide, 25 points between the hands will be enough to make a game contract. Here North holds 19 points and expects his partner to hold at least 6 points for his response.) North jumps to 4♠ because this will be worth 120 points and is therefore a game contract.

The next three players pass and the auction is over. The "final contract" is 4♠ and South will be the declarer since he was the first player to bid spades. West, the player to the dealer's left, will make the opening lead.

Right: Bidding game in spades. North's bid of 4♠ is followed by three passes and so becomes the final contract. South will become declarer, since he was the first player to bid spades. West will make the opening lead and the North hand will be laid out as the dummy.

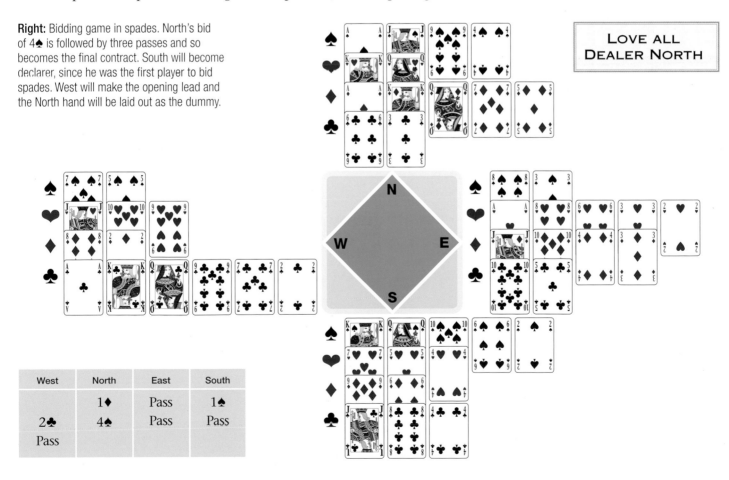

LOVE ALL
DEALER NORTH

West	North	East	South
	1♦	Pass	1♠
2♣	4♠	Pass	Pass
Pass			

We will now see the play of the cards. South, the declarer, must attempt to score ten tricks with spades as trumps. West, the player to declarer's left, makes the "opening lead" of the ♣A. North lays his cards on the table, displaying the dummy. From now on, declarer will play a card from the dummy to each trick as well as a card from his own hand.

Trick 1: The other three players follow with lower clubs and West's ♣A wins the trick.

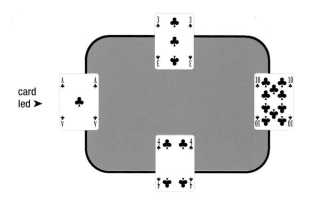

Above: Trick 1. West wins the first trick with the ♣A, the other three players following suit.

Trick 2: Since West won the trick he will lead to the second trick. He leads the ♣K and again the other three players follow with lower clubs. East–West (known as the "defenders") now have two tricks.

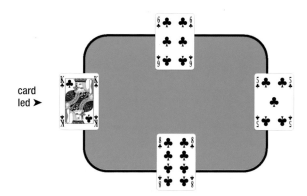

Above: Trick 2. West leads the ♣K, everyone following, and wins the trick.

Trick 3: West leads the ♣Q. Since the dummy has no clubs left, declarer can "ruff in the dummy". If he carelessly ruffs with the ♠4, East (who also has no clubs left) will overruff with the ♠8. That will be three tricks for the defenders and the ♥A would then give them a fourth trick to defeat the contract. Declarer therefore ruffs with the ♠9. He knows that neither defender holds a higher trump than this, so he has prevented an overruff.

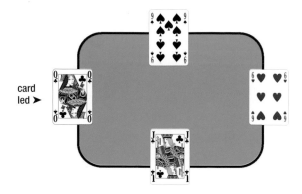

Above: Trick 3. West leads the ♣Q and declarer ruffs with the ♠9. East cannot overruff and discards a heart.

Trick 4: Declarer now starts to "draw trumps". In other words, he will play sufficient rounds of trumps to remove the defenders' trumps. They will not then be able to ruff any of his tricks. Declarer leads dummy's ♠4 to his ♠K and both defenders follow.

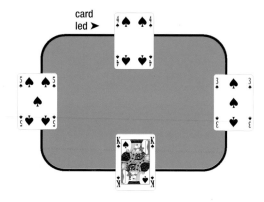

Above: Trick 4. Declarer leads dummy's ♠4 to his ♠K and both defenders follow suit.

Trick 5: Declarer leads the ♠2 to dummy's ♠A and both defenders follow again. Since there were only four trumps missing, he has now drawn trumps.

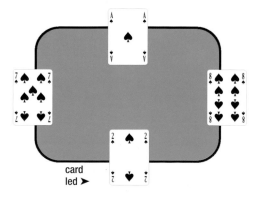

Above: Trick 5. Declarer draws a second round of trumps, everyone following suit.

Tricks 6/7/8: Declarer scores tricks with the ace, king and queen of diamonds. On the third round he has no diamond to play from the South hand and discards one of his hearts. West also "shows out", discarding a club. If the diamond suit had "broken 3–2" (in other words, one defender had held three diamonds and the other had held two), the ♦7 and the ♦5 would have scored two further tricks and declarer would have been able to discard his two remaining hearts.

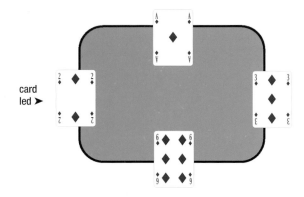

Above: Trick 6. Declarer scores a diamond trick by leading dummy's ace.

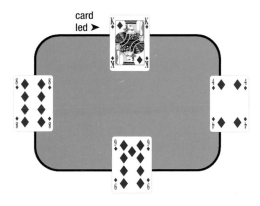

Above: Trick 7. Declarer continues with dummy's ♦K, scoring a second diamond trick.

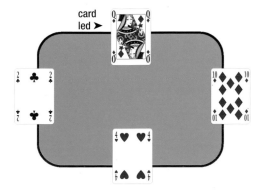

Above: Trick 8: Declarer discards a heart on the dummy's ♦Q and is disappointed to see West show out, throwing a club.

Trick 9: As it is, declarer leads the ♥K and East wins with the ♥A. Declarer has "knocked out" the ♥A, as bridge players say, and "established" the ♥Q as a winning card.

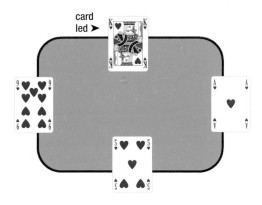

Above: Trick 9: Declarer leads the ♥K to East's ♥A, thereby setting up the ♥Q as a winner.

Trick 10: East leads a heart and the trick is won with dummy's ♥Q.

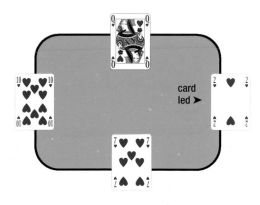

Above: Trick 10. Declarer wins East's heart return in the dummy.

The last three tricks will be taken with the three trumps remaining in declarer's hand. In total, declarer scored ten tricks: five trump tricks, one club ruff in the dummy, three diamond tricks and one heart trick. He therefore made his game contract of four spades. We will look at scoring in some detail, later in the book. For the moment, we will just say that North–South will score 120 for making four spades and a bonus of 300 for bidding and making a game. That is a score of +420 for North–South. The defenders, East–West will score -420 because the game was made against them. Scorepads (social bridge) and scorecards (competition bridge) have a plus column and a minus column.

CHAPTER 2

THE HISTORY OF BRIDGE

Contract bridge has existed as a game only since 1925. It evolved over a long period of time, beginning in the early 17th century with the trick-taking game of "whist". In that game, the choice of trump suit was determined by the turn of the dealer's last card. Towards the end of the 19th century, variants known as "bridge whist" and "auction bridge" introduced elements of bidding into the game, to choose the trump suit. In 1925, Harold Vanderbilt proposed some further changes. The most important of these was that a partnership must actually bid a "game contract" to score the bonus points that such a contract attracted. (The same applied to "slam contracts", where a target of 12 or 13 tricks was set.) The new game was called "contract bridge". Millions were drawn to it and all previous similar games were swept aside. The history section contains some exciting deals, played in various world championships. If you are new to the game, you may wish to read the early instructional sections on bidding and play first.

Right: A famous hand held by Charles Goren, who followed a brilliant line of play in the ensuing 6♥ contract.

PREDECESSORS OF THE GAME

Nearly all games and sports develop gradually, sometimes over many decades or even centuries. The same is true of contract bridge (or, more simply, bridge – as it is known today). A hand of bridge consists of a bidding auction followed by the play of the cards. The format of the play, 13 tricks contested by four players in two partnerships, comes directly from the ancient game of whist.

Whist

This game originated in England at the start of the 17th century and was derived from an earlier game, known variously as "ruff and honours", "triumph" or "trump".

There is no bidding in whist and the trump suit is determined by the turn of the dealer's final card. The scoring is simple. The partnership that scores the majority of the tricks is awarded one point for each

Above: Whist in progress. Since the game is whist, rather than bridge, all four players are holding their own cards during the play. (In bridge, one of the hands is displayed face-up, as the dummy.)

trick made in excess of the six-trick "book". If they make nine tricks, for example, they score three points. To win a "game", you had to score nine points in early versions of the game, later increased to ten points.

The earliest works that touched on whist were Charles Cotton's *Compleat Gamester* (1674) and Richard Seymour's *Court Gamester* (1719). However, it was not until 1728 that the rules of whist were formalized. The first book entirely devoted to whist was *Short Treatise on The Game of Whist* (1742) by Edmund Hoyle. The book was such a success that counterfeit copies began to appear. The next major authority on the game was "Cavendish" (Henry Jones). His book *Cavendish on Whist* (1862) sold prodigiously and ran to 30 editions.

Whist was not a game played in high society; it was more of a social pastime in the coffee houses of the day. A writer in the mid-18th century described whist as being "only fit for hunting men and country squires, and not for fine ladies or people of quality". Elsewhere it was described as "the game of the servants' hall".

In many ways the play of the hand at whist was considerably more difficult (or, at any rate, contained more guesswork) than the play in bridge today. There was no bidding to guide the players, of course; neither was any "dummy hand" exposed. Various conventions in the play became established, such as leading the fourth-best card from a strong suit. If you signalled with a high card, followed by a low card, known as a "high-low signal", you showed strong trumps and suggested that your partner should lead a trump when he gained the lead. As in bridge today, a player who had just won his partner's lead with an ace was expected to return the higher of two remaining cards and the original fourth-best from any longer holding.

In the last decade of the 19th century, whist became bogged down with a plethora of conventions in the play of the cards, as well as arguments about which signal should be made from a given card combination. Such intricacies deterred players of moderate ability from playing the game. They were attracted instead by a new and apparently simpler game, known as "bridge whist" – or in those days, "bridge".

Bridge whist

In the game of bridge whist, for the first time, one of the four hands (known as the "dummy", the hand of the declarer's partner) was exposed to view. Also, play in no-trumps was permitted. Another change was that the trump suit was chosen by the dealer or his partner rather than being determined by the last card to be dealt. The scoring was more complicated too, with the trick value depending on which suit was trumps. Spades were the lowest value suit, then clubs, diamonds and hearts. No-trumps was the highest scoring denomination. The trick values were 2, 4, 6, 8, 12 respectively. If the dealer held no great length in the high-scoring heart suit, he was likely to pass the decision on choosing trumps to his partner. Thirty points were required to make game, so 11 tricks in diamonds would produce game (5 times 6), as would ten tricks in hearts (4 times 8) or nine in no-trumps (3 times 12).

Either the dealer or his partner had to choose a trump suit, however weak they both might be. The penalties for failing to make a contract were ferocious – 50 points for every trick by which you fell short (for each "undertrick", as bridge players say). For the first time, the notion of doubling and redoubling became

THE FRUSTRATIONS OF BRIDGE WHIST

♠ ♥ ♦ ♣

Bridge whist was played for around 12 years, at the end of the 19th century. You can imagine how infuriating it must have been for a player to pick up ♠3 ♥A K Q J 10 8 2 ♦A K Q 7 ♣A, only to find that the dealer, on his right, would then choose spades as trumps! If the other side held the majority of the spades, as was very likely, they would probably score at least seven tricks. The fine hand, worth a small slam if its owner had the chance to makes hearts the trump suit, would therefore come to nothing.

part of the game. So much so, in fact, that bridge whist was regarded as a serious gambling game, much to the horror of its more staid followers.

Below is a typical hand of bridge whist, as described by the great American writer of the time, J. B. Elwell. Note the order of the suits, which is different from that used nowadays for contract bridge. The highest-scoring suit (hearts) was positioned at the bottom of the hand.

Right: A deal of bridge whist. The player called "Z" (nowadays he would be called "South") chooses to play the deal in no-trumps. That is all the bidding that was allowed in this form of the game.

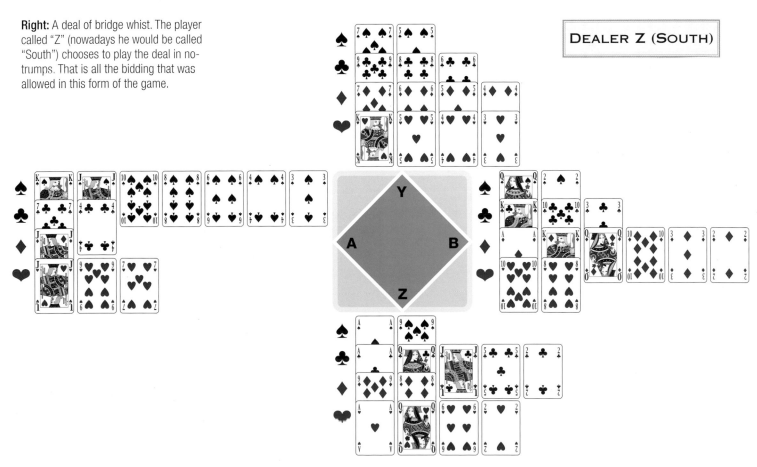

DEALER Z (SOUTH)

The players we now call West and East were referred to as A and B. Similarly, North and South were called Y and Z. Elwell's description begins: *Z deals and makes it "no-trump"*. In other words, the dealer (sitting South, as we know it) exercised his privilege to choose a trump suit or, in this case, to play the hand in no-trumps.

There was no further bidding in bridge whist, so it was West to lead and the play would take place in no-trumps. We are told that West led the ♠10 and declarer won with the ♠A. He played the ace and queen of hearts, both defenders following, and now needed to enter dummy twice to finesse in the club suit. (The term "finesse" means to lead towards a card, hoping that a higher card lies with the defender playing second to the trick. Here declarer leads towards his ♣Q, hoping that East holds the ♣K.)

Cleverly, declarer led the ♥6 (rather than the ♥2) to dummy's ♥K. A finesse of the ♣Q proved successful and declarer was then able to lead his carefully preserved ♥2 to dummy's ♥5 to finesse the ♣J. In this way he made five club tricks, four heart tricks and the ♠A. Elwell concludes: *The dealer wins four odd tricks*. By this strange-sounding phrase, he meant that declarer had scored ten tricks, four tricks over the book. Nowadays, we would say that declarer had scored ten tricks in no-trumps. In contract bridge, North–South would also need to bid to the game-level.

Auction bridge

In both whist and bridge whist, the play of the cards was exactly as it is in contract bridge. The main difference from the game today was that there was no auction before the play started. This was the major innovation of auction bridge, the next stepping stone on our journey. In this version of the game, the dealer could start the auction with a bid in one of the suits or he could opt to pass. Each player in turn could then do the same until one side was unwilling to bid any higher. If the highest bid was, say, three hearts, then hearts became trumps and declarer would have to make at least nine tricks.

The ranking of the denominations changed to that of today, with clubs (lowest), followed by diamonds, hearts, spades and no-trumps (highest). The trick value was 6, 7, 8, 9, 10 respectively and you needed to accumulate 30 points to make a game. As in contract bridge, contracts of 5♣ or 5♦ would suffice for game; so would 4♥ or 4♠. Playing in no-trumps, a contract of 3NT would yield the necessary 30 points.

The first side to score two games was said to have "won the rubber" which attracted a bonus of 250 points. In contract bridge, you need to actually bid a game or slam to receive the appropriate bonus. This was not the case in auction bridge. Even if you won the auction at just 1♠, you would still receive a game bonus if you made 10 tricks and a small slam bonus for 12 tricks.

Left: When several tables of whist are in play at one venue, this is known as a "whist drive". The players change tables every few deals and therefore face several different pairs of opponents. These sociable events were often held in church halls.

To get a flavour of auction bridge, here is a deal described in Denison's *The Play of Auction Hands* (1922). Again, the diagram looks strange to modern eyes because the diamond suit is placed at the bottom of each hand, despite the ranking of the suits being the same as it is today. This was so that the red and black colours of the suits were alternated.

Right: A deal of auction bridge, described by Denison in 1922. More than one player can make a bid but there is no necessity to carry the auction to the game-level in order to score a game bonus.

North opened 1♦ and South responded 1NT. It was natural for him to lay claim to the highest-scoring denomination since his side held the balance of the high cards. There was no reason to bid any higher, because you did not need to bid a game or slam in order to enjoy the bonus that those levels attracted.

West led the ♣J, East winning with the ♣K and returning the suit to dummy's bare ace. Declarer took a successful finesse of the ♥Q and then ran the ♦J. Denison now describes East's clever defence: *East refuses to take the Jack as declarant will then probably place the Queen with West and finesse dummy's 10 on the second round. Then if he has no more diamonds, he cannot make dummy's suit. While holding up the Queen will lose a trick if declarant does not again finesse, it is worth trying on the chance of saving game.*

As you see, if East wins with the ♦Q, declarer will score four diamonds, two hearts, two clubs and the ♠A, making game in no-trumps. If instead declarer falls for East's deceptive play and finesses the ♦10 on the second round of the suit, he will score only one diamond trick and fall short of the nine tricks required.

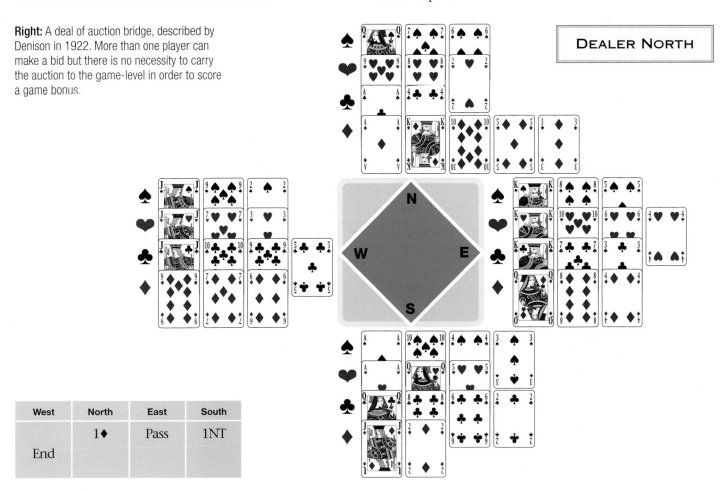

DEALER NORTH

West	North	East	South
	1♦	Pass	1NT
End			

THE ARRIVAL OF CONTRACT BRIDGE

The modern game of contract bridge is the result of changes to the scoring method suggested by Harold Vanderbilt in 1925. The most important of these, which transformed the whole game, was that you could count tricks towards a game or a slam only if you had contracted to score them during the auction.

Above: Harold S. Vanderbilt, the originator of contract bridge. The great grandson of a famous sea captain, he was a brilliant yachtsman and defended the America's Cup successfully in 1930, 1934 and 1938.

The value of each trick bid and made was set at 20 points per trick if trumps were diamonds or clubs and 30 points per trick if trumps were spades or hearts. If you played in no-trumps, you would score 40 for the first trick and 30 for each subsequent trick. Ten tricks (four above the "book") with spades as trumps would be enough for game, but only if you had bid 4♠ during the auction. If you stopped in 2♠ and scored ten tricks, you would score only 60 points (2 times 30) below the line on the score-sheet. The remaining 60, for the two overtricks, would go above the line and would not count towards game.

It is hard to over-emphasize the difference that this made to the game. Much more skill was required in the auction because a partnership had to assess accurately the trick-taking potential of their two hands together. Previously they had only to choose their most profitable trump suit and to outbid the opponents, should they have competed. On many deals there was a considerable risk involved with bidding a game, even more so if you contracted for a slam. That is because you would end with a minus score if you failed to achieve your objective. If you bid 4♠ (contracting for ten tricks) and then made only nine, you would score nothing and your opponents would receive an award for each "undertrick". As all contract bridge players know, it is a very skilful business to assess the combined playing strength of two hands, solely by making bids based on the sight of just one of these hands. This is one of the great attractions of the game.

Vanderbilt also introduced the notion of becoming "vulnerable" after you had won a game, which increased the penalties if you subsequently failed to make a contract. Within a few years, contract bridge had become so popular that it displaced bridge whist and auction bridge almost completely. The term "bridge" became synonymous with "contract bridge". Although there have been some minor changes made to the scoring of contract bridge, the game has remained largely untouched from the 1920s to this day.

Opposite is a typical deal of contract bridge – one that involves bidding by both sides:

CONTRACT BRIDGE SCORING

When you make a part score (a contract below the game level) you score the trick value, plus a bonus of 50. So 2♠ made with an overtrick is worth 3 x 30 + 50, for a total of 140. Games, bid and made, attract a bonus of 300 (non-vulnerable) and 500 (vulnerable), so ten tricks in 4♥ when non-vulnerable gives you 4 x 30 + 300, for a total of 420. Vulnerable, you would score 620. When you bid and make a small slam (12 tricks) you score an additional bonus of 500 (non-vulnerable) and 750 (vulnerable). A vulnerable 6♠ is therefore worth 6 x 30 + 500 + 750 = 1430. A grand slam (13 tricks) attracts a bonus of 1000 (non-vulnerable) and 1500 (vulnerable). 7NT, vulnerable, is worth 2220.

Right: A deal of contract bridge. In order to qualify for a game bonus, North–South have to bid the heart game as well as make it. Note that the auction is competitive, with East–West bidding in spades.

LOVE ALL
DEALER SOUTH

West	North	East	South
			1♥
1♠	2♥	2♠	4♥
End			

South opens 1♥ and West overcalls 1♠. North raises the opener to 2♥, showing heart support and a fairly weak hand. East raises to 2♠, similarly. At auction bridge, South would now bid just 3♥ because there would be no point whatsoever in bidding more. If he happened to score ten tricks, as was likely, he would receive the game bonus even when playing in 3♥. Playing contract bridge, however, South bids 4♥ because he needs at least 100 points below the line to give his side a game. (Here 4 x 30 = 120, enough for game.)

West leads the ♦A against the final contract of 4♥ and East has the chance to "signal", by following with an appropriate spot-card. Because East holds the ♦Q he plays a high card, the ♦9, to encourage a diamond continuation from his partner. West leads the ♦K next, winning the second trick, and plays a third diamond, which declarer ruffs. Declarer can see five trump tricks, three certain club tricks and the ♠A. That is a total of nine tricks. If he draws trumps next, he will need the defenders' clubs to divide 3–3. Dummy's ♣8 would then be worth a trick on the fourth round.

Rather than rely on luck, declarer plans to ruff a spade loser in dummy. He delays drawing trumps and leads a low spade from his hand. West wins the trick and leads a fourth round of diamonds,

ruffed by declarer. He can now cash the ♠A, ruff the ♠9 in dummy and draw trumps. Declarer scores ten tricks: five trump tricks, three top winners in clubs, the ♠A and a spade ruff in dummy. He therefore makes his contract of 4♥ exactly and will score 420 points for the non-vulnerable game in a major suit.

PENALTIES FOR GOING DOWN
♠ ♥ ♦ ♣

When you are not vulnerable (you have not yet won a game), each undertrick at contract bridge costs you 50. If the defenders have doubled the contract – see later section on penalty doubles – the penalty is 100 for the first undertrick, 200 each for the next two, and 300 each thereafter. Four down doubled would result in an 800 penalty (100+200+200+300). When you are vulnerable the penalties are more severe, with undoubled undertricks costing 100 each. If you are doubled, the first undertrick costs you 200 and each subsequent undertrick costs 300. So, going four down doubled would now result in an 1100 penalty (200+300+300+300).

POPULARIZING THE GAME

Ely Culbertson was born in 1891 in Romania, the son of an American engineer and a Cossack princess. He eventually became the leading authority on contract bridge in America and was largely responsible for making the game popular worldwide. This was no easy task, even in America, because at that time card-playing was regarded as a pastime for the idle and even reckoned by some to be sinful.

Above: Ely Culbertson. The most brilliant self-publicist the game of bridge has ever known. Three of his phenomenally popular bridge books reached the USA's top ten best-seller lists for non-fiction.

Largely self-educated, Culbertson was fluent in Russian, English, French, German, Italian, Spanish and Czech. He also had a fair knowledge of several other languages, including Latin and Greek. His family's considerable fortune had been lost in the Russian Revolution of 1917. Culbertson fled to Paris and earned a living there as a skilful player of several card games.

After World War I, Culbertson moved to New York and he married Josephine Murphy Dillon, a leading bridge teacher, in 1923. He soon realized the business opportunity that the emerging game would offer and attempted to install himself as the country's leading authority. In 1929 he founded the *Bridge World*

magazine and began to publish a string of best-selling books on bridge, which had reached the peak of its popularity in the 1930s. In 1937 alone, *Bridge World* made a profit of over a million dollars, from which Culbertson collected royalties of more than $200,000.

In the Culbertson bidding system the requirements for opening bids and responses were not measured in terms of the point-count system that is familiar today (where an ace is worth 4 points, a king 3 points, a queen 2 points and a jack 1 point). The emphasis was instead on "honour tricks". This was Culbertson's Table of Honour Tricks:

Ace/King	2 honour tricks
Ace/Queen	1½ honour tricks
Ace	1 honour trick
King/Queen	1 honour trick
King/Jack/10	1 honour trick
King/x	1½ honour tricks
Queen/Jack/x	1½ honour tricks
Queen/x and Jack/x	½ honour trick

To open the bidding with one of a suit, you required 2½ honour tricks. For example, you might hold:

♠ A Q 8 6 2 ♥ J 9 2 ♦ K Q 5 ♣ 8 6

This hand contains 1½ honour tricks in spades, 1 honour trick in diamonds and no further honour tricks in hearts and clubs. That is a total of 2½ honour tricks, so the hand would be deemed worth an opening bid of 1♠.

If you held 2½ honour tricks but no suit worth bidding, you could open 1NT. With 5 honour tricks, you would open 2NT.

As a player, Culbertson was one of the leading lights in the 1930s, winning several domestic events including the prestigious Vanderbilt Trophy. He took an international team to England, winning several matches there, and won the Schwab Cup in 1933 and 1934. Opposite is a deal from the 1933 event is shown, along with some of Culbertson's comments.

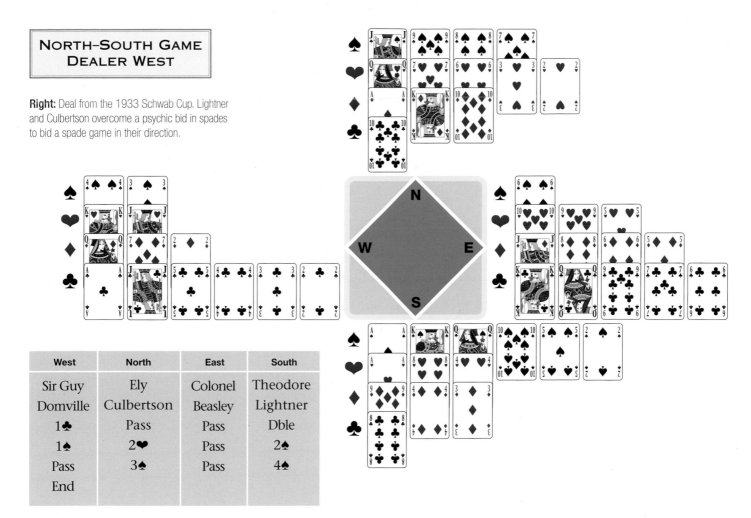

NORTH–SOUTH GAME DEALER WEST			

Right: Deal from the 1933 Schwab Cup. Lightner and Culbertson overcome a psychic bid in spades to bid a spade game in their direction.

West	North	East	South
Sir Guy Domville	Ely Culbertson	Colonel Beasley	Theodore Lightner
1♣	Pass	Pass	Dble
1♠	2♥	Pass	2♠
Pass	3♠	Pass	4♠
End			

Culbertson wrote: *Very interesting bidding. North is vulnerable and an overcall of 1♥ is dangerous against the keen opponent who is quick on the trigger. South precedes his Spade bid by a Take-out Double to show 3 or more Honour tricks. At this stage Sir Guy Domville makes a fine psychic Spade bid* (in other words, bidding 1♠ when he did not hold spades in an attempt to mislead the opponents). *He fears the opponents might get together on a game in spades. Note that Domville's Spade bid is safe because he has already warned his Partner that his best suit is clubs. Domville's brilliant psychic proves to be a dud. Unfortunately for him, South's Spade suit is too strong. The spade game is bid and made.*

Culbertson's name became synonymous with the game of bridge itself. He transformed a previously elitist game into an entertaining pastime for millions.

JOSEPHINE CULBERTSON
♠ ♥ ♦ ♣

Ely Culbertson's wife, Josephine was a fine player, described in the 1930s as "the modern miracle – the woman who can play on even terms with the best men". She played high-stake set games in partnership with Ely and achieved fame in the Culbertson–Lenz match. Her trend-setting clothes and the chic way in which she wore them drew the attention of the nation's fashion magazines. She and Ely were divorced in 1938 but continued to work as business partners. She died of a stroke three months after Ely's death in 1958.

Above: Josephine married her bridge partner Ely Culbertson in 1923.

THE CULBERTSON–LENZ MATCH

Towards the end of 1931, Culbertson felt that his position at the pinnacle of bridge was being threatened by another authority, Sidney Lenz. In the *Bridge World* magazine, and in several national newspapers, he challenged Lenz (and his chosen partner) to a grand match. This would determine which player's methods were superior and should therefore be adopted by the millions of bridge players in the USA.

Vast numbers of reporters relayed details of the daily play to their newspapers. By today's standards, the quality of the bidding and play was unexceptional. Culbertson and his partner, von Zedtwitz, did however fare well on the deal shown below.

Culbertson, sitting North, suggested a slam with his jump to 2♥ and von Zedtwitz indicated strong heart support with his rebid of 4♥. Aware that his heart suit was of moderate quality, Culbertson then suggested diamonds as an alternative trump suit for the small slam. Von Zedtwitz was happy to accept and the partnership had reached a fine contract.

West led the ♥10 and declarer played low from dummy, capturing East's ♥Q with the ♥K. He could not play for a spade ruff in dummy by conceding a spade trick, since he would then suffer a heart ruff. Von Zedtwitz cashed the ♣K, drew trumps in three rounds and crossed to the ♥A. After throwing a spade on the ♣A, he ruffed a club and crossed to dummy with the ♥J. At this stage West was down to ♠K–8–5 and the ♥9. He was thrown in with a heart and then had to lead away from his ♠K. Declarer therefore made both the ♠A and the ♠Q, scoring the 12 tricks that he needed. It was a fine piece of card play.

Making psychic bids (those that bear little relationship to your hand, such as opening 1♠ with only two spades in your hand) was a large part of the game in those days. On one deal, Jacoby overcalled 1NT on just 5 points, rather than the 16–18 points normally required. Lenz was furious at yet another psychic bid from a partner who had supposedly agreed to decline from such action. "Why do you make such rotten bids?" he cried. "You're having a lot of fun.

Below: A well-bid diamond slam. Culbertson's rebid of 6♦ offers partner a choice of slams and von Zedtwitz leaves it in diamonds.

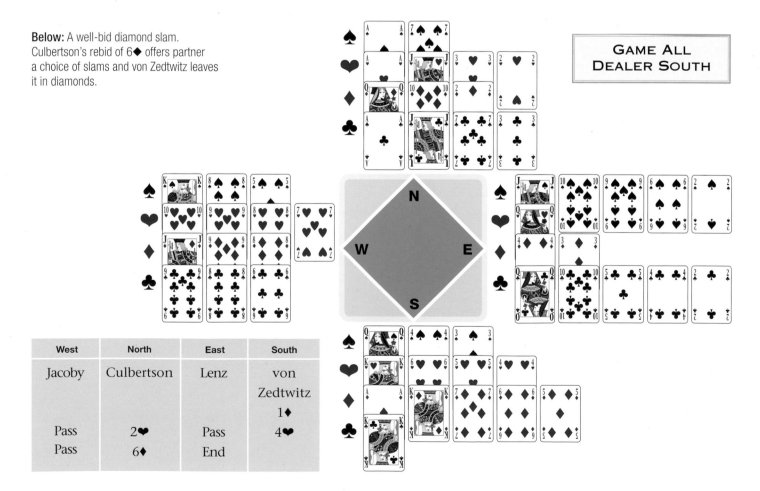

GAME ALL
DEALER SOUTH

West	North	East	South
Jacoby	Culbertson	Lenz	von Zedtwitz
			1♦
Pass	2♥	Pass	4♥
Pass	6♦	End	

Right: An ill advised penalty double. Liggett and Lenz did well to reach the club game and received an extra reward when Mrs Culbertson chose to double.

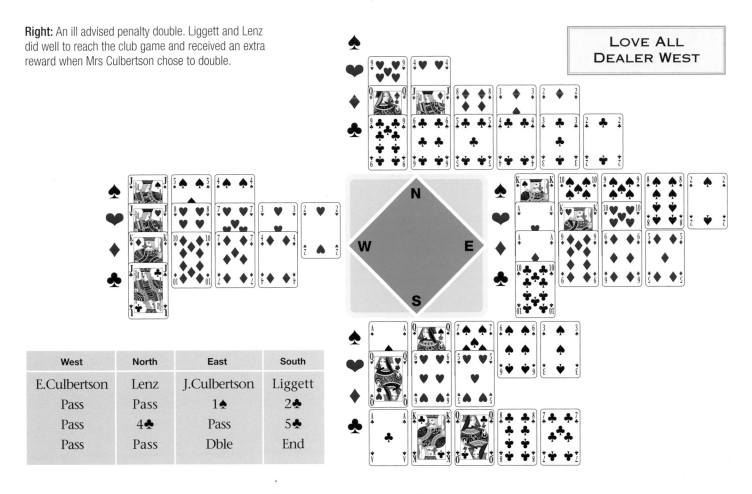

LOVE ALL
DEALER WEST

West	North	East	South
E.Culbertson	Lenz	J.Culbertson	Liggett
Pass	Pass	1♠	2♣
Pass	4♣	Pass	5♣
Pass	Pass	Dble	End

Give me a chance. I can't tell whether you have anything or not when you bid." Jacoby, who had played very well to this point, left the match the following day and was replaced by Winfield Liggett. The newcomer had an early success on this board, which featured an unwise penalty double.

West had passed throughout on the deal shown above and there was no reason for Josephine Culbertson to place him with any values. No one had forced South to bid the club game and he presumably had distributional values (a shapely hand) to make up for the missing two aces and two kings that were in the East hand. Few players would double 5♣ on the East cards nowadays.

When Ely Culbertson led the ♠J, Liggett threw a heart from dummy and won with the ♠Q. He drew trumps in one round and discarded dummy's other heart on the ♠A. He then ruffed three spades and two hearts in the dummy, meanwhile ruffing four diamonds in his hand. When diamonds broke 4–4, dummy's ♦Q became established and declarer made all 13 tricks.

Right: Culbertson-Lenz match. The contestants discuss a deal after the cards have been played.

The Culbertson team, which had at one stage led by over 20,000 aggregate points, eventually won by 8,980 points. As a result of huge publicity for the match in the press, sales of Culbertson's books rocketed. Indeed, two of his books on bidding featured in that year's national non-fiction Top Ten best sellers.

Charles Goren's influence

Charles Goren was born in Philadelphia in 1901 and graduated in law at McGill University, Montreal. While studying there, a girlfriend expressed amusement at his lack of bridge-playing ability. This triggered him to study existing books on the game and he rapidly became a top-class player. In the 1930s the huge success of Ely Culbertson eventually persuaded Goren to abandon the law and pursue a career in bridge.

The strength of a bridge hand had previously been measured in honour tricks (where, for example, an ace–king combination counted as 2 honour tricks). Goren favoured a point-count system developed by Milton Work, where 4 points were counted for an ace, 3 for a king, 2 for a queen and 1 for a jack. In 1936 he wrote his first book, *Winning Bridge Made Easy*, in which he publicized this method. Players found the point-count system easier to use than counting honour tricks. The 4–3–2–1 method is still in universal use today, when most players would scarcely know what an honour trick is.

Goren produced several more best-selling bridge books, also writing a syndicated bridge column that appeared in dozens of newspapers from coast to coast. Between 1959 and 1964, he increased his reputation further with the first successful bridge programme on television – *Championship Bridge with Charles Goren*.

As a player, Goren was a member of the winning American team in the inaugural Bermuda Bowl (open world championship) in 1950. He won 34 national titles, many of them in his famous partnership with Helen Sobel. On eight occasions he won the McKenney Trophy, which is awarded to the player who collects the most master points in each season. (Master points are awarded by national bridge organizations for success in tournaments at all levels. For winning a session at your local club, you might win 30 master points; for winning a national championship the award would be several thousand.) As a result of this regular tournament success, Goren had the highest master point total in America throughout the period 1944–62.

As well as being a top-rank player, Goren was a very successful teacher and lecturer. He enhanced the 4–3–2–1 point-count system to assign extra values for long suits and shortages. Once a trump fit had been found, 5 points were added for a void and 3 for a singleton. Goren also pointed out that there were advantages to be gained from opening in a four-card major suit. Previously it had been common practice to insist on a five-card suit for an opening bid of 1♠ or 1♥. Players debate the benefits of five-card majors and four-card majors to this day. In most parts of the world the pendulum is swinging towards five-card majors.

Left: Charles Goren. His name was synonymous with the game of bridge for many decades in the USA. "Do you play Goren?" players would ask.

Right: A brilliant winner-on-loser play. Goren makes 6♥ by playing a losing club, throwing West on lead, and throwing a winning spade.

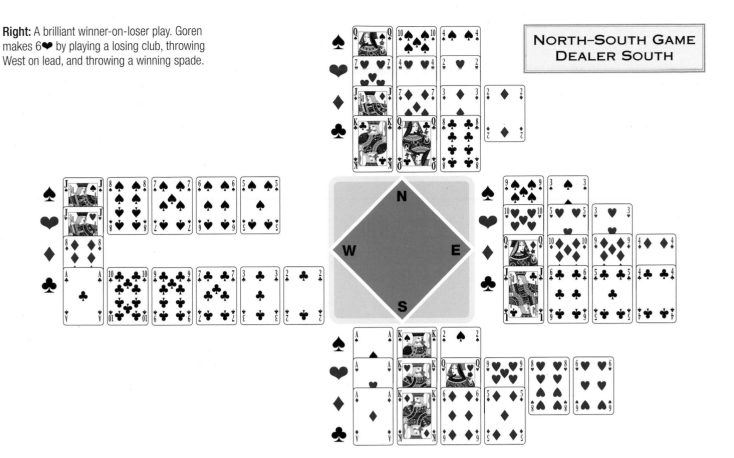

Above is one of Charles Goren's most famous hands. After a bidding sequence that has not survived (neither have the names of the other three players), he arrived in a small slam in hearts.

West decided to lead his singleton jack of trumps. Goren won and drew a second round of trumps. If the trump suit had broken 2–2, he would have led the ♥6 to dummy's ♥7 and played the ♣K, discarding a diamond loser. West would have been welcome to score his ♣A because declarer could subsequently throw his other diamond loser on the established ♣Q.

When trumps broke 3–1, Goren drew East's last trump. All would still be well if the diamond suit produced three tricks. This was an excellent prospect, requiring a 3–2 break, West to hold the ◆Q or East to hold a singleton ◆Q. However, when Goren cashed the two top diamonds West showed out on the second round.

Few players would realize that any hope remained. Goren could see a chance, however, if he could reach dummy twice in order to play clubs. Seeking an extra entry to dummy, he cashed the ♠A and then led the ♠2, finessing the ♠10. When this card won, he led dummy's ♣K, discarding the ♠K from his hand! West won with the ♣A but had only black

cards left. If he played a club, Goren would win with dummy's ♣Q. If instead he played a spade, Goren would win with dummy's ♠Q (which was the point of throwing the ♠K from his hand on the previous trick). Whatever was played by West, declarer would reach the dummy and be able to discard his two losing diamonds.

Did the American maestro gain a big swing when this result was compared with the score at the other table of the match? No, indeed. When the board was replayed, North–South overbid to a contract of 7♥. West made the uninspired lead of the ♣A, ruffed by declarer, and there were now two discards available on the king and queen of clubs.

BIDDING GUIDELINES
♠ ♥ ♦ ♣

A good general guideline is to bid boldly when a game contract is possible but to be more cautious when considering a possible slam. Failure at the slam level causes you to lose the game bonus you would otherwise have won. Be particularly wary of bidding uncertain grand slams, where failure to make the contract will cause you to lose the small slam bonus as well as the game bonus.

BRIDGE CHAMPIONSHIPS

THE BERMUDA BOWL

The first world championship for the Bermuda Bowl was held in 1950. The three invited teams were the USA, Europe and Great Britain. The USA won by a good margin, represented by six players whose names are well known in bridge circles even today: John Crawford, Charles Goren, George Rapee, Howard Schenken, Sidney Silodor and Sam Stayman. The trophy for the winners was presented by the government of Bermuda.

The next six Bermuda Bowls were two-team challenge matches between the USA and the winners of the European Championship. The USA retained the trophy for the next three holdings until Great Britain won in 1955. After a win by France in 1956, there followed a long dominance by Italy, who remained unbeaten until 1970. Their team, known as the Blue Team, included such great names as: Massimo d'Alelio, Walter Avarelli, Giorgio Belladonna, Eugenio Chiaradia, Pietro Forquet, Benito Garozzo and Camillo Pabis-Ticci.

During this period the number of teams was gradually increased. In 1958, the South American champions joined. In 1966 the South Pacific zone sent their champions. In 1979 the Central America and Caribbean Zone winners were admitted, joined in 1981 by the champions of Asia and the Middle East. Also, in 1981, a second European team was admitted.

From 1976 until the present day the Bermuda Bowl has been dominated by the USA. In total, the USA have won the event 16 times, while Italy has won

it 15 times. France has won twice and four teams have won on a single occasion: Great Britain, the Netherlands, Iceland and Brazil. The Bermuda Bowl had begun as an exclusive event, with a gladiatorial atmosphere. Nowadays the character of the championship has changed and around 20 teams take part. They compete in two mini-leagues, with the top four teams from each section advancing to the knock-out quarter-finals. As a result of the advent of other world championships – the Olympiad and the Rosenblum transnational world championship – the Bermuda Bowl is now held only on odd-numbered years.

AN OLYMPIC SPORT
♠ ♥ ♦ ♣

In 2000 the President of the International Olympic Committee, Jacques Rogge, declared that bridge had been accepted as a sport by the Olympic movement. To retain this classification, non-smoking restrictions had to be introduced. Also, players at the two world championships in 2000 were randomly selected for drugs tests. Drugs such as steroids, which carry advantage in track and field events, are of little benefit to bridge players. However, there is a limit on the amount of caffeine that is allowed and bridge players are known for their heavy consumption of coffee! A demonstration bridge event was held at the 2002 Winter Olympics in Salt Lake City.

Right: Unbeaten in the World Championship between 1958 and 1970, the Italian Blue Team are regarded as the most successful team in bridge history.

Above: The Bermuda Bowl. Awarded for the open world championship every two years, it is the ultimate prize in bridge.

The deal below comes from the 1954 Bermuda Bowl, with France facing the USA. In matches of this sort, each deal is played twice (to reduce the luck factor). At one table the USA sat North–South and stopped in 4♠, making 12 tricks after a diamond lead. At the other table France sat North–South and their pair

bid to 6♠. If this could be made, France would gain a huge swing. (The scoring for each board is based on the difference between the two results.) West led the ♥2, hoping that his partner could win and deliver a club ruff. Declarer won with the dummy's ♥A and continued with the ace and queen of trumps, the suit breaking 3–2.

The world championship book of that year gives the play only for the first three tricks. Yet it states that the slam went one down. Declarer presumably drew the last trump and then needed to score four club tricks. A low club to the queen is the correct safety play, because it wins against any lie of the suit. Here West would show out on the first round of clubs and East would take the ♣Q with the ♣K. Declarer could then ruff the heart return, cross to the ♣J and finesse the ♣9. After cashing the ♣A, he would cross to the ◆A to discard his potential diamond loser on dummy's fifth club. We can assume that declarer cashed the ace of clubs on the first round, after which there was no way to recover. East would then be assured of two club tricks.

Moving forward to 1965 marks the middle of the period of Italian dominance. Although the Italians were all fine card players it was perhaps their bidding that attracted the greatest admiration.

Right: Declarer misses the safest play. To pick up the 4–0 club break, declarer must refrain from cashing the ace on the first round.

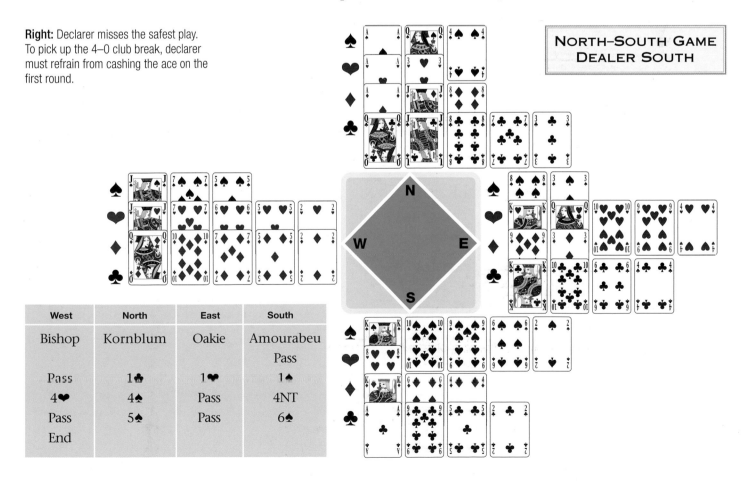

NORTH–SOUTH GAME
DEALER SOUTH

West	North	East	South
Bishop	Kornblum	Oakie	Amourabeu
			Pass
Pass	1♣	1♥	1♠
4♥	4♠	Pass	4NT
Pass	5♠	Pass	6♠
End			

Right: A brilliantly-bid grand slam. When South bids so strongly, missing three aces, North deduces that his partner's trumps must be solid.

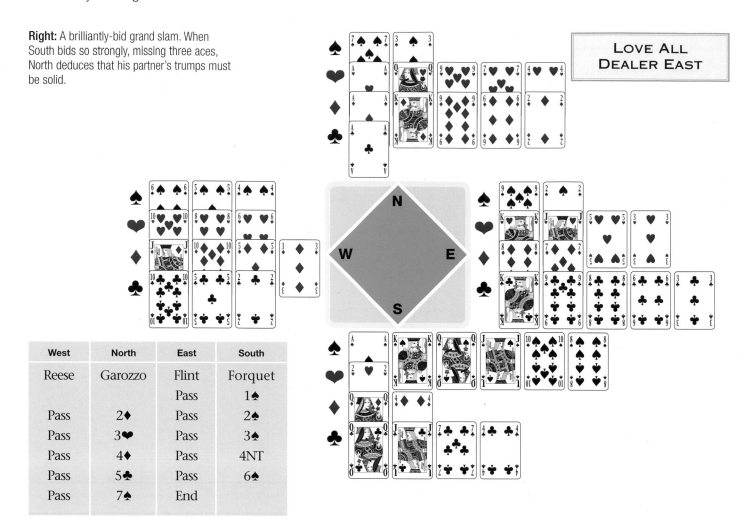

LOVE ALL
DEALER EAST

West	North	East	South
Reese	Garozzo	Flint	Forquet
		Pass	1♠
Pass	2♦	Pass	2♠
Pass	3♥	Pass	3♠
Pass	4♦	Pass	4NT
Pass	5♣	Pass	6♠
Pass	7♠	End	

The deal shown above was played in the 1965 world championship, during the ten-year period when Italy dominated world bridge. Here is a grand slam, bid by the Italians and missed by the British.

On a strong responding hand, it was part of the Italian system to make a canapé response – in other words, to bid the second longest suit first. Although Garozzo's (North) suits were of equal length, this method implied that he would bid diamonds before hearts. Forquet (South) rebid his spades twice and Garozzo then rebid his diamonds, to show 5–5 in these suits. South was too strong to sign off in 4♠, so he made a natural slam try of 4NT. When Garozzo showed a club control with 5♣, he leapt to a small slam in spades. Garozzo had so many controls in the side suits, he could judge South's spades to be solid and therefore raised to the grand slam.

Without a trump lead, declarer can simply ruff two clubs in dummy and discard the remaining club loser on the third round of diamonds. West did lead a trump, however, and now declarer had a little more work to do. After winning the trump lead, Forquet crossed to the ♣A. He re-entered his hand with the ♦Q

Above: Benito Garozzo. Now resident in the USA, Garozzo is thought by many to be the best bridge player of all time.

and led the ♣Q, ruffing with dummy's remaining trump. He then cashed the ♦A and ruffed a diamond, establishing the suit against the 4–2 break. After drawing trumps, he could then claim the remaining tricks. The king and nine of diamonds were good for two club discards and the ♥A would provide the necessary entry to dummy.

At the other table Albert Rose opened 4♠ on the South cards, raised to 6♠ by Harrison Gray. In tournament play the difference in aggregate scores is converted to International Match Points (known as IMPs) according to a standard table. Here the Italians scored 1,510 for their grand slam, the British scoring only 1,010 for an overtrick in the small slam. The difference of 500 gave the Italians a "swing" of 11 IMPs.

We will see next the deal that decided the 1974 Bermuda Bowl. The final, between Italy and North America, was nearing its close when a potential slam deal (shown below) arose.

Forquet bid 4♣ to set clubs as the trump suit. The next two bids (4♦ and 4♠) were cue-bids that showed a control in that side suit. A cue-bid can be made on an ace or a king, also sometimes on a singleton or void. Bianchi won the heart lead with the ace and played a

	SCORING IN DUPLICATE MATCHES
	♠ ♥ ♦ ♣

To reduce the effect of slam hands, where luck can have a huge effect, the difference in scores (when a hand is played twice in a duplicate match) is reduced by converting it to International Match Points, known as IMPs. For example, a difference of 1,000 points converts to 14 IMPs, while a difference of 500 points converts to 11 IMPs. The relatively small difference of 100 points, meanwhile, is worth a full 3 IMPs.

trump to the ace, West showing out. He then played two rounds of diamonds, throwing his heart loser, and led another trump. East won with the king and returned a third round of trumps. When the king and ace of spades stood up, Bianchi was able to ruff a spade with the ♣J, return to hand with a ruff and draw East's last trump to make the slam.

If East had held only one spade, declarer's intended safety play of a trump to the ace would have misfired. East would then have been able to ruff the second round. The commentators at the time

Right: A slam deal from the 1974 Bermuda Bowl. Bianchi shows that his play of a trump to the ace was safe even against a 4–0 trump break.

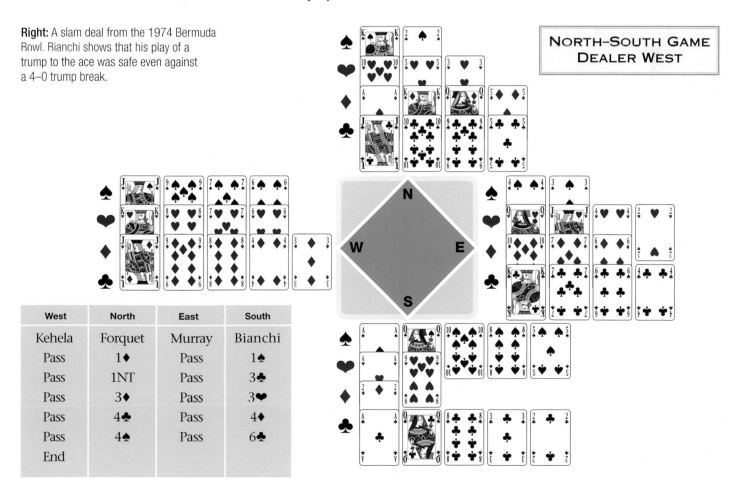

	NORTH–SOUTH GAME
	DEALER WEST

West	North	East	South
Kehela	Forquet	Murray	Bianchi
Pass	1♦	Pass	1♠
Pass	1NT	Pass	3♣
Pass	3♦	Pass	3♥
Pass	4♣	Pass	4♦
Pass	4♠	Pass	6♣
End			

suggested that it would have been better to discard the heart loser before drawing trumps, and then to run the ♣J. If this lost to the ♣K with West, declarer would be able to draw trumps in two more rounds at worst. He could then ruff one spade loser and discard the other.

The USA's Bob Hamman and Bobby Wolff stopped in 4♠ on these cards. They lost 12 IMPs on the board and the Italians eventually won by 196–166.

In the 1983 Bermuda Bowl, an unfortunate bidding misunderstanding by Belladonna and Garozzo, on the penultimate board of the final against the USA, handed victory to their opponents. Italy led by 8 IMPs with two boards to play and had two seemingly favourable results already obtained in the other room, where play had finished. The fatal board for the Italians in the Open Room is shown below.

Belladonna's 2NT was artificial, showing good spade support and a side-suit singleton. He might make the bid either when seeking a game contract or when he had a slam in mind. The opener was expected to rebid 3♣, after which responder would bid 3♦, 3♥ or 3♠ to show a game-try hand with a diamond, heart or club singleton. With a slam-try hand, opener would rebid at the four-level. Garozzo had opened on a 10-count and attempted to indicate this by rebidding 3♠, not even

asking partner to define his hand further. The bid appeared to confuse Belladonna, who was no doubt exhausted after playing for so many days. The report in USA's *Bridge World* stated that he had interpreted 3♠ as a "trump-asking bid" and that his six-step 4NT response showed his six trumps to the ace–king. He then took 5♦ as a control-showing cue-bid, after which he bid a small slam. Garozzo said instead that 4NT had been Blackwood, asking how many aces his partner held, and Belladonna had suffered from a momentary aberration. Whatever the explanation, the pair who at that time were rated the strongest in the world had given away a world championship by bidding a slam with two aces missing. At the other table the Americans stopped in 5♠, which they duly made.

Moving to more recent times, we will end with a dramatic slam deal from the final of the 2003 Bermuda Bowl, between Italy and the USA. Italy's Giorgio Duboin probably still has nightmares about the board opposite.

After no fewer than nine rounds of bidding, Duboin (South) arrived in 6♠ redoubled. The Americans doubled this contract and the Italians redoubled. (When one partnership has been doubled in a contract and think they can make it nevertheless, they have the right to redouble.)

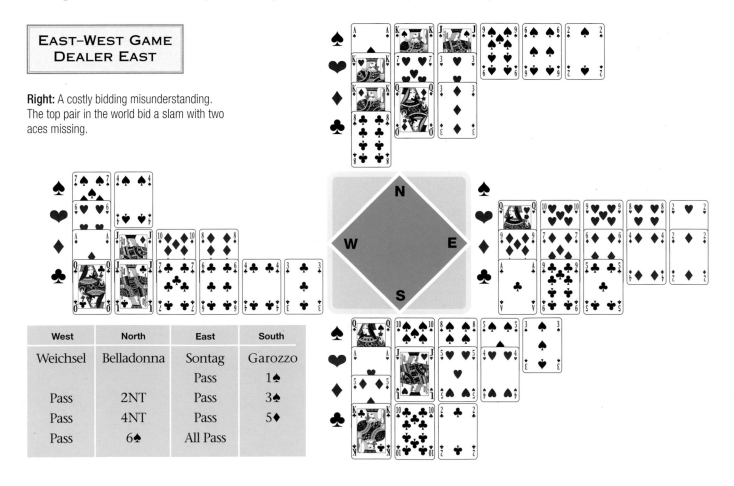

EAST–WEST GAME	
DEALER EAST	

Right: A costly bidding misunderstanding. The top pair in the world bid a slam with two aces missing.

West	North	East	South
Weichsel	Belladonna	Sontag	Garozzo
		Pass	1♠
Pass	2NT	Pass	3♠
Pass	4NT	Pass	5♦
Pass	6♠	All Pass	

Although the ♥K was offside (lying over the ♥A–Q) and the trumps were breaking 4–0, it seemed to the onlookers that there was every chance of landing the contract.

Bob Hamman (West) led the ♦10. Duboin won with dummy's ♦A and led a heart towards his hand without first cashing a top trump from dummy.

Below: A costly mistake. One of the world's top players, Giorgio Duboin, goes down in 6♠ redoubled.

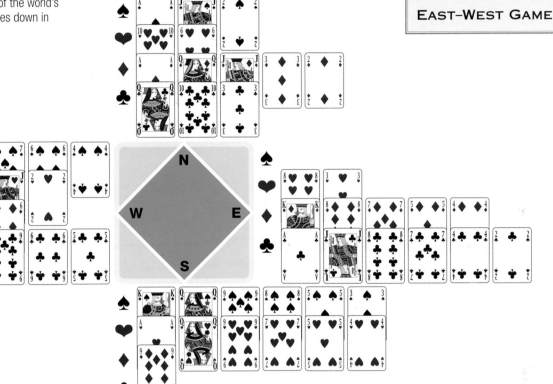

MAKE SURE IT ADDS UP!
♠ ♥ ♦ ♣

Eddie Kantar, the American expert and teacher, tells his students: "Count your losers and then count your winners. If the answer does not come to 13, count your cards!"

EAST–WEST GAME

The commentators in the auditorium expected him to finesse the ♥Q, but Duboin rose with the ♥A and returned a second round of hearts. Hamman won with the ♥J, East following, and promptly placed the ♥K on the table. Declarer knew that East held no more hearts and had to decide whether to ruff with a low trump or one of dummy's trump honours. Because he had not cashed an early round of trumps, to investigate the situation in that suit, Duboin did not yet know that trumps were breaking 4–0. It was natural for him to ruff the third round of hearts with dummy's ♠J, to avoid an overruff. Imagine his thoughts when he continued with the ♠A and East showed out! West now had to score a trump trick and the redoubled slam went one down.

At the other table the American North–South pair, Jeff Meckstroth and Eric Rodwell had bid 1♠ – 2♦ – 2♥ – 4♠, making 12 tricks. Duboin had therefore lost 12 IMPs where he might have gained 17. The Americans eventually won the final by 303–302!

Above: Giorgio Duboin, photographed in 2007, when he was first ranked as the world's best player. He had won 12 European and world championships.

THE VENICE CUP

The women's world championship, the Venice Cup, was first contested in 1974 and is now held every two years. The USA has a fine record in the event, with no fewer than nine wins. Great Britain and Germany have each won the event twice, with France and the Netherlands recording a single win.

The original holding, in 1974, was a two-team affair. Italy, champions of Europe and the Olympic champions, challenged the USA, and lost by 35 IMPs. Again in 1976 only two teams played: the USA were challenged by Great Britain, European champions. In 1978 the event was brought in line with the Bermuda Bowl, with one team representing each continent: USA, Italy, Argentina, Australia and the Phillippines. Nowadays the entry is much larger, as in the Bermuda Bowl. Twenty-two teams contested the 2005 event.

The deal shown below features an excellent piece of card play by the USA's Carol Sanders, playing South in the very first Venice Cup in 1974. She arrived in 4♠ and appeared at first to have four losers: one heart, two diamonds and one club.

North's 2NT showed a sound raise of spades to the three-level. Had she instead bid 3♠ directly over the double, this would have shown a weak hand with four-card spade support.

The Italian West led a top club against the spade game and switched to ace and another diamond. East won the second diamond with the king and played back a club, ruffed by declarer. All now depended on not losing a heart trick and South knew from West's take-out double that the ♥Q was likely to be offside. She drew trumps, ruffed her diamond loser in dummy and then played her remaining trumps. West had to find one more discard from ♣K and ♥Q-10-7. Whatever she threw, declarer would have her tenth trick. The play was identical at the other table, for a classy flat board.

The narrowest winning margin in any world championship came in the 1999 Venice Cup, with USA facing the Netherlands. With one board to be played, the atmosphere in the VuGraph theatre was electric, as the Dutch led by just 0.5 of an IMP. (The fraction was due to a 2.5 IMP penalty applied on the Americans for finishing five minutes late in one session.) This was the last board of the final:

Right: A well played contract of 4♠. Carol Sanders catches her Italian opponent in a major-suit squeeze.

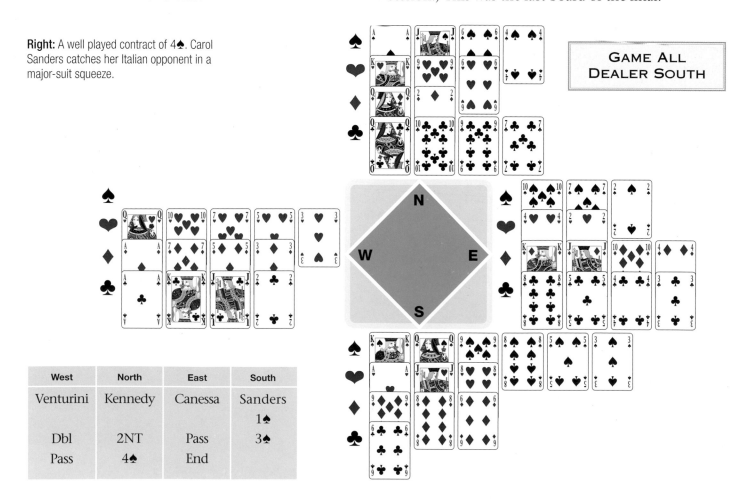

GAME ALL
DEALER SOUTH

West	North	East	South
Venturini	Kennedy	Canessa	Sanders
			1♠
Dbl	2NT	Pass	3♠
Pass	4♠	End	

Right: With only 0.5 IMPs separating USA and Italy, one extra overtrick could decide the championship.

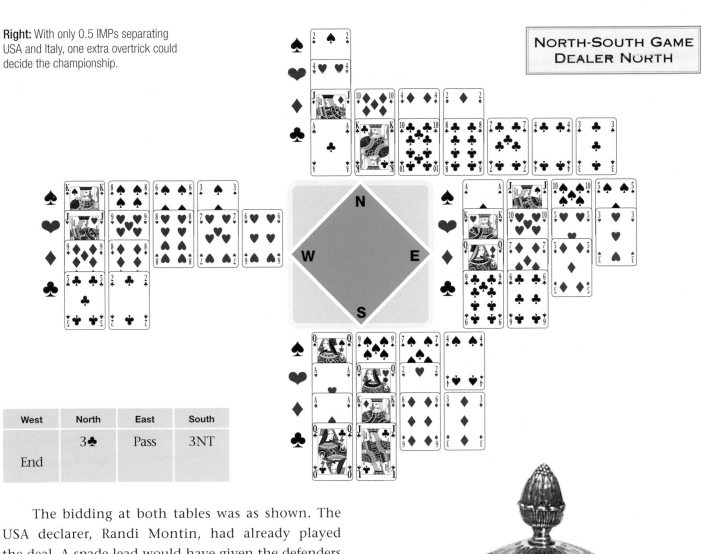

West	North	East	South
	3♣	Pass	3NT
End			

The bidding at both tables was as shown. The USA declarer, Randi Montin, had already played the deal. A spade lead would have given the defenders the first three tricks, holding declarer to +630. The Netherlands West had led the normal ♥7, however. Declarer had won East's king with the ace, cashed the ♦A and run seven rounds of clubs. When no diamonds were thrown, she declined to risk the diamond finesse and collected +660 for 3NT made with two overtricks. So, if the USA West led a spade, restricting declarer to ten tricks, the USA would gain 1 IMP and win the championship by 0.5 IMPs.

To the anguish of the American spectators watching VuGraph, West led a heart instead of a spade. The Netherlands declarer duly took the same 11 tricks as in the other room, thereby retaining their 0.5 IMP lead and winning the world championship by the narrowest conceivable margin. Had they avoided the earlier penalty for slow play, the Americans would have been world champions instead.

Right: The Venice Cup is awarded for the women's world championship, held every two years. Each team member receives a miniature version of the trophy.

Who would have guessed then that there would be a similarly exciting Venice Cup final only two years later? Germany faced France in the final and with only 16 boards to be played, the French led by a full 46.5 IMPs. The Germans played strongly and were within touch when the board shown below hit the table.

At both tables West opened with a weak two-bid and North doubled for take-out. Both Souths responded 3♦ and there was no more bidding at the other table, where the French declarer scored +130 for ten tricks. Here 3♦ had suggested around 8–10 points

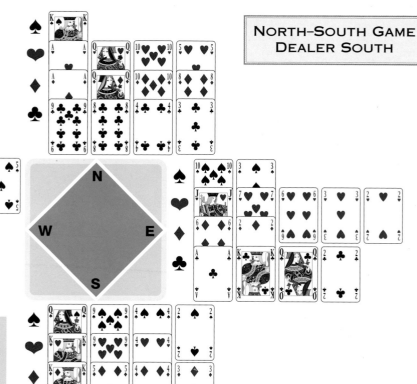

USA TEAMS IN THE VENICE CUP
♠ ♥ ♦ ♣

By virtue of its number of bridge players, the USA enters two teams for the Venice Cup whereas all other countries may have a maximum of one (if they qualify from their continental championship). In the Venice Cups where two American teams have participated, their second team has in fact won three times and the first team has won once.

Right: A brave player and a spectacular recovery. Daniela von Arnim deduces the lie of the heart suit, thereby winning the world championship.

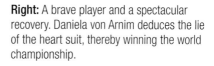

West	North	East	South
Bessis	Auken	D'Ovidio	von Arnim
			Pass
2♠	Dbl	Pass	3♦
Pass	3♠	Pass	3NT
End			

(because South would have bid a conventional 2NT to show a hand of 0–7 points). Auken probed with 3♠ and the Germans duly arrived in 3NT.

After an unlikely club lead, the French defenders would have claimed the first five tricks. This would have defeated the contract and given the French team the world championship. West, however, made the natural lead of the ♠7. Dummy's ♠K won the trick and declarer now needed eight red-suit tricks to make her game. She played three rounds of diamonds and East discarded a heart on the third round. All now depended on how von Arnim played the heart suit. West had shown up with nine cards in spades and diamonds to East's four,

so East figured to hold the heart length. East would scarcely discard a heart if she had begun with four cards in the suit, so von Arnim correctly deduced that East must have started with five hearts. She crossed to the ace of hearts and boldly finessed the nine of hearts on the second round. She could then cash the king of hearts and enter dummy with the fourth round of diamonds to score the heart queen.

Germany moved into a 2.5 IMP lead and, when the last board proved to be flat, that was their eventual winning margin. The German women had won the last set 51–2, making it one of the most exciting fight-backs on record.

THE BRIDGE OLYMPIAD

Following the tradition, the Bridge Olympiad is contested every four years, in different locations around the world. The event was first held in 1960, with France winning the open championship and the United Arab Republic the women's championship. Since then, France has won the open event a further three times. Italy has won five times and there are three one-time winners: USA, Poland and Brazil. The USA has had four wins in the women's event, Italy two wins and several countries have enjoyed one win: Great Britain, Sweden, Denmark, Austria and Russia.

Twenty-nine teams contested the first Open Olympiad in 1960, including two from Sweden and no fewer than four from the USA. (The USA Spingold 2 team was packed with big names: Charles Goren, Harold Ogust, Paul Allinger, Lew Mathe, Helen Sobel and Howard Schenken.) Nowadays only one team is permitted from each country. To get a flavour of the 1960 event, we will look at a slam deal from the match between Italy and USA Vanderbilt I.

It was the Italian style of bidding to respond in their second-best suit (here clubs) when they held a strong hand, a method known as "canapé responses".

Chiaradia's 3♦ rebid showed long diamonds and the Italians then wasted little time in reaching a small slam in the suit. The USA West led the ♠A, winning the first trick. He then found the best switch of a heart, forcing the Italian declarer to decide immediately whether to finesse in hearts (before he could see whether he had four club tricks and therefore a discard for his potential heart loser). With little to guide him, Chiaradia eventually decided to finesse the ♥Q and went one down.

At the other table the American declarer, Norman Kay, played in just 5♦ from the North hand. After a spade to the ace and a heart switch, he could not afford to finesse in case he lost a heart trick and a heart ruff. He rose with the ♥A playing safe, and duly made an overtrick when clubs proved to be 3–3.

**EAST–WEST GAME
DEALER NORTH**

Right: A sharp defence forces the Italian declarer to a critical guess.

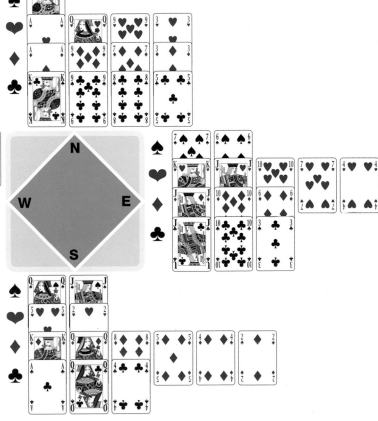

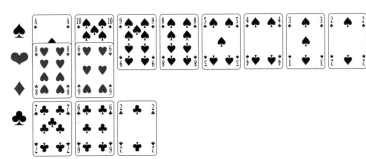

West	North	East	South
Rapee	Forquet	Silodor	Chiaradia
	1♥	Pass	2♣
2♠	3♣	Pass	3♦
Pass	3♠	Pass	6♦
End			

Twenty years later, in the 1980 Olympiad event, France and the USA qualified for the final. The Americans were desperate for their first win in the event but the French, led by Paul Chemla, had other ideas. The deal below received much publicity. Robert Hamman (USA) found himself on lead against a grand slam with two aces in his hand. He had to decide which ace to lead and the fate of the grand slam rested on his choice.

Right: Bob Hamman faces an important decision on which ace to lead against a vulnerable grand slam.

> ## THE VANDERBILT TROPHY
> ♠ ♥ ♦ ♣
> Every four years the winners of the Open Olympiad receive the Vanderbilt Trophy. It was presented for the first time at the 1960 Olympiad in Turin, by Harold S. Vanderbilt, to the victorious French team.

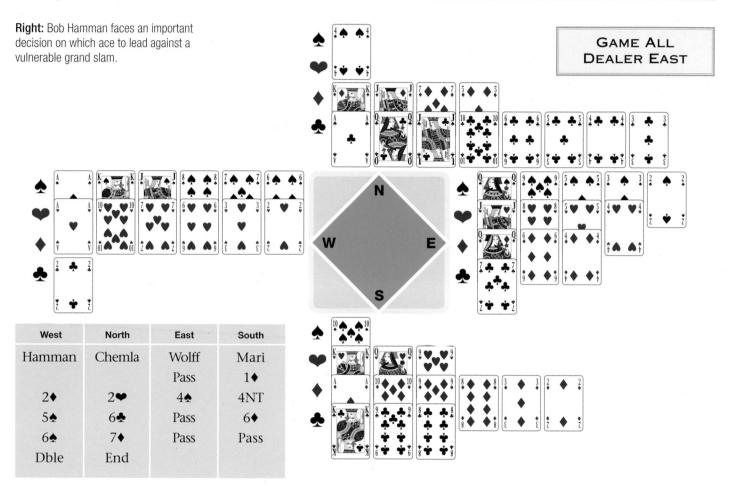

> GAME ALL
> DEALER EAST

West	North	East	South
Hamman	Chemla	Wolff	Mari
		Pass	1♦
2♦	2♥	4♠	4NT
5♠	6♣	Pass	6♦
6♠	7♦	Pass	Pass
Dble	End		

Hamman's 2♦ overcall was a Michaels cue-bid, showing at least five cards in each of the major suits. Chemla's 2♥, also a bid in an opponent's suit, showed strong diamond support. Wolff raised to the game-level in spades and Mari indicated a hand that was suitable for a slam with his bid of 4NT. Hamman attempted to buy the contract at the six-level eventually by bidding only 5♠ for the moment. Chemla showed his second suit of clubs and Mari corrected back to diamonds. Hamman continued with his plan by bidding his spades one more time.

At the other table the auction went no higher. The American North–South pair doubled the French in 6♠ and took the contract one down after a lead of the ♣A. At this table the great French player, Paul Chemla, aimed for greater things by bidding the grand slam in diamonds. Hamman doubled and all now depended on his choice of opening lead. His partner had raised spades to the four-level and would therefore hold longer spades than hearts. This suggested that the ♥A was more likely to stand up (in other words, not be ruffed). Hamman duly led this card and had to suffer the agony of seeing Mari ruff in the dummy. Knowing that West was long in both major suits and therefore likely to be short in diamonds, Mari cashed the ♦K on the first round. When West showed out, declarer was able to finesse the ♦J, draw trumps and claim the doubled grand slam. The swing was 2,130 aggregate points, which converts to 19 IMPs. France eventually won the match by 131–111.

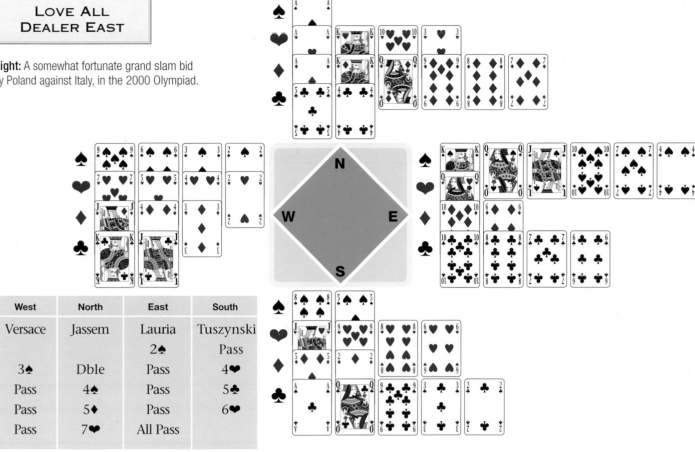

LOVE ALL
DEALER EAST

Right: A somewhat fortunate grand slam bid by Poland against Italy, in the 2000 Olympiad.

West	North	East	South
Versace	Jassem	Lauria	Tuszynski
		2♠	Pass
3♠	Dble	Pass	4♥
Pass	4♠	Pass	5♣
Pass	5♦	Pass	6♥
Pass	7♥	All Pass	

Continuing to sample the great action over the years, we will move forward another two decades. The grand slam shown above arose in the 2000 Open Olympiad with Italy facing Poland.

The Italian East opened with a weak two-bid, raised to the three-level, and Jassem made a take-out double. When partner responded 4♥ North might well have passed (indeed, in the Women's Olympiad, Mildred Breed did pass for the USA). He continued with 4♠ (once trumps have been agreed, hearts here, a bid in a new suit at this level is a "control-showing cue-bid", usually showing the ace of the suit bid). After two further cue-bids, Tuszynski leapt to 6♥. Placing partner with the ♣A and hoping that his hearts were headed by the queen, Jassem raised to 7♥.

Versace, West for Italy, led a trump and East's queen fell under dummy's king. Declarer cashed the ♠A, crossed to the ♥8 and ruffed his last spade with the ♥A. He then overtook the ♥10 with the ♥J, drew trumps and ran dummy's diamond suit to discard the four club losers in his hand. Grand slam made! At the other table the Polish East opened 3♠, raised defensively to 4♠. North doubled and there was no further bidding. The Italians collected only 300, losing 15 IMPs on the board.

Above: The Vanderbilt Trophy. Due to the generous provision made by Harold S. Vanderbilt, each member of the winning team receives a silver replica of the trophy.

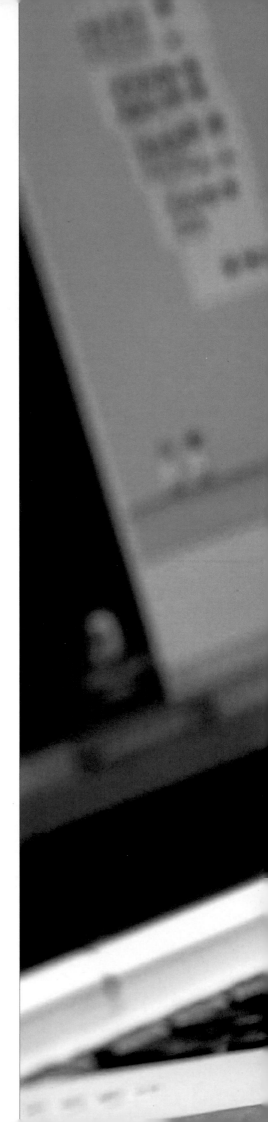

CHAPTER 3

BRIDGE ON THE COMPUTER

There are two main ways in which you can play bridge on your computer. You can install a bridge-playing program and then compete against three robot players, whose bids and plays are calculated by the computer. Alternatively, you can join one of several Internet sites that allow you to play bridge with and against human players from around the world. The screen appearance will be similar in both cases. You will click on a bidding table to select your bid and click on one of your cards to select which one to play. These bridge-playing programs fight amongst themselves to determine which can win the world computer bridge championship. Finally, it is now possible (using the free software: Bridge Base Online) to watch many of the world's top tournaments on the Internet. The cards and bids are shown in the same way as when you are playing bridge yourself. International commentators add their comments and analysis so you can follow the passage of play.

Right: Playing bridge on the Internet is popular because you do not have to plan a session in advance. With an hour to spare, you can log on and join a game immediately.

PLAYING BRIDGE AGAINST THE COMPUTER

By using the Internet, you can play with human players from around the world. Alternatively, without needing to access the Internet, you can play bridge on your own computer. Your partner and your opponents will be provided by software that runs on your machine. They will bid and play their cards automatically. The early bridge-playing programs were disappointingly weak, making poor bids and even worse plays. However, they have greatly improved in the last few years and can now give you an entertaining game.

There are many such software packages on the market (including Jack, Q-Plus, Bridge Baron and GIB). The saved screen below reflects the bidding of a hand on GIB. The human player (South) was playing

with three computer-generated players, and the deal came from a supplied library of deals from real tournaments. In this case it was from the 2002 Cap Gemini tournament. The human player decided to double 3♠ at this stage. He led the ♥Q against 3♠ doubled and declarer lost two clubs, a diamond and three trump tricks, going two down for a 500 penalty.

Below: A screen from the GIB computer-playing software, taken at a moment South is about to bid.

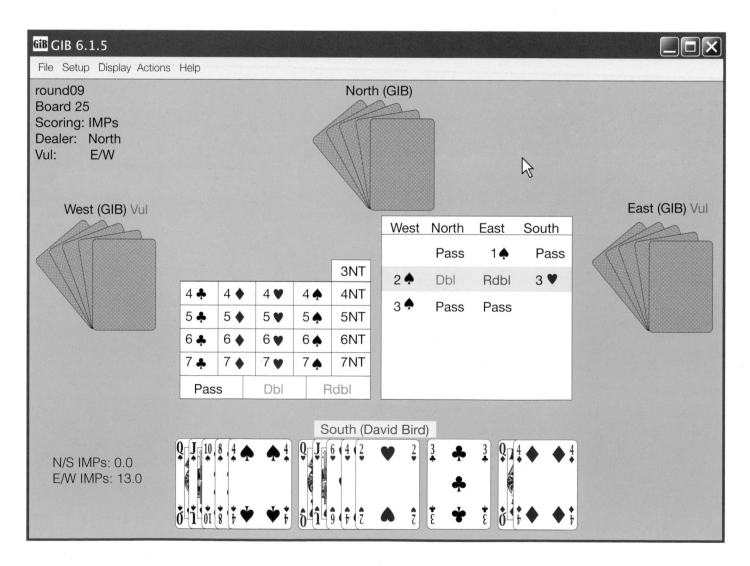

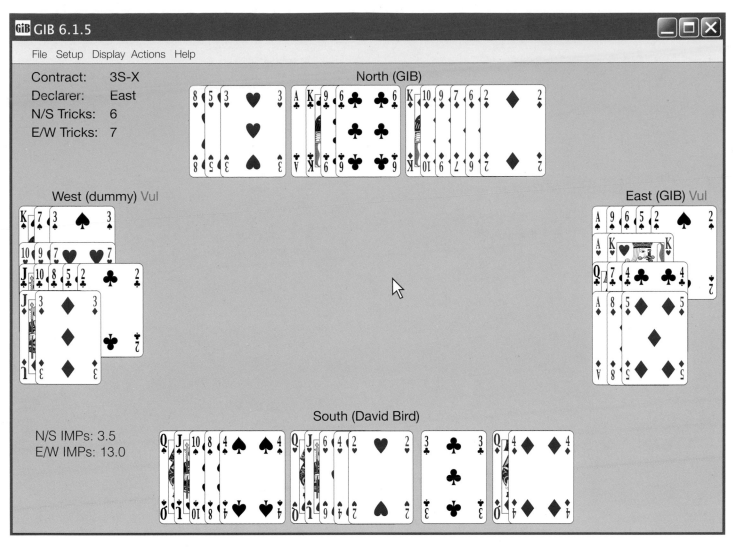

Above: A screen from the GIB computer-playing software, just after completion of the play.

This was the screen at the end of play (above). The score-sheet from the original event reveals that +500 is worth +3.5 International Match Points (IMPs) when compared with the average result. A good bridge-playing package will offer you some means of judging how well you have performed. In other words, you need other scores for a comparison. Either the software can replay the deal, with four computer players, or it can use deals from real tournaments, as we have just seen.

You may wonder how such packages are programmed. GIB decides which card to play by creating several sets of random hands for the two unseen players – hands that match the bidding and the play so far. It then sees which card will produce the best result, by playing each random deal to its conclusion. For example, if playing the ♠9 wins on 15 of the 20 random deals and playing the ♠Q wins on only 12, it will play the ♠9. This is much more effective than trying to program general rules such as "second hand low". Indeed, when a super-powered version of GIB competed against world-class players at

a recent world championship, it was placed halfway up the field. This was a phenomenal achievement when you bear in mind how weak bridge-playing programs were in the early days.

North	East	South	West	Contract	Declarer	Result	Score	IMPs
Chagas	Pszczola	Brenner	Kwiecien	3S-X	East	down 3	+800	+9.5
SaelensmindeSacul	Brogeland	Versace	Karwur	3S-X	East	down 2	+500	+3.5
Ravenna	Gawrys	Madala	Jassem	3C-X	West	down 2	+500	+3.5
Westra	Stansby	Leufkens	Gitelman	3S-X	East	down 2	+500	+3.5
GIB 6.1.3	GIB 6.1.3	David Bird	GIB 6.1.3	3S-X	East	down 2	+500	+3.5
Garozzo	Muller	Versace	De Wigs	2H	South	made 3	+140	-5.37
Robson	Auken	Mahmood	Reps	2D	North	made 4	+130	-5.87
Verhees	Gromov	Jansma	Peturin	2D	North	made 4	+130	-5.87
Helness	Weinstein	Helgemo	Gamer	2D	North	made 3	+110	-6.37

Board Results

Click OK to continue to next deal.
click on a line to see the hand record
or select from the menus.

Above: By comparing your own result with those obtained by the players in the original tournament, you can assess how well you fared.

WATCHING BRIDGE ON THE INTERNET

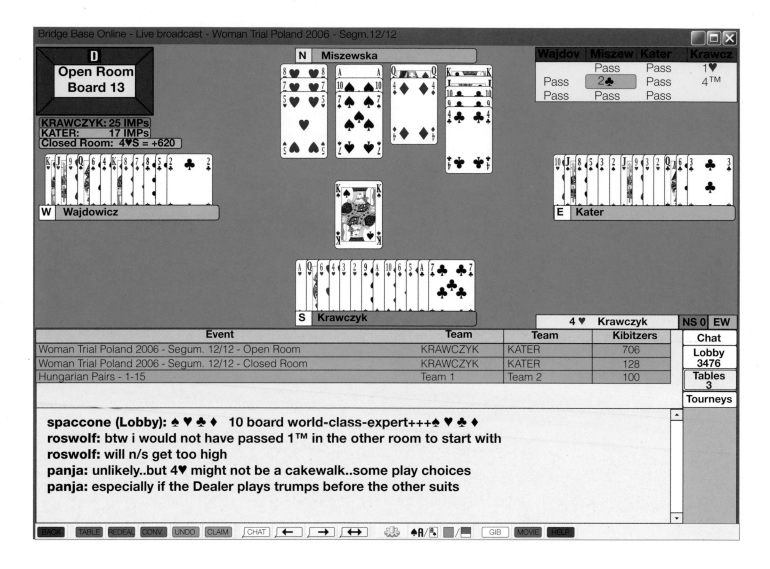

Above: A screen from Bridge Base Online, taken just after the opening lead has been made.

Once upon a time it would cost you a fortune in air fares and hotel bills to watch the world's top bridge tournaments. Not now! The Internet site Bridge Base Online, web address: http://online.bridgebase. com, allows you to watch all the world championships and many big tournaments, internationals and trials absolutely free. You can also play bridge online yourself, on the same site.

The screen capture above shows a live broadcast in progress from the 2006 Women's Trials in Poland. During the auction the bids gradually appear in a bidding table in the centre of the dark green baize. When the auction is over and play begins, the auction is reduced in size and moved to the top-right corner. You can see there that Krawczyk, the South player, opened 1♥ in the third seat. Her partner responded 2♣.

This is shown with a different colour background because it was a conventional bid (Drury, to show a maximum pass with three-card heart support). South then leapt to the heart game and West has just led the ♠K.

As the bidding and the play progress, expert commentators add their thoughts in the grey space at the bottom of the screen. The commentator whose BBO identifier is "panja" has just expressed the view that declarer may be in trouble if she decides to play trumps straight away. Kibitzers (watchers) are not allowed to add comments to this box. Only the approved expert commentators are "switched on", as it is called. However, the kibitzers frequently send their questions and views to the commentators, who may then reply within a private conversation.

At the top left, just below the red box, you can see the current score in the match. Krawczyk has 25 IMPs and Kater has 17. Also given is the result from the other room (the Closed Room) for this particular deal. South bid to 4♥ and made ten tricks for a score of +620. If the South player here, in the Open Room, can achieve the same result, it will be a flat board and there will be no swing in International Match Points (IMPs). (In duplicate matches, the aggregate difference between the scores at the two tables is converted into IMPs.)

You can see from the position of the white-arrow cursor that the BBO user who made this screen capture had just clicked on the "Tables" icon. That is why the three lines shaded in pale green appear. They inform the user that there are three broadcasts currently being transmitted, two from different tables at the Polish Women's Trials and one from the Hungarian pairs championship. As you see, a total of some 934 viewers are logged on. During a major championship such as the Bermuda Bowl, there will be many thousands of viewers.

Finally, look at the icons on the bottom row of the screen. Pressing BACK would take you out of the VuGraph room. You would use this if you perhaps wanted to play bridge on BBO, rather than watch this match. Or you might choose to look through the large record of VuGraph presentations from tournaments over the past few years. Further along is the CHAT button. You would press this if you wanted to ask one of the commentators a question, or talk to a friend of yours who was also watching. A box would then pop up into which you could type your question or comment, also the identity of the person you wanted to talk to.

Further icons allow you to change the appearance of the playing cards or to reduce in size the comment portion of the screen. Pressing the GIB button sets software in motion that will analyze the present hand double-dummy and show which plays will be successful for the current player. Finally, the MOVIE button allows you to see a scorecard of the entire session. You can look back on any deal from the session and remind yourself how the bidding and the play went.

It is a great piece of software. When a big tournament is being shown from, say, China, there might be English commentary from one table and Chinese commentary from the other. Flip to the Chinese table and all the experts' comments would appear in Chinese characters!

VUGRAPH OPERATORS

You may wonder how all the bids and plays appear on the screen. A "Vugraphic operator" attends the tournament being relayed, sitting close to the players with a laptop computer. He types in all the bids and plays and the Bridge Base software then sends the information over the internet to all the spectators who are watching online.

Right: To watch or play bridge online, you need to download and install the free Bridge Base Online software, from http://online.bridgebase.com.

PLAYING BRIDGE ON THE INTERNET

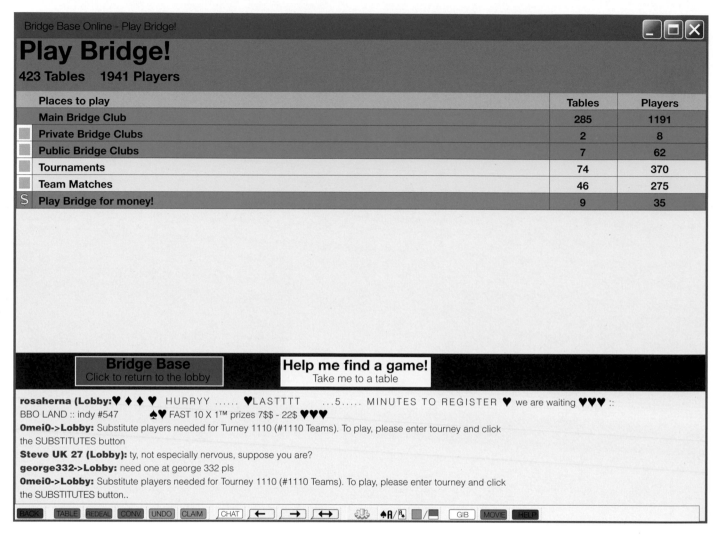

Above: A screen from Bridge Base Online, offering various types of bridge to the user.

The same Internet packages that allow you to watch top-class tournaments will also allow you to play bridge yourself. You can play with a partner and opponents from any part of the world. Each player invokes the software on his own machine and the magic of the Internet allows all the players to see the bids and plays that everyone makes. You might, for example, play with an Australian partner against two opponents from the Netherlands.

The saved screen above shows the various types of bridge game that might be offered. You could choose to play in a friendly, social game. Perhaps you would prefer to play in a teams-of-four or pairs tournament. The software, Bridge Base Online in this illustration, arranges many such tournaments each day. Perhaps you even want to play for money. That is possible too, as with the similar poker sites. Once you have entered a tournament, or joined a social table, the deals appear one at a time on the screen. If it is a

social game, you can leave the game at any stage, allowing a new player to take your place. The software will maintain records of all the boards you have played and will provide statistical evaluation of your long-term success (or otherwise!) If this makes you nervous, you can always decline to make your true identity known to other players.

MOMENT OF REALIZATION
♠ ♥ ♦ ♣

Edgar Kaplan, one of the USA's greatest ever players, said: "I decided I was a good bridge player when I found out that people whose names I had heard all my life, people I respected, did the same dumb things that I did."

We are looking at the screen (below) as the East player will see it. Only his own cards are visible at this stage because the bidding is in progress. His partner opened 1NT and he is about to respond 2♦, a transfer bid that shows at least five hearts. He does this by clicking on the "2" (he has already done this, so it is shown in yellow) and then clicking on the diamond symbol just below. To alert the opponents, he has also typed in the meaning of his bid ("transfer") and will mouse-click on the "Alert" button, so that they are made aware of his conventional bid. Once the auction is completed and the play of the cards begins, declarer and the defenders will click on the card that they wish to play to each trick. Declarer may also CLAIM a contract, to save time. In some types of game, the players are allowed to request an UNDO if they have selected some bid or play erroneously.

As when watching a session, a player can press the MOVIE button, bottom right, to look at the scoresheet. He may then select one of the deals to see again the hands, the bidding and how the play went. He may also press the CHAT button to type in a message to the other three players at the table. It will appear in the currently empty grey space in the bottom half of the screen.

When you first log on to such a site you are prompted to choose a name by which you will be known as a player. You can choose a representation of your actual name or a fictional name such as "Cloudy" or "simpleboi", as we see here. It is up to you whether, in your profile, you give your personal details or prefer to remain anonymous.

One of the advantages of playing online is that you do not have to pre-plan a session or arrange a partner. If you feel like playing bridge for an hour or so, you simply log on and join three other players for a few hands.

Most players like to play against opponents of a similar standard to themselves. You may therefore see messages on the Home Panel such as "Two experts needed at table Alan109, please."

Below: A screen from Bridge Base Online, as seen by East when he is about to make a transfer bid.

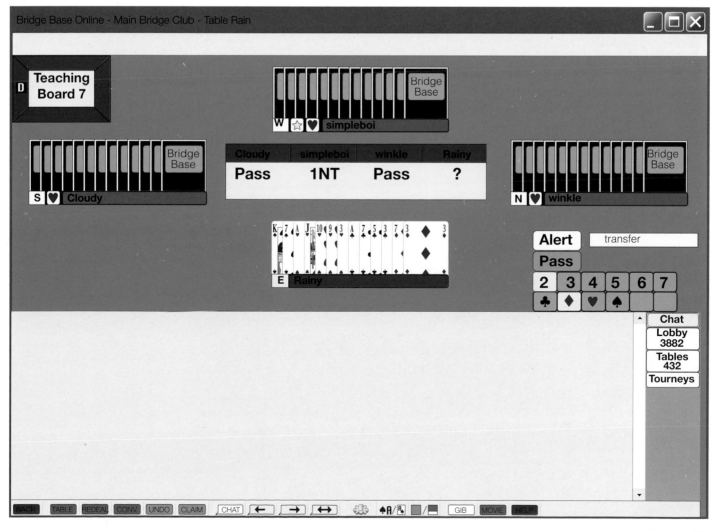

CHAPTER 4

BASIC BIDDING

To bid well with your partner, you must each strive to paint a clear picture of your hand as quickly as possible. This section covers various opening bids that begin this process, including one no-trump (1NT) and suit openings at the one-level. You will also see how to respond to such opening bids. The objective for both players will be to make a "limit bid" as soon as possible, so that partner can add his strength to that shown and calculate whether a game should be bid. The opener's rebid (his second bid) and the responder's rebid come next. Finally it will be explained how such auctions are completed. Strong openings of 2♣ and 2NT will be described, also weak (pre-emptive) openings at both the two-level and the three-level. After a discussion of higher pre-emptive bids, you will see how to bid accurately after the opponents have opened the bidding.

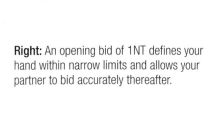

Right: An opening bid of 1NT defines your hand within narrow limits and allows your partner to bid accurately thereafter.

OPENING ONE NO-TRUMP (1NT)

An opening bid of 1NT shows that your hand is balanced. It defines the high-card strength to within a couple of points. The shape will be 4–4–3–2 (in other words: two four-card suits, one three-card suit and one two-card suit), 4–3–3–3 or 5–3–3–2 with a five-card minor. Occasionally some players will venture a 1NT opening with 5–3–3–2 shape and a five-card major. There are two main variations, so far as the number of points is concerned. You can either play a "strong 1NT" of 15–17 points or a "weak 1NT" of 12–14 points.

The strong 1NT

A strong 1NT of 15–17 points has a very large following worldwide and that is the method assumed in other chapters of this book. This chapter will look at some examples of both types of 1NT. The first three hands shown below are all prime examples of the strong 1NT:

1

Hand (1) is suitable in every way. It has 16 points (an ace is worth 4 points, a king 3 points, a queen 2 points and a jack 1 point). It also has 4–4–3–2 shape and a "stopper" in every suit. (A stopper is a card combination, such as K–2 or Q–9–3, that may stop the defenders from scoring several immediate winners in the suit.)

2

You would open 1NT on hand (2) as well. Do not be deterred by the fact that you hold a low doubleton in one of the suits. The problem with opening 1♣ instead is that after a response of 1♠ you would have no satisfactory

rebid (as we will see later, a rebid of 1NT would show 12–14 points).

3

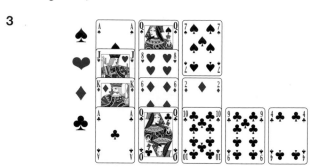

Hand (3) is a strong 1NT that contains a five-card minor. Again you would not open 1♣ instead because this might cause a problem with your rebid. When you play the strong 1NT, look for a different opening bid when you hold 12–14 points and a balanced hand. Suppose you have to choose a bid on this hand:

4

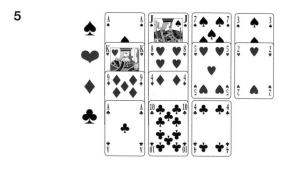

Many players who use the strong 1NT also favour five-card majors (where an opening bid of 1♠ or 1♥ promises at least five cards). This does not cause any problem on (4) because you can open 1♣. If partner responds 1♦ or 1♠, you will rebid 1NT to show 12–14 points.

5

Hand (5) is more difficult. You cannot open a strong 1NT because you are too weak. Neither can you open 1♠ or 1♥ because you do not hold a five-card major. You are therefore forced to open 1♣ on a three-card suit.

6

Hand (6) is even more awkward. There are two schools of thought on the best way to treat it. Some players use a method known as "better minor" and are willing to open 1♦ (as well as 1♣) on a three-card suit. Others prefer an opening bid of 1♦ to promise at least four diamonds and are therefore willing to open 1♣ even when they hold only a doubleton in the suit.

The weak 1NT

Exponents of the weak 1NT favour the bid because hands in the 12–14 point range arise more frequently and they like to open 1NT as often as possible. It is not a clear-cut advantage because when you hold the lower range there is more chance that someone will open in front of you. You would open a weak 1NT on any of these hands:

7

You would be right in thinking that (7) is not much of a hand and is barely worth an opening bid. Although that is true you should think of the weak 1NT as being similar to a pre-emptive bid. By opening 1NT, you could make it much harder for the opponents to bid accurately, should they hold the majority of the points.

8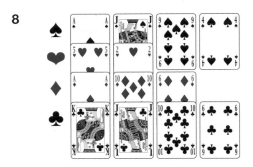

Open a weak 1NT on (8) too. Do not be deterred by the low doubleton in hearts.

9

Hand (9) is an example of a weak 1NT that contains a five-card minor.

When you are playing a weak 1NT and you hold a balanced hand of 15–17 points, you open one of a suit with the intention of rebidding in no-trumps. If you play a five-card major system, you may (as with the strong 1NT) sometimes have to open on a three-card minor suit.

FACING THE CHAMPIONS
♠ ♥ ♦ ♣

Bridge is unique among all games and sports in that it gives you a chance to compete directly against the most famous players in the world. If you enter a big tournament in London, Paris or New York, for example, there is every chance that you and your partner may find yourselves facing a pair of world champions. This could never happen in games like golf or tennis, where expert players compete only against each other.

RESPONDING TO 1NT

When your partner has opened 1NT, you have an excellent picture of his hand and will immediately have a good idea whether the combined hands will produce a part score, a game or a slam. If you are playing a strong 1NT of 15–17 points, you will want to be in game when you hold 10 points or more in the hand opposite. With 17 points upwards, or a strong hand with one or more long suits, your thoughts will turn towards a slam. Sometimes you will be uncertain whether to bid a game or a slam and will therefore seek some way to invite your partner's cooperation.

Responding on a weak hand

On most hands in the range of 0–7 points, you will either want to pass 1NT or to suggest playing at the two-level in a suit where you hold at least five cards. We will see in a moment that a response of 2♣ has a special meaning. These are your options on a weak hand:

Pass	no interest in game and no long suit (except, possibly, clubs)
2♦	no interest in game, at least five diamonds
2♥	no interest in game, at least five hearts
2♠	no interest in game, at least five spades.

These three two-level responses are known as "weakness take-outs". Partner will not bid again. A 1NT opening is an example of a "limit bid", a bid that defines the hand very accurately. It is a sound principle that you should allow partner to control the auction, once you have made a limit bid.

Above: Stayman auction. Partner has invited a game and, with a maximum of 17 points, you accept.

The Stayman convention

When you hold at least enough strength to invite a game (8+ points opposite a strong 1NT), you can bid 2♣ (the Stayman convention) to ask partner if he holds a four-card major. Your objective will be to find a 4–4 major suit fit, allowing you to make that suit trumps. After a start of 1NT – 2♣, the opener rebids as follows:

2♦	"I have no four-card major."
2♥	"I have four hearts (and may also have four spades)."
2♠	"I have four spades."

This is a typical Stayman auction:

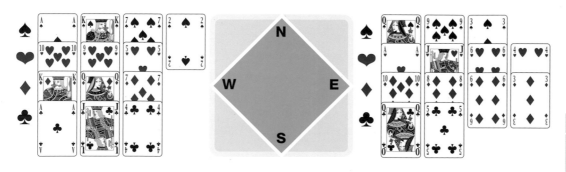

West	East
1NT	2♣
2♠	2NT
3NT	

East bids Stayman to look for a 4–4 heart fit. If West were to rebid 2♥, he would invite a heart game by raising to 3♥. When West instead rebids 2♠, East invites game in no-trumps by bidding 2NT. Since West's hand is in the top half of the 15–17 point range, he bids 3NT.

Inviting a game

When you hold 9 points, or a good 8 points, you can invite game by raising 1NT to 2NT. The opener will accept the invitation when he is in the upper range for his opening bid. On a 15-count he would usually pass. We saw in the previous section that you can also invite a game after partner has responded to your Stayman bid.

Bidding game

When you hold 10 points or more, and therefore want to be in game even opposite a minimum strong 1NT, you can bid a game contract immediately. If you are sure you want to play in no-trumps, you raise 1NT to 3NT. If you hold at least six spades or six hearts, you can bid game in that major. Occasionally you might want to bid game in a minor, but remember that it is usually easier to make nine tricks in no-trumps.

When you have enough for game or slam, and a suit of at least five cards, you can seek trump support by making a forcing bid at the three-level. This is a typical auction:

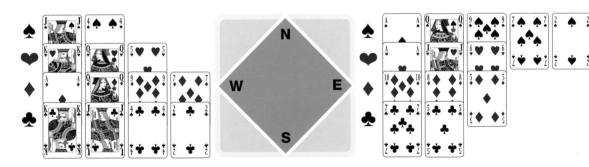

West	East
INT	3♠
3NT	

East's 3♠ shows enough points for game, at least, and a five-card spade suit. Since West has only two spades, he bids 3NT. With three or more spades, he would know that the partnership held at least eight trumps and would bid 4♠ instead.

East has enough points for a game contract but not sufficient to consider a slam. He therefore passes 3NT and that becomes the final contract. If instead he held around 18 points, he would raise 3NT to 6NT.

BIDDING A MINOR SUIT
♠ ♥ ♦ ♣

Suppose your partner opens a 15–17 point 1NT and you hold a six-card minor suit and around 10 points. It is much more likely that you can make 3NT than 5♣ or 5♦. You should therefore respond 3NT rather than jumping to three of your suit.

OPENING ONE OF A SUIT

When your hand is unsuitable for an opening bid of 1NT, either because it is unbalanced or because it is not within the three-point range that you have chosen, you will usually open with a one-bid in one of the four suits. Many people use a bidding system where a five-card suit (or longer) is needed to open 1♥ or 1♠. When their only four-card suit is a major suit, they will therefore be forced to open 1♣ or 1♦ on a three-card suit. The range of an opening one-bid is very wide. You might sometimes open on as few as 10 points with a very good suit. On other occasions you might open a one-bid on as many as 20 points. It is with your second bid (the rebid) that you will define the strength of your hand more closely.

Choosing which four-card suit to bid

When you have no suit of five cards or more, you must choose which four-card suit to open. This choice may be influenced by whether you are playing a five-card major system. Suppose you are playing a strong 1NT and have to open on one of these hands:

1
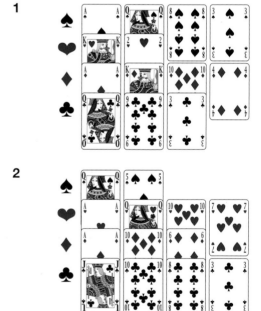

2

Hand (1) is too strong to open 1NT. You would open 1♦, if playing a five-card major system. Playing a four-card major system, such as Acol, you would open 1♠. Hand (2) is too weak for a strong 1NT. You would open 1♣ in a five-card major system and might do the same in Acol. You would open 1♥ only if your partnership treats the sequence 1♥ – 2♦ – 2NT as showing 12–14 points.

3
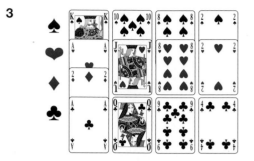

When you hold a hand of 4–4–4–1 shape, such as (3), don't follow any particular "rule" that you may have heard. Satisfy yourself that you will have a convenient rebid, should partner happen to respond in your short suit. Here you see that you can open 1♣. If partner responds 1♦, which is likely, you can rebid 1♥.

Choosing which five-card suit to bid

When you have two five-card suits, you normally open the higher suit (except when you hold both black suits). Again the choice of suit is based on ensuring a convenient rebid. Suppose you have to choose an opening bid on one of these hands:

4
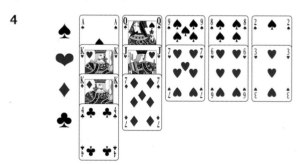

You open 1♠ on hand (4), planning to rebid 2♥. On a weak hand your partner will then be able to give preference to spades at the same level (rebidding 2♠).

5
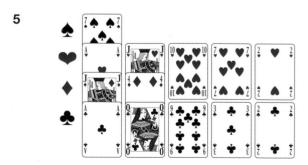

Similarly, you open 1♥ on (5). If partner responds 1♠ or 1NT, you will rebid 2♣ and again allow partner to return to your first suit at the same level of bidding.

6

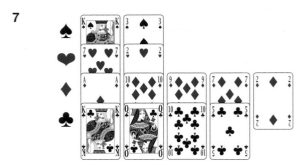

On (6) you would open 1♣, planning to rebid 1♠ and then to bid spades again on the following round (if applicable). However, if the hand was weaker and would not justify so many bids, you might open 1♠, to make certain that partner heard about your five-card spade suit.

COMPUTER DEALT HANDS
♠ ♥ ♦ ♣

From 1970 onwards, tournaments began to use computer-dealt hands. There was an immediate outcry that the deals were much more distributional than normal, with many more voids. Subsequent research showed that the deals were in accordance with the frequencies to be expected mathematically. The problem was that humans tended to deal hands from inadequately shuffled packs. For example, a trick containing four hearts might remain intact in the pack and each player would then receive one heart. This resulted in much more balanced hands being dealt than should be the case.

Left: Riffle shuffle. In the riffle shuffle, the two halves of the pack are interleaved, by running the thumbs from the bottom of each half to the top.

Opening on a 5–4 hand

When your shape is 5–4 in the two longest suits, it is generally best to open the five-card suit. This is the case even when the five-card suit is quite weak. The important point about choosing a trump suit is the length of the suit. You want to have as many trumps as possible. Look at these three hands:

7

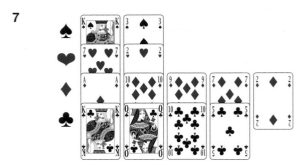

Hand (7) offers no problems at all. You open 1♦, planning to rebid 2♣.

8

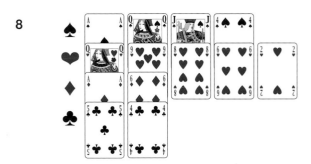

On (8) you should open 1♥. If partner responds 2♣ or 2♦, you are not strong enough to rebid 2♠ (we will see in a later section that such a rebid, carrying you past the safety level of two of your longest suit, is a strong bid). You would rebid either 2NT, if that shows 12–14 points in your system, or a simple 2♥.

9

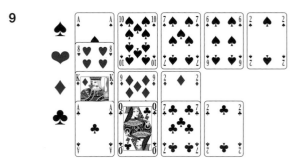

Similarly, on (9), you would open 1♠, planning to rebid 2♠ over a response of 2♥. A rebid of 3♣, carrying you to the three-level would show much greater strength.

RESPONDING TO ONE OF A SUIT

Responder has many options facing a one-level opening in a suit. With trump support, he can raise partner's suit. With a balanced hand, he can bid no-trumps at some level. If he follows either of these paths, he will give an accurate picture of how strong his hand is. The higher he bids, in general terms, the stronger he will be. A third option is to respond in a new suit. You will recall that an opening bid at the one-level covers a very wide range, about 10–20 points. Similarly a response in a new suit may be made on 6 points, also on 20 points. The first priority is to find a good trump suit. There will be an opportunity on the second round to show the strength of the two hands.

Raising partner's minor suit

When partner has opened 1♣ or 1♦, it is normal to respond in a four-card major even when you hold good support for partner's suit. That is because game in a major suit needs only ten tricks, whereas game in a minor suit requires 11 tricks. Suppose partner has opened 1♦ and you hold one of these hands:

1

2

On (1) you respond 1♠. Such a change of suit is forcing (in other words, partner must bid again). If partner rebids 2♣, you will give preference to 2♦.

You have no major to bid on (2) and will raise directly to 2♦, showing 6–9 points.

Hand (3) is stronger and you would raise to 3♦, showing 10–11 points.

3

Raising partner's major suit

When partner opens 1♥ or 1♠ and you have a fit, you raise to the level that you expect will be successful opposite a minimum hand. This is a rough guide, opposite a bid of 1♠:

2♠	6–9 points, maybe only three-card support
3♠	10–11 points, at least four-card support
4♠	12–14 points, at least four-card support.

The term "rough guide" was used because shape is important as well as high-card points. If you hold four-card trump support and a side-suit singleton, partner will be able to score some ruffs in the short-trump hand. The singleton is likely to be valuable and, on average, it is worth 2 or 3 points extra. A void is even more valuable, some authorities assigning it a value of 5 extra points. Suppose partner has opened 1♠ and you hold one of these hands:

4

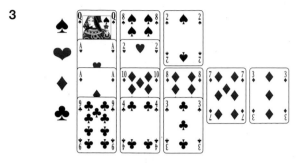

On (4) you should raise to 2♠, even if you play a four-card major system and partner may hold only four spades. He is likely to hold five spades, even so, and he may well be able to ruff a heart in your hand. Hand (5) contains a valuable singleton in clubs. This elevates the 9 point-count into a raise to 3♠. On hand (6) you are worth a raise to 4♠.

5

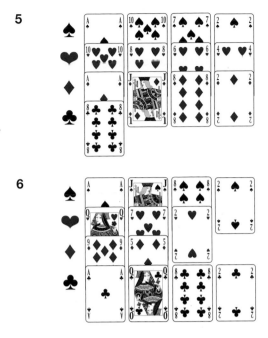

6

Above: With 13 points and a four-card spade fit, responder raises partner's 1♠ opening to 4♠.

Tournament players use various conventional bids to show game-strength hands with good trump support and we will see these in later sections. When such methods are used, a direct raise to 4♠ becomes pre-emptive, showing very good trump support but relatively few points.

JUMPING TO 3NT

♠ ♥ ♦ ♣

When partner opens with a one-bid in a suit, it is not attractive to leap all the way to 3NT. If the opener has a strong hand, you have robbed him of the space to describe it. It is better to make a low-level response in some other suit. If the opener shows a minimum hand, you can bid 3NT then.

Responding in no-trumps

When you respond in no-trumps, you give an accurate account of the number of points that you hold in your hand. A response of 1NT suggests about 6–10 points, 2NT shows 11–12 points and 3NT around 13–15. If you have space to show a four-card major at the one-level you should do that instead of responding in no-trumps.

Suppose partner has opened 1♦ and you hold one of these hands. We will see in a moment that hand (7) is not strong enough for a 2♣ response.

7

Since you have no suit to bid at the one-level, you respond 1NT.

8

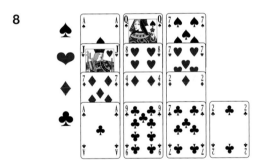

Hand (8) is stronger and you would respond 2NT. This is not forcing and partner is allowed to pass if he holds a minimum hand. With 14 or more points, he will advance to a game contract.

9

On (9) there is no hurry to bid no-trumps and you should respond 1♥ in case there is a 4–4 fit in that suit. You should bid 3NT if appropriate on the next round.

When partner has opened 1♥ or 1♠, there is no hurry to respond 2NT or 3NT. You can make a simple response in a minor at the two-level, intending to rebid in no-trumps on the next round. In this way you may find a fit, either in your suit or in the opener's. Suppose partner has opened 1♠ and you hold one of these hands:

10

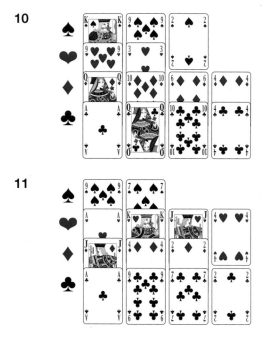

11

12

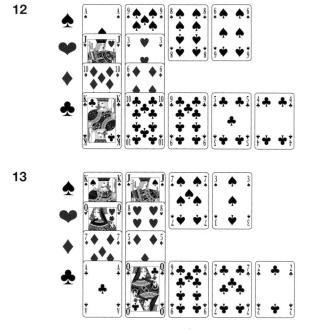

13

Above: With 13 points opposite an opening bid, a game should be bid. To discover more about partner's hand, you respond 2♣.

There are two reasons why you would not respond 2NT on (10). Firstly, you have no guard in hearts. Secondly, there is every reason to think that the hand will play well in spades, where partner is likely to hold a five-card suit (even if you play a four-card major system). You respond 2♣, showing the cheaper of your four-card suits. If the opener bids 2♥ or 2♦ next, you can be sure that he holds five spades

and will invite a game by jumping to 3♠. If you chose to respond 2NT instead, and partner passed on a minimum hand, you would have missed your 5–3 spade fit.

Similarly, on (11) you would not leap straight to 3NT. By doing so, you might miss a 4–4 heart fit. The correct response is 2♣, which leaves space for partner to introduce a four-card heart suit. Note that a response of 2♥ is nearly always based on a five-card heart suit.

Responding in a new suit

You can respond in a new suit at the one-level on 6 points or more. If you hold a five-major suit you can respond on only 5 points. A two-level response requires greater strength, since you will be carrying the bidding higher. In most bidding systems you need around 10 points for such a response.

Suppose partner has opened 1♦ and you must find a response on one of these hands:

You respond 1♠ on (12) because you are not strong enough for a two-level response. Also, you do not want to miss a 4–4 fit in spades. Hand (13) contains 12 points and you are therefore worth two bids. On such a hand you should show your longest suit first and then bid your other suit. You respond 2♣, intending to invite game by continuing with 2♠ over partner's 2♦ rebid.

14

When you have two four-card suits, as in (14), you respond in the cheaper suit. Here you respond 1♥. If the opener has four hearts with you, he will raise the hearts. If instead he holds four spades, you have given him the space to rebid 1♠ (which you will raise to 3♠, inviting a game).

When you hold two five-card suits in response, you bid the higher suit first. Suppose partner has opened 1♦ and you hold one of these hands:

15

You respond 1♠ on (15). Over a rebid of 2♦ you can bid 2♥ next. Partner will then be able to give preference to spades at the same level, rebidding 2♠.

16

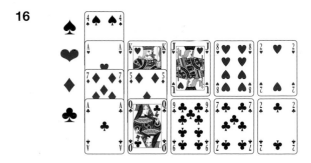

Similarly, you respond 1♥ on (16), intending to continue with 3♣ on the next round.

The jump shift

When you hold a hand that is so strong that you suspect a slam may be possible, you may give a jump response in a new suit (for example 1♥ – 3♣). This is known as a "jump shift". Because it uses up so much bidding space, the bid is used only on two types of hands: those that contain a powerful suit and those that contain very strong support for the opener's suit.

Suppose your partner has opened 1♥ and you hold one of these hands:

17

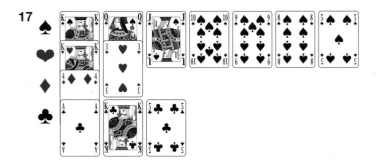

Hand (17) is fine for a jump shift of 2♠. You plan to rebid 3♠ on the next round to let partner know your jump shift was based on a very powerful suit.

18

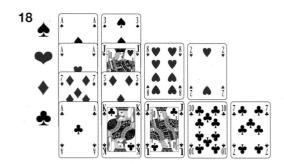

Hand (18) contains excellent support for partner's hearts and you will begin with a jump shift of 3♣, supporting hearts later.

19

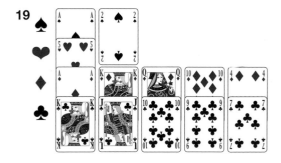

Hand (19) is very strong but it does not belong to either of the categories for a jump shift. You need time to find the best fit and cannot afford to waste space by jumping to 3♦ on the first round. Respond 2♦, intending to continue with a game-forcing 3♣.

OPENING 2♣ AND 2NT

When your hand is so strong that you have enough (or nearly enough) to make game on your own, you cannot afford to open with a one-bid. If your partner held fewer than six points, he might then pass and a game would be missed. There are two opening bids at the two-level that show a very strong hand:

2♣	shows (i) an unbalanced hand of game-going strength
	or (ii) a balanced hand of at least 23 points
2NT	shows a balanced hand of 20–22 points.

By opening with one of these bids, you ensure that you do not play a game hand at the one-level.

Opening 2♣

An opening bid of 2♣ is the strongest bid that you can make. It is an artificial bid and says nothing whatsoever about your holding in clubs. Partner will usually respond 2♦, to allow you to describe your hand further. If you rebid 2♥, 2♠, 3♣ or 3♦, you are showing your best suit and the bidding must continue to the game-level at least. If instead you rebid 2NT, you indicate a balanced hand of 23–24 points. Your partner is allowed to pass this when he has no more than 1 point in his hand. This is the only time that the bidding may stop short of game after a 2♣ opening.

You would open 2♣ on any of the three hands shown below:

1

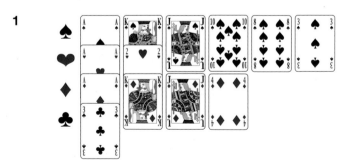

Even with a weak hand opposite, you are very likely to make 4♠ on hand (1). If you opened only 1♠ and this was passed out, you would be worried indeed that game had been missed. You open 2♣, intending to rebid 2♠ and the bidding will continue to the game-level at least.

Hand (2) is a balanced 23-count. You will rebid 2NT over 2♦, allowing partner to pass when he holds a valueless hand. If he makes any further bid over 2NT, the bidding must continue to game.

2

Hand (3) is stronger, with 26 points. You will rebid 3NT to make sure that game is reached. Knowing you hold such a strong hand, your partner will often advance to a slam. The range for a 3NT rebid is 25–27. On the rare occasions when you hold a balanced hand of 28–30 points, you will indicate this by rebidding 4NT.

3

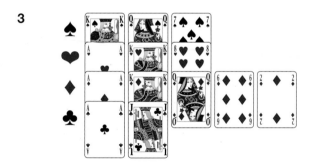

OLD FASHIONED
TWO BIDS
♠ ♥ ♦ ♣

In the first decades of contract bridge, opening bids of 2♦, 2♥ and 2♠ showed a powerful hand with a strong holding in the suit that had been bid. Hands that would justify such a "strong two bid" arose infrequently. It was eventually thought preferable to use "weak two bids", which show a hand of around 6–10 points and a six-card suit. Such hands arise much more frequently. When you do pick up a powerful hand with a long suit, you must either open at the one level or bid 2♣.

Responding to 2♣

On most hands responder will bid 2♦. This keeps the auction low and does not preclude strong bidding thereafter. When responder has a good suit, such as ♥K–Q–J–8–3 and perhaps another good card outside, then a positive response of 2♥ is best. You can also make a positive response in no-trumps (2NT) when you hold a balanced hand of 9 points or more. Usually the two hands will be worth a slam when a positive response is made.

Opening 2NT

You open 2NT with a balanced hand of 20–22 points. It would not be safe to open with a one-bid on such a hand because partner might pass with 4 or 5 points and you would miss a game. These hands are all suitable for a 2NT opening:

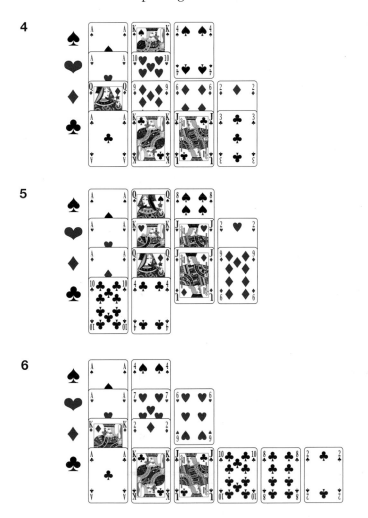

Hand (4) is a typical example, with a stopper in every suit. You may be worried about the clubs on hand (5) but go ahead and open 2NT. You give an excellent description of your hand by doing so. If partner raises to 3NT, the most likely place for his

honours is in clubs (because four of the missing eight picture cards are in that suit). Hand (6) is well worth 2NT too. Only 19 points, but that club suit entitles you to add a point or two. If you opened only 1♣ you might miss a game. Even if partner responded, you would have difficulty in describing such a strong hand.

Responding to 2NT

With fewer than 4 points and no particularly long suit, the responder should pass 2NT. A response of 3♣ is Stayman, asking for a four-card major. Responses of 3♦, 3♥ and 3♠ are game-forcing and show at least a five-card suit. The opener will generally raise the suit when he has three-card support and rebid 3NT otherwise.

> ### BIDDING OPPOSITE A 1NT OVERCALL
> ### ♠ ♥ ♦ ♣
>
> So far as is possible, it is a good idea to play the same methods in different circumstances. If you use Stayman and transfers opposite a 1NT opening, it makes good sense to use the same methods opposite a 1NT overcall. The same methods that you use facing a 2NT opening should be used after a start of 2♣ – 2♦ – 2NT, also opposite a natural 2NT overcall.

Above: A typical balanced 26-point hand. You would open 2♣ and rebid 3NT.

THE OPENER'S REBID

A player who has opened with a one-bid in a suit may regard his hand as belonging to one of three categories. Expressed solely in terms of point-count, they are (a) minimum, 12–15 points, (b) medium, 16–18 points and (c) strong 19–20 points. With his first rebid, he will usually specify into which of these classifications his hand falls. That is particularly the case if the responder's first response was a limit bid – either a raise of the opener's suit or a bid in no-trumps. We will look at the opener's rebid in the various situations that may arise.

Responder bid no-trumps

After a start such as 1♠ – 1NT, the opener may pass when he has a minimum hand with only five spades and no other suit of at least four cards. With six or more spades, he may rebid 2♠ on a minimum hand and a non-forcing 3♠ on a medium hand. On the deal below East has only one spade and decides to pass 3♠.

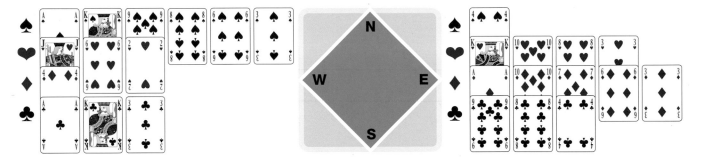

West	East
1♠	1NT
3♠	

The opener may rebid in a different suit (for example, 1♠ – 1NT – 2♦) on a suit of at least four cards. This is non-forcing, so when the opener sees a chance of game opposite a 1NT response he should consider bidding 2NT, or a game-forcing 3♦ instead.

A rebid of 2♣ would have led nowhere on the West hand shown below. Since West is strong enough to invite a game, but not strong enough to insist on one by rebidding 3♣, he chooses a raise to 2NT. On this occasion, East is happy to raise to 3NT.

West	East
1♠	1NT
2NT	3NT

After a start such as 1♠ – 2NT, a rebid of a new suit (such as 3♣) is forcing. A rebid of the opener's suit at the lowest level (3♠) shows a minimum hand and is non-forcing.

Responder raised the opener's major suit

When the responder raised opener's major suit (1♠ – 2♠), the opener will have a good idea whether a game is possible. If his hand is in the middle range and he cannot make up his mind whether to bid game or not, he will usually bid his second longest suit – a trial bid – to ask whether partner thinks a game is worth bidding. The responder can then see how well his own hand fits with the opener's second-best suit. A shortage opposite this suit will be beneficial.

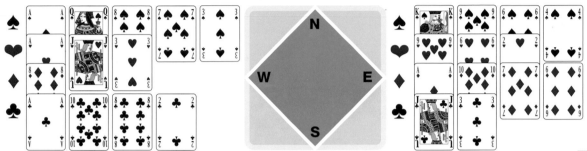

West makes a trial bid in clubs. East accepts the try because he holds a sound 8 points and a ruffing value in West's second longest suit. He expects West to score some club ruffs.

West	East
1♠	2♠
3♣	4♠

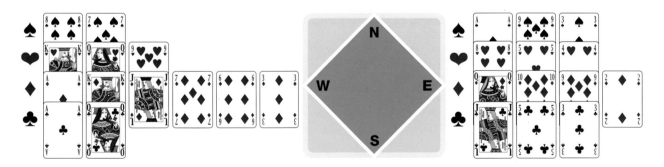

Responder raised the opener's minor suit

After a start of 1♦ – 2♦, or 1♦ – 3♦, the most likely game target (if any) will be 3NT. To this aim, a bid in a new suit shows a good stopper in that suit and requests partner to cooperate towards a no-trump contract. This would be a typical auction:

West	East
1♦	2♦
2♥	2♠
3NT	

Holding 19 points, West can visualize a game in no-trumps. He can hardly rebid 3NT with only a low doubleton in spades, so he consults his partner with a stopper-showing bid of 2♥. As you see, this does not promise four cards in the suit. Indeed, East is most unlikely to hold four hearts because he responded 2♦ instead of 1♥. East shows his spade stopper, by bidding 2♠, and West is sufficiently emboldened to leap to the no-trump game.

If East had rebid 3♣ or 3♦ instead, this would deny a spade stopper. Knowing that the spade suit was not stopped, West would rule out a no-trump contract. Game in diamonds might still be possible if East held the ♥A and West would invite a game by bidding 4♣.

The response was one of a suit

When the bidding starts with a bid in two different suits (such as 1♦ – 1♠), neither player has limited his hand; the final contract could be a part score or a grand slam. The opener will now usually limit his hand by making some bid in his own suit or the responder's suit, or by bidding no-trumps. These are the options that limit the opener's hand:

1NT	shows a balanced hand of the opposite range to a 1NT opener (15–17 points when 1NT is 12–14, and 12–14 points when 1NT is 15–17)
2♦	minimum hand with at least five diamonds
2♠	minimum hand with four-card spade support
2NT	18–19 points, balanced hand
3♦	medium hand, 16–18 points and at least 6 diamonds
3♠	medium hand with four-card spade support
3NT	strong hand with long diamonds, expecting to make nine tricks.

The opener may also bid a new suit. The point-count range for such rebids depends on whether the safety level of two of opener's suit has been breached:

2♣	wide range, 12–18 points
2♥	a "reverse", 17+ points and forcing
3♣	forcing to game.

Both 2♥ and 3♣ carry the bidding past the safety level of 2♦. They therefore show significantly more than a minimum opening bid.

Suppose the bidding starts 1♦ – 1♠ and you hold one of these hands:

1

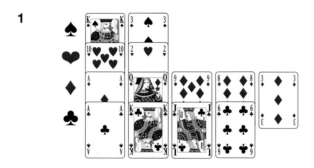

On (1) you would rebid a wide-range 2♣. You are not strong enough to force to game with 3♣.

2

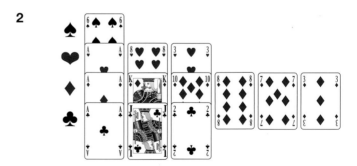

With hand (2) you would rebid a medium-range 3♦. This is non-forcing but partner can consider advancing to game with 9 points or more.

3

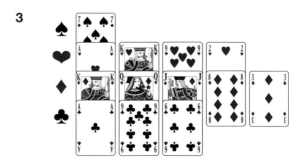

Hand (3) is strong enough for a reverse. You rebid 2♥.

The response was two of a new suit

A two-level response promises at least 10 points. It follows that the opener will want to reach a game contract when his hand is medium range or better. Remember that a medium-range opening hand will contain about 15–17 points. When the responder holds 10 points upwards, the total will be at least 25 points, which is enough for game. All the rebids that show extra strength are forcing to game.

Although a rebid of a new suit below the "safety level" (for example, 1♠ – 2♣ – 2♥) may be based on a minimum hand, it is convenient to play it as forcing for one round. (This is a fairly recent modification and you would have to discuss it with your partner.)

If you play a weak 1NT, it is normal to play a non-jump 2NT rebid as 15–17 (1♠ – 2♣ – 2NT). Since it is logical to play this as forcing to game, with at least 15 points facing 10, many players are willing to rebid 2NT on 15–19, leaving more space to find a fit. If instead you play a strong 1NT, then most players treat a 2NT rebid as weak (12–14).

These are the possibilities for the opener's rebid after a start of 1♠ – 2♦:

2♥	12–19, forcing for one round
2♠	12–14, minimum hand
2NT	15+ if you play a weak 1NT, 12–14 if you play a strong 1NT
3♣	15+, a "high reverse", game forcing
3♦	minimum hand with diamond support
3♠	15+, game-forcing with good spades.

Suppose, after a start of 1♠ – 2♦, you have to find a rebid on one of these hands:

4

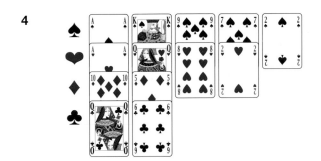

On (4) you expect to reach game eventually, with 15 points opposite partner's minimum of 10. For the moment, you should bid a simple 2♥, which is forcing for one round. You hope that partner can show support for one of your suits. If not, the most likely game will be 3NT.

5

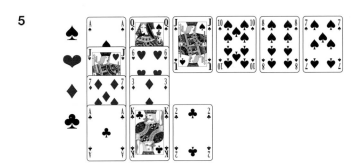

Since you want to reach game on hand (5) also, you cannot afford to rebid 2♠, which would show a minimum hand. You rebid 3♠ instead, forcing the bidding to the game level. This rebid shows a six-card spade suit, so partner will often raise to 4♠. When he is very short in spades, he may prefer to bid 3NT.

6

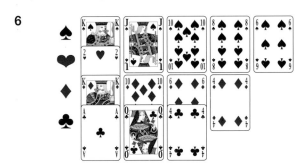

Hand (6) is suitable for a raise to 3♦, showing a minimum hand. If partner continues with 3♥, showing good values in hearts, your good stopper in clubs will allow you to bid 3NT. When partner has a strong hand with no heart stopper and cannot bid 3♠ to show spade support, you will have to play in diamonds. The final contract will be 5♦ (or maybe 6♦).

THE RESPONDER'S REBID

By the time three bids have been made – two by opener and one by responder – the auction will have been limited (except in the case where three different suits have been bid). It will often be possible for the responder to announce the final contract or, at any rate, his opinion on what it should be. He will add the strength of his hand to that indicated by the opener. When the opener has shown a minimum hand, the responder will need an opening bid himself to contract for game. When he has around 11 points, he may invite a game. With anything less, he will pass or sign off somewhere.

The opener rebid his own suit

Suppose the bidding started 1♦ – 1♠ – 2♦, the opener showing that he has a minimum hand. The responder may take one of these actions:

Pass	no game ambitions
2♥	showing a second suit (forcing for one round)
2♠	no game ambitions and a six-card spade suit
2NT	balanced, about 11 points, inviting a game
3♣	showing a second suit (game-forcing)
3♦	diamond support, about 11 points, inviting a game
3♠	six spades, about 11 points, inviting a game.

He may also bid any game contract that appears to be a reasonable prospect, in particular 3NT.

The opener rebid 1NT

After a start of 1♦ – 1♠ – 1NT, the opener may take one of these options:

Pass	no game ambitions
2♦/2♥/2♠	no game ambitions
2NT	inviting a game in no-trumps
3♣/3♥	second suit (game-forcing)
3♦	diamond support, inviting a game
3♠	six spades, inviting a game.

Many players use a bid of 2♣ (the "other minor") as an artificial bid, asking for further information.

The opener showed support

When the opener gave a single raise of the responder's suit (1♦ – 1♥ – 2♥, for example), the responder knows he is facing a minimum opening and will be well placed to announce the final contract. Similarly, after a double raise (such as 1♣ – 1♠ – 3♠), the responder knows that he is facing a medium hand and will advance to game when he is a queen better than a minimum response.

When the raise was in a minor suit, the most likely game contract will be 3NT. Any bid in a new suit will therefore show a stopper.

Left: A typical invitational hand for responder. After a start of 1♦ – 1♠ – 2♣, you would give "jump preference" to 3♦, inviting partner to proceed to game.

Left: Responder accepts the invitation. After a start of 1♦ – 1♠ – 3♠, you would place partner with a medium hand of around 16 points. With 9 points yourself, rather than a minimum 6, you would raise to 4♠.

In the auction 1♠ – 2♦ – 3♦ – 3♥, the responder shows good heart values and hopes that the opener has a club stopper and can bid 3NT. The opener would have rebid 2♥ if he held four cards in the heart suit, so there would not be much point in responder's 3♥ rebid showing a four-card suit (rather than a stopper).

Three suits have been bid

The most difficult and least limited situation is when three suits have been bid (a start such as 1♦ – 1♠ – 2♣). The opener's range is about 12–18 and the responder must now show his own strength: minimum, game-try, or "at least game". These are the responder's options:

Pass	weak and prefers clubs to diamonds
2♦	weak and prefers diamonds
2♥	"fourth suit forcing", see the next section
2♠	weak with long spades
2NT	about 10–12 points, inviting game
3♣	about 10–12 points, club support, inviting game
3♦	about 10–12 points, diamond support, inviting game
3♠	about 10–12 points, six spades, inviting game
Game bids	when the responder knows which game is best.

As you see, there are three actions that are weak. When you hold a near-minimum response, you can pass the opener's rebid when you prefer his second suit to his first. You may also give preference to his first suit at the minimum level or rebid your own suit.

When you are somewhat stronger and wish to invite game, you have four options. You can raise the opener's second suit, give jump preference to his first suit, jump one level in your own suit or bid 2NT.

When you are strong enough to insist on a game, you can either bid such a contract directly or ask for further information to help you to decide which denomination will be best. You do this by bidding the fourth suit (2♥ here). Such a bid is artificial and says nothing whatsoever about the heart suit. The device is in general use around the world and is known as "fourth suit forcing".

GIVING PREFERENCE

♠ ♥ ♦ ♣

When the opener has shown two suits (for example, in the auction 1♦ – 1♥ – 2♣), the responder will often want to choose which of them should become trumps. With a weak responding hand he can "give preference" by passing 2♣ or correcting to 2♦. When responder wants to invite a game, he can instead bid 3♣ or 3♦. Bidding 3♦ is an example of what is known as "jump preference".

FOURTH SUIT FORCING

As was mentioned in the previous section, the most wide-ranging start to an auction is when three different suits are bid (for example: 1♦ – 1♠ – 2♣). If the responder now makes any two-level or three-level bid in one of those suits, this will be a limit bid. Sometimes he is strong enough to insist on a game contract, at least, but does not yet know what denomination will be best. In that case the responder must make an artificial bid in the fourth suit – 2♥, here. The meaning is: "I have enough strength for a game contract. Please continue to describe your hand."

Bidding the fourth suit to investigate the best game

Let's see some examples of auctions that contain a "fourth-suit forcing" bid.

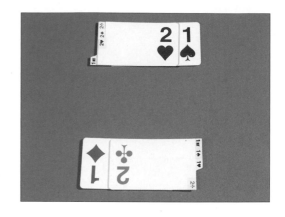

Above: Fourth suit forcing sequence. These bidding cards (from a duplicate game) show that after a start of 1♦ – 1♠ – 2♣, North has rebid a fourth-suit-forcing 2♥.

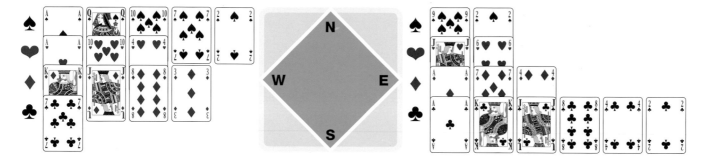

As you see, East's 2♥ bid says nothing whatsoever about his holding in hearts. Indeed, if he held four hearts (or even a good stopper in the suit) he would doubtless have made some bid in no-trumps instead of his fourth-suit bid. Here West has a stopper in the fourth suit, so he rebids 2NT. Remember that the bidding is forced to game, so there is no need whatsoever for West to jump to 3NT. Without the "fourth-suit forcing" method, East would be stuck for a bid at his second turn. A rebid of 3♣ would be non-forcing. A rebid of 4♣ would be unsatisfactory, since it would carry the bidding past the 3NT level.

West	East
1♠	2♣
2♦	2♥
2NT	3NT

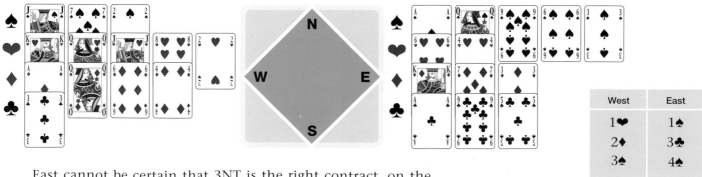

East cannot be certain that 3NT is the right contract, on the second round. He bids a fourth-suit 3♣ instead and is delighted to hear that West has some spade support. If West held one spade and ♣Q–x–x, he would have bid 3NT instead.

West	East
1♥	1♠
2♦	3♣
3♠	4♠

Bidding the fourth suit to make your next bid forcing

Sometimes the responder bids the fourth suit so that he can make his next bid forcing, rather than a limit bid.

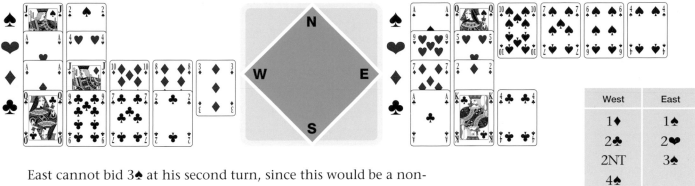

West	East
1♦	1♠
2♣	2♥
2NT	3♠
4♠	

East cannot bid 3♠ at his second turn, since this would be a non-forcing limit bid. He bids a fourth-suit forcing 2♥ instead and then bids 3♠, thereby making this bid forcing. Since West has already bid diamonds and clubs, and shown a heart stopper, he knows that his partner cannot be looking for more than two-card spade support. He is therefore happy to raise to the spade game. With only one spade and a secure heart stopper, he would have bid 3NT instead.

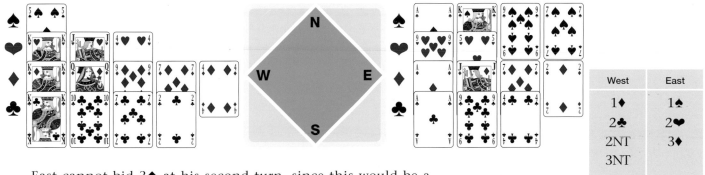

West	East
1♦	1♠
2♣	2♥
2NT	3♦
3NT	

East cannot bid 3♦ at his second turn, since this would be a non-forcing limit bid. As on the previous hand, he bids a fourth-suit forcing 2♥ with the intention of making a forcing diamond bid on the next round. The purpose of showing the diamond fit is to investigate a possible slam in the suit. When West can only bid 3NT on the fourth round, East abandons his thoughts of a slam.

Below: Too strong for a limit bid. After a start of 1♦ –1♠ – 2♣, you cannot bid 3♠ because this would suggest around 11 points. Instead you must bid a fourth-suit-forcing 2♥, intending to bid a forcing 3♠ on the next round.

USA v USA
♠ ♥ ♦ ♣

The 1977 Bermuda Bowl is unique because the final was contested by two teams from the same country, the USA. Robert Hamman, Bobby Wolff, Billy Eisenberg, Eddie Kantar, Paul Soloway and John Swanson eventually won the trophy, despite being more than 80 IMPs behind at one stage. It was deemed unsatisfactory to have the two American teams meeting in the final. Since then they have been forced to play each other in the semi-final, should they both survive to that stage.

COMPLETING THE AUCTION

When the players have made two bids each, a considerable amount of information has been exchanged. It remains only to put the finishing touches to the auction. When responder's rebid was a limit bid, the opener must assess whether he is strong enough to advance to game. When responder's rebid was a forcing bid in a new suit, the opener will generally be able to give his view of which game will be best.

Responder's rebid was a limit bid

Let's see a couple of complete auctions that follow a limited rebid by the responder:

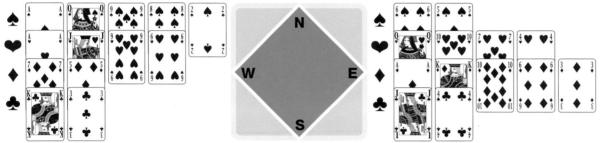

West	East
1♠	2♦
2♥	3♥
4♥	

East's 3♥ was non-forcing, suggesting about 11 points. Since West holds 14 points rather than a minimum 12 points, he decides to bid game. Since there is a big bonus for bidding and making game, most players are fairly adventurous in this area. A game needs to have only a 40 per cent chance of being made for it to be worth bidding.

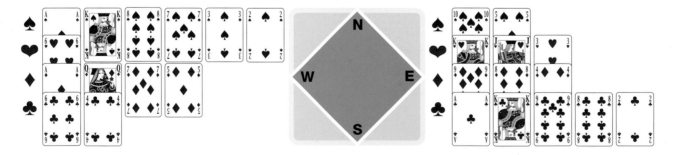

West	East
1♠	2♣
2♦	2NT
3♠	4♠

East's 2NT suggested around 11 points and showed a good stopper in hearts, the unbid suit. Holding six spades, West decided to bid the suit once again. East then judged it best to bid game in that suit. As you see, ten tricks are by no means certain in spades. Nevertheless, it is a contract worth attempting.

Suppose one of West's low spades had been a low heart instead, giving him 5–2–4–2 shape. Since he had already indicated five spades and four diamonds by opening in one suit and rebidding in a lower suit, there would be no reason to bid the spades again. West would rebid 3NT instead.

Responder introduced a new suit

When the responder bids a new suit at the two-level, this is forcing for one round (except when the opener rebid 1NT). Here is a typical auction:

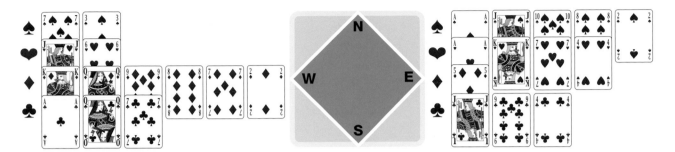

West is happy to bid no-trumps as he has an excellent stopper in clubs, the unbid suit. Since he has a minimum hand he bids only 2NT, which East would sometimes pass. Here East holds 13 points opposite an opening bid, so he raises to 3NT. East has already indicated that he holds five spades and four hearts. If he held four spades and four hearts, he would have responded 1♥ on the first round.

West	East
1♦	1♠
2♦	2♥
2NT	3NT

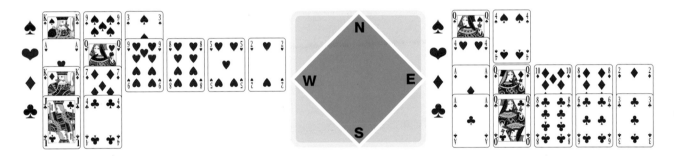

East's bid of 3♣, a new suit at the three-level, is forcing to game. West has a stopper in spades, the unbid suit, so he suggests 3NT as the final contract. East is happy to accept. If West had not held a spade stopper, he would have had to bid his heart suit again (3♥) or give preference to partner's diamonds (3♦).

West	East
1♥	2♦
2♥	3♣
3NT	

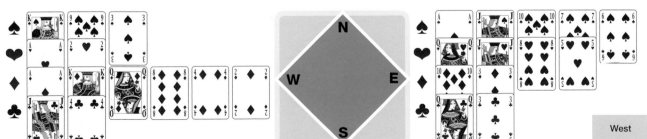

West's rebid of 3♦ is not forcing but it shows a hand in the intermediate range (16–18 points). Since East has 10 points, he has enough for game. He advances with the forcing bid of 3♥ and West gives preference to spades. Game in spades is a sound contract. In 3NT there would have been no stopper in the club suit.

West	East
1♦	1♠
3♦	3♥
3♠	4♠

WEAK TWO-BIDS AND RESPONSES

In the early days of bridge, opening bids of 2♦, 2♥ and 2♠ were forcing and showed a very powerful hand. Such openings arose very infrequently and a new form of two-bid gradually became popular, one that showed a six-card suit and 6–10 points. The classical form of the weak two-bid is based on a good six-card suit. These are all worthy examples:

1

2

Hand (1) is an obvious 2♦ opening. Hand (2) is a standard 2♥ bid, despite the four-card club suit on the side. However, you would not usually open with a weak two-bid when you held a four-card major on the side.

3
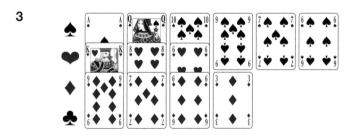

Most players would open 2♠ on hand (3). Partner will not expect the void club, though, and might pass when he holds enough in the red suits for a game contract to be made.

One of the objects of such openings is to take away the opponents' bidding space when they hold the balance of the points. Some players are therefore willing to open with a weak two-bid on hands that do not fit the classical requirements:

4
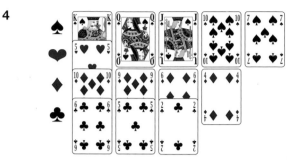

It is tempting to open 2♠ on hand (4), if only to tell your partner that you have a suit that will be worth leading.

5

Hand (5) does not contain the recommended "good suit" but many players would open 2♥, even so, in an attempt to make life awkward for the opponents.

6
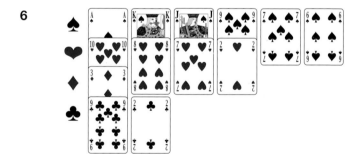

Similarly, some players would open 2♠ on (6), despite holding four cards in the other major. You and your partner can decide whether you want to keep your weak two-bids disciplined or a bit on the wild side!

SOUND WHEN VULNERABLE
♠ ♥ ♦ ♣

When you are vulnerable, you should keep your weak two-bid openings fairly disciplined. If you have a strong trump holding, there is little reason to fear a bad result from being doubled.

Responding to a weak two-bid

On most moderate hands, including balanced hands of up to 13 points, you will usually pass. Remember that partner has shown a weak hand. These are the responses available to you when partner has opened 2♥:

2♠	natural and invitational
2NT	relay bid, asking for more information (see below)
3♣/3♦/3♠	natural and forcing
3♥	pre-emptive
game bids	to play.

So, a raise to the three-level is an attempt to increase the pre-emption. The opener is not invited to bid game. When you can see a reasonable chance of game, if partner has values to spare, you normally respond 2NT. This asks the opener to describe his hand further and he will then rebid along the following lines:

3♣	lower-range without two of the three top honours in his suit
3♦	lower-range with two of the three top honours
3♥	upper-range without two of the three top honours
3♠	upper-range with two of the three top honours
3NT	the long suit is headed by the ace-king-queen.

Above: Not enough for game. Many players overbid opposite weak two-bids. Suppose partner opens 2♠ and you hold this hand. You should pass. Indeed, you should be quite glad if partner managed to make eight tricks eventually!

SKIP BID WARNING
♠ ♥ ♦ ♣

When an opponent makes a "skip bid", in other words a bid that is one or more levels higher than the minimum legal bid in that suit, it may take you a while to decide whether your hand is worth a bid at that level. To avoid giving away information by thinking for a few seconds about bidding and then passing, it is correct etiquette to pretend to think for around eight seconds, whether or not your hand is worthy of such consideration. The opponent should warn you to be ready to pause by saying "skip bid", or displaying the skip-bid card from the bidding box, before making his jump bid.

This would be a typical auction:

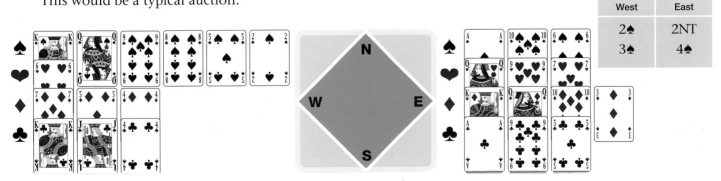

West	East
2♠	2NT
3♠	4♠

With 15 points and three-card support, East decides he will play in game opposite an upper-range opening. He makes the relay bid of 2NT and West's 3♠ response shows that he is upper-range (8–10) and holds two of the three top spade honours. East bids the game and it turns out to be a worthwhile prospect.

WEAK THREE-BIDS AND RESPONSES

An opening bid at the three-level shows a weak hand, usually with a seven-card suit. When you are vulnerable, the suit needs to be fairly strong to offer some safety against a large penalty. Suppose you are dealt one of these hands:

1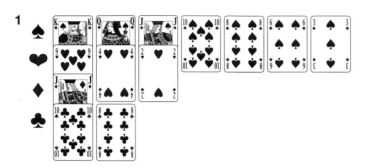

A good guideline for a pre-emptive bid is that you will score many more tricks if you play the contract than you would when defending. Hand (1) fits this requirement admirably. Playing in spades, you are almost certain to score six tricks. Defending a contract by the opponents, you might score none at all; the second round of spades might well be ruffed. So, open 3♠ even when vulnerable. Do not worry that you might go for 800 if you are doubled and partner has nothing. First of all, it will be difficult for the opponents to double you, since a double is nearly always for take-out. Secondly, you will be making life very difficult for the opponents by opening with such a high bid. It is worth taking a small risk to this effect.

2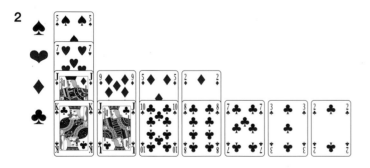

Similarly, you should open 3♣ on hand (2). Don't worry that you might miss a better contract in diamonds. If your partner has good diamonds, the opponents will have a big fit in one of the majors anyway. It is generally advised that you should not pre-empt when your long suit is accompanied by four cards in a major suit. In the first or second seats, when partner may still be strong, it is true that opening 3♦

3

on (3) might cause you to miss a fit in hearts. When you are in the third seat, you should open 3♦ nevertheless. The player on your left is marked with a big hand. Also, if your partner does hold heart length, the opponents will have a great fit in one of the black suits. Don't be one of those players who always find an excuse not to pre-empt.

Above: It is reasonable to open 3♦ on this hand, despite holding four cards in a major suit.

Responding to a three-bid

The purpose of the three-bid is to remove the opponents' bidding space. When it is your partner who holds a good hand, you will have little space to manoeuvre yourselves. The best method is to play that a new suit at the three-level is natural and forcing. Remember, though, that your partner's hand may be very little use to you unless you choose his seven-card suit as trumps.

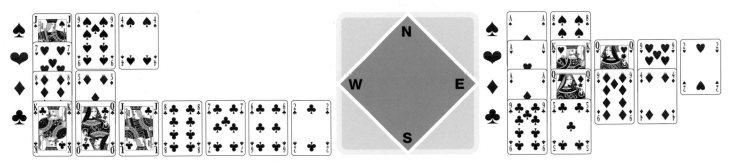

East makes a forcing response in hearts and West shows a stopper in spades. It may be tempting for East to bid 3NT now. The contract may make on a good day, but there is every chance that only one club trick will be available. (On the present hands, for example, the defenders will hold up the ♣A for one round.) It may well be better for East to bid game in clubs. The hope is that West's clubs will provide six tricks and that East can add five top winners. Remember that you need a big hand, or a good trump fit, to make game opposite a pre-emptive bid.

West	East
3♣	3♥
3♠	5♣

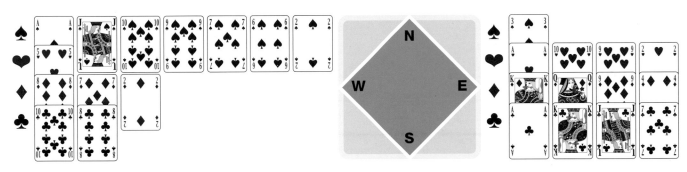

With 17 points, it is reasonable for East to attempt a spade game. Opposite the actual West hand, there is a good chance of losing just two spades and one diamond. Note that it would be very poor to respond 3NT. In all probability, you would score only one spade trick and would finish well short of your target.

The time to respond 3NT to a pre-empt in a major is when you have a good fit for the major and think that nine tricks may be easier to score than ten:

West	East
3♠	4♠

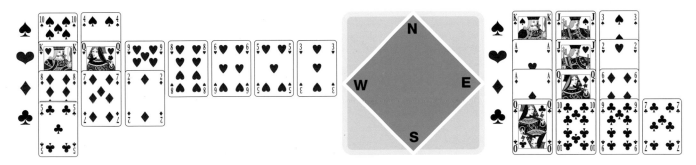

East reckons that nine tricks in no-trumps may be easier than ten in hearts. He hopes to make seven heart tricks and the ♦A. A spade or a diamond opening lead will give him a ninth trick. Even on a club lead you would expect to make 3NT. Playing in 4♥, you would have every chance of four losers in the side suits.

West	East
3♥	3NT

HIGH-LEVEL PRE-EMPTS

We have already looked at weak two-bids and pre-emptive three-bids. To complete the picture, we look now at the Gambling 3NT and at four-level pre-emptive bids. An opening bid of 4♣ can be played as natural, showing clubs and more shape than an opening 3♣ (often an eight-card suit). Another popular treatment is to use 4♣ to show a strong four-level pre-empt in hearts. Similarly, 4♦ shows a strong pre-empt in spades. This method is known as South African Texas.

The Gambling 3NT

The most popular meaning for an opening bid of 3NT is that it shows a solid seven-card minor with no card higher than a queen in the other suits. The responder will pass only when he thinks that 3NT is the best available contract. That will be the case, of course, when the responder holds stoppers in the other three suits. Even when he does not, it may be best to pass and perhaps hope that the weakest suit is not led. This is a typical situation:

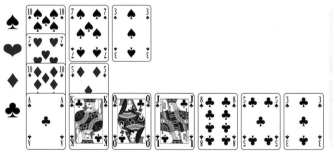
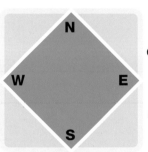

West	East
3NT	Pass

East decides to pass the Gambling 3NT, even though he holds no stopper in the diamond suit. He reasons that a major suit may be led, in which case seven club tricks and two aces will produce the game. Even if a diamond is led, partner may hold a doubleton diamond and a 4–4 break would then limit the defenders to four tricks. On a lucky day West might hold three diamonds. A final reason for passing is that the alternative contract of 4♣ would not yield a game bonus and might not be any easier to make.

When responder does choose to bid 4♣ (or 5♣), this is a request for the opener to pass if his suit is clubs and to correct to 4♦ (or 5♦) if his suit is diamonds. This caters for the case where East holds no minor-suit honour and cannot therefore tell which seven-card suit his partner has.

Responder can count on seven tricks from the opener's solid suit. Therefore, if he is confident that he has the three three-side suits under control and can contribute another five tricks, he will be able to bid a slam.

Right: With a solid seven-card minor suit, and very little outside, you open with a Gambling 3NT.

South African Texas

To distinguish between weak and stronger pre-empts in a major at the four-level, many pairs use 4♣ and 4♦ to show strong pre-empts in hearts and spades, respectively. An opening bid of 4♣, for example, would suggest a one-loser heart suit and an ace outside, or perhaps a solid heart suit and no ace outside.

Suppose you had to find an opening bid on these hands:

1

Hand (1) is too strong for 3♠, even when vulnerable, and merits a 4♠ opening.

2
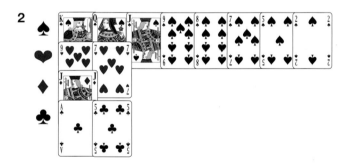

Hand (2) fits exactly the meaning of a 4♦ South African Texas opening. There is only one loser in the 8-card spade suit and an ace is held outside.

3
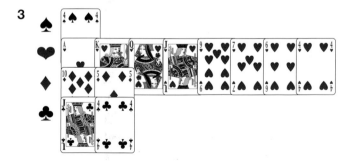

Hand (3) is worth an opening bid of 4♣, since it contains a solid 8-card suit.

The purpose of distinguishing between a strong and a weaker four-level pre-empt is so that the responder can judge whether a slam may be possible. He will have a better idea what to do if an opponent contests the auction with an overcall such as 5♣.

Five-level openings

An opening bid of five of a minor is quite rare and will usually be based on a suit of at least eight cards. With a seven-card suit, particularly opposite an unpassed partner, you would be wary of bypassing a possible game in no-trumps.

Since four of a major is a game contract, an opening bid of 5♥ or 5♠ (also very rare) tells partner you are solid except for the two top trumps. Partner can then raise to a small slam with one top trump and to a grand slam with two top trumps.

1
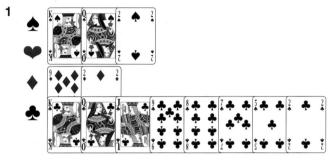

You would open 5♣ on (1). As you see, the hand follows the guidelines for a pre-emptive bid. If you had only two top losers, and a more powerful hand, you would open 1♣ or perhaps an artificial 2♣.

2

On (2) you would open 5♦. Again, your aim is pre-emptive – to make life difficult for the opponents, who will no doubt have a big fit somewhere.

3
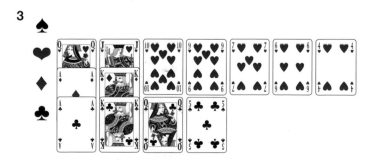

Hand (3) illustrates the rare opening of five of a major. You would like partner to raise to 6♥ if he held the ace or king of hearts, to raise to 7♥ with both these cards.

TAKE-OUT DOUBLES AND RESPONSES

In the early days of bridge a double had just one meaning: that you thought the opponents had bid too high and you wanted to double the stakes, thereby increasing the penalty if they failed in their contract. Gradually it was realized that a more useful meaning of a double, particularly at a low level, was to show that you had a good hand but no particularly long suit to bid. This became known as a "take-out double", because you wanted your partner to take out the double into his longest suit. Nowadays, most doubles at a low level are for take-out.

Take-out doubles of a one-bid

This is a typical auction after a take-out double of a one-bid:

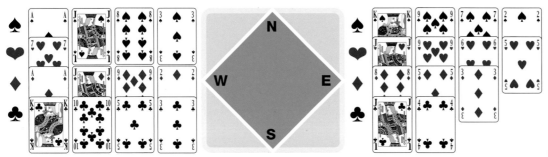

South opens 1♥ and West has the strength for an opening bid, along with a shortage in hearts. He cannot tell which suit will be best as trumps and therefore makes a take-out double.

In responding to the take-out double, East has two duties. The first is to choose a trump suit (or to bid no-trumps). The second is to indicate the strength of his hand. With about 0–7 points, he will bid his best suit at the minimum level. With around 8–11 points, he will jump one level in his best suit. With more than 11 points, the bidding should be forced to game. The responder will either bid a game directly or show his strength with a cue-bid in the opponents' suit (here it would be 2♥).

West	North	East	South
			1♥
Dble	Pass	1♠	End

East has 9 points, so he jumps one level in his best suit. West has a minimum double, with only 12 points, so he passes. If West had 17 points, he would know that he and his partner had 25 points between them. He would bid again, looking for a game contract.

West	North	East	South
			1♠
Dble	Pass	3♣	End

Let's see an example of the cue-bid response:

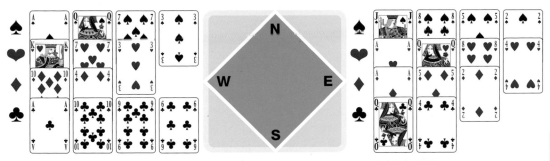

West	North	East	South
			1♦
Dble	Pass	2♦	Pass
2♠	Pass	4♠	End

With 13 points opposite West's take-out double, East wants to reach a game contract in one of the major suits. Rather than guess which one to bid, he shows his strength with a cue-bid in the opponent's suit. The players now bid their suits in ascending order, searching for a trump fit. When West shows four spades, East is happy to choose that suit as trumps.

Take-out doubles on other auctions

Whenever the opponents have bid one or two suits and the bidding is below the game level, a double is for take-out.

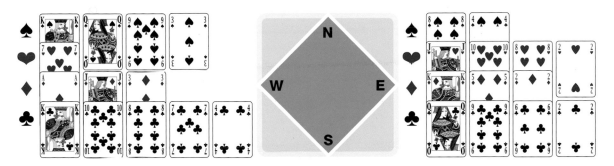

West	North	East	South
	1♥	Pass	2♥
Dble	Pass	3♣	End

West is strong enough to compete at the two-level. Rather than guess which suit to make trumps, he enters the auction with a take-out double. East chooses clubs as trumps and bids them at the minimum level, since he is too weak to look for a game contract.

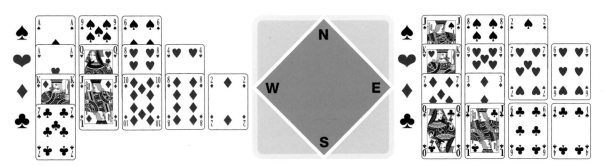

West	North	East	South
	1♣	Pass	1♠
Dble	2♣	2♥	End

The opponents have bid spades and clubs, so West's take-out double shows hearts and diamonds. When North bids again, East can pass when he has nothing worth bidding. Here he has 7 points and four-card support for partner's indicated heart suit. He rightly competes with 2♥.

OVERCALLS AND RESPONSES

An overcall at the one-level (for example, 1♥ over an opponent's 1♣) shows a good five-card suit. To overcall at the two-level (for example, 2♦ over 1♠), you need a good six-card suit. These are the main purposes of making an overcall:

• you suggest a good opening lead to partner
• you take away the opponents' bidding space
• you can bid to a worthwhile part score or game.

Suppose your right-hand opponent has opened 1♦ and you hold one of these hands:

1

Hand (1) is well worth a 1♠ overcall. You have a good suit, so you are happy to suggest a spade opening lead. You also take away bidding space, preventing your left-hand opponent from responding 1♥.

2

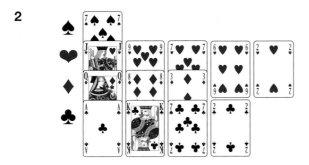

Hand (2) contains a point more but you would be less inclined to overcall. You do not want a heart lead and you will not be taking away any bidding space.

3

On Hand (3) you would bid 2♣, although somewhat hesitantly when vulnerable. You have a very good club suit and are keen for partner to lead it. Also, the overcall will prevent the next player from making a cheap response in one of the major suits. As you see, you can overcall on less strength than would be needed for an opening bid.

The choice between an overcall and a double

Roughly speaking, an overcall tells partner what suit you want to make trumps, whereas a take-out double asks partner to choose trumps. When your hand contains a good five-card major, you will often choose to overcall in that suit, rather than doubling. Suppose your right-hand opponent has opened 1♣ and you hold one of these hands:

4

On (4) you have the values for an opening bid and a shortage in clubs. You are therefore strong enough for a take-out double. However, you are fairly sure that spades will be the best trump suit and should therefore overcall 1♠. If the next player bids 2♣ and two passes follow, you could make a take-out double on the second-round, asking partner to choose a trump suit.

5

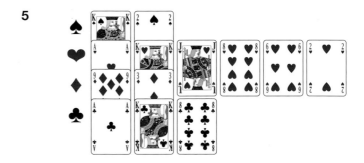

It would be dangerous to overcall 1♥ on (5) because partner might pass when you had a game available. So, you should start with a double and then bid hearts on the next round.

6

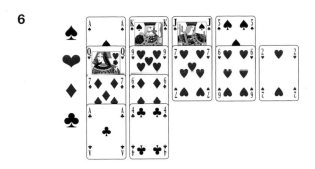

On (6) your five-card heart suit is fairly weak. You cannot be at all sure that hearts will make a better trump suit than spades, so begin with a double, asking partner to choose trumps.

West	North	East	South
	1♠	2♣	Pass
2♥	Pass	3♣	End

Responding to an overcall in a new suit

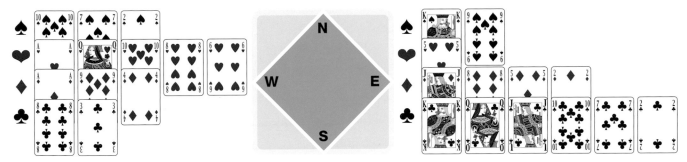

When you bid a new suit in response to an overcall, this should be constructive but non-forcing. In other words, you think that a game may be possible. Do not bid a new suit as a rescue bid, just because you do not like the suit that partner has bid.

With ten points and a good five-card major, West sees the chance of a game if partner has a maximum overcall or a good heart fit. He responds 2♥, non-forcing but constructive. East, on this occasion, has a minimum overcall. If he held two hearts, he might pass. As he has only one heart and a solid club suit, he prefers to bid 3♣.

Raising an overcall

When you have a three-card or four-card fit for partner's overcall, you should raise even on quite a weak hand. Your objective is to remove bidding space from the opponents. If instead you are genuinely interested in game, you can bid the opponent's suit rather than raising directly. Suppose the bidding has started 1♦ – 1♠ – Pass (where your partner has made an overcall of 1♠) and you hold one of the hands opposite.

Raise to 2♠ on (7). There is little chance that your side can make game but the opener probably holds a strong hand and you will make life difficult for him. On (8), with four-card support and a side-suit singleton, you are worth a pre-emptive raise to 3♠.

Hand (9) is a different type entirely. You are genuinely interested in game and should cue-bid 2♦ (bidding the opponent's suit) to show partner that you have a strong hand with a good spade fit.

7

8

9

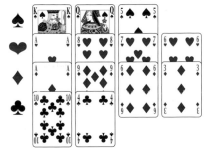

THE REDOUBLE

When your partner's opening bid has been doubled by the opponents, you can redouble to show that your side has the balance of the points and that you are interested in playing for penalties. If instead you bid a new suit over a double, this is generally treated as forcing (a method known as "ignoring the double"). However, it is popular in the USA for a two-level bid in a new suit, over a double, to be non-forcing.

Suppose the bidding has started 1♦ – Dble and you are sitting in the third seat with one of the hands shown on the right:

Hand (1) is a classic redouble. You hold 11 points and shortage in partner's suit. Some players would redouble on (2) as well, but it is a poor idea. You have no intention of defending 1♥ doubled, should your partner double this bid by the fourth player. It is best to bid a simple and forcing 1♠. You can then develop the auction in the same way that you would have done without the double. Similarly on (3) you do best to bid a forcing 2♣. However, if your method is to play a non-forcing 2♣ over a double, you would have to begin with a redouble.

1

2

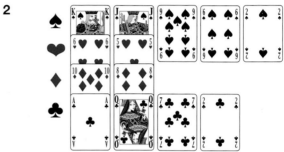

3

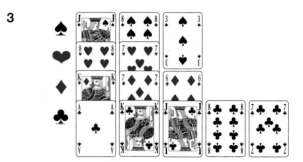

The opener's rebid facing a redouble

It is commonly agreed that if the opener rebids before his partner has had a chance to double the opponents, he is showing a weak hand with some shape.

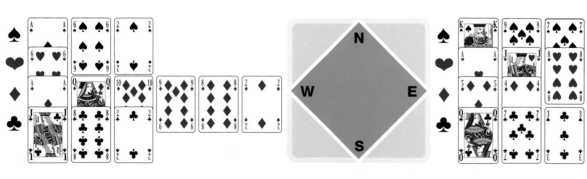

West has a minimum distributional opening bid, with no interest in defending a contract of 1♥ even if it is his partner's intention to double this contract. He announces this by rebidding 2♦ before his partner has even had a chance to double the opponents. Knowing that his partner has a minimum opener, East is not tempted to bid again.

West	North	East	South
1♦	Dble	Rdble	1♥
2♦	End		

If West held a stronger hand with the same shape, he could rebid 3♦ immediately or pass initially and then remove partner's double (if it comes) to diamonds.

Since the redoubler has announced willingness to defend, the opener should double the fourth player's escape freely:

West	North	East	South
1♠	Dble	Rdble	2♦
Dble	End		

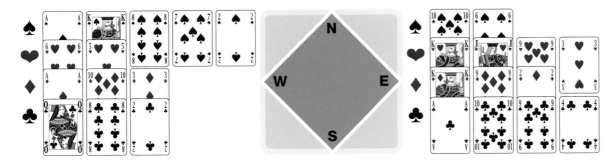

West does not need to wait until he holds four trumps to double. He is unlikely to hold four trumps, in fact, since the redoubler has indicated a willingness to double and is therefore likely to hold at least three diamonds himself.

The SOS redouble

The situation is different when a part score contract (other than 1NT) has been doubled for penalties. Since you will normally get a good result for making a doubled contract, there is no need to use a redouble merely to increase the score even further. Many players use redouble in a conventional way, to ask partner to choose another suit. It is a rescue manoeuvre known as the SOS redouble.

FIVE-SUIT BRIDGE
♠ ♥ ♦ ♣

A game called "five-suit bridge", played with a 65-card pack, was devised in 1937. The fifth suit, called Royals in England and Eagles in the USA, ranked above no-trumps and was worth 50 points a trick. Since the four hands each contained 16 cards, the "book" was set at eight tricks and success in a one-level contract therefore required declarer to make nine tricks. The 65th card, originally undealt, was placed face-up and known as the "widow". The eventual declarer was allowed to replace any card in his hand with the widow card before play began.

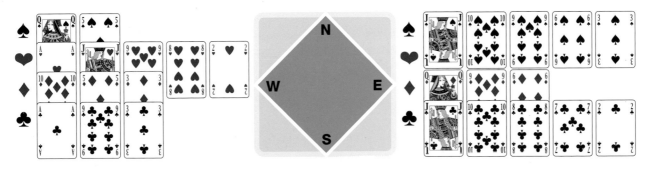

North's double of the 1♥ overcall was for penalties. Since East is void in hearts, he decides that the partnership would be better off choosing one of the black suits as trumps. Because the contract is a part score in a suit, his redouble is SOS and asks for rescue into one of the unbid suits. West chooses clubs and North will now have to decide whether to double this contract or to make some other call.

West	North	East	South
			1♦
1♥	Dble	Rdble	Pass
2♣			

PENALTY DOUBLES

I n an earlier section it was mentioned that most low-level doubles are nowadays played for take-out. In this section we will see the main categories of double which are still treated as being for penalties, by most players.

Penalty doubles of 1NT and subsequent rescues

It would not make much sense for a double of 1NT to be for take-out, since no suit has been bid. Indeed, it is standard for a double of a 1NT opening to be for penalties. This is particularly so when the opening is a weak 1NT. (There are some conventional defences to a strong 1NT that include an artificial meaning for a double.) Here is a typical example:

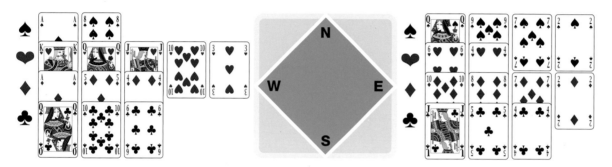

West doubles the 12–14 point 1NT for penalties. He has 16 points, which is more than the maximum count for the weak 1NT. He also has a promising opening lead in the heart suit. East does not hold very much but he has no reason whatsoever to take out his partner's double. Only if he were very weak and held a five-card suit, would he consider removing the penalty double. If North were to attempt an escape to some suit at the two-level and East were to double, this would also be a penalty double.

West	North	East	South
			1NT
Dble	Pass	Pass	Pass

Penalty doubles of an overcall

In traditional bidding, a double of an overcall is for penalties:

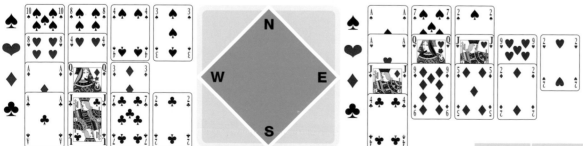

West does not expect 2♣ to be made. Since a game for East–West is uncertain, with 11 points facing an opening bid, he makes a penalty double to suggest defending against 2♣. East has no reason to remove the double.

West	North	East	South
		1♥	2♣
Dble	Pass	Pass	Pass

We will see in a later section that most tournament players now prefer to use a double of an overcall for take-out. This method is known as the "negative double".

Penalty doubles of game contracts

When the opponents bid to a game contract and you have an unpleasant surprise for them, such as an unexpected trump holding, you can double them for penalties.

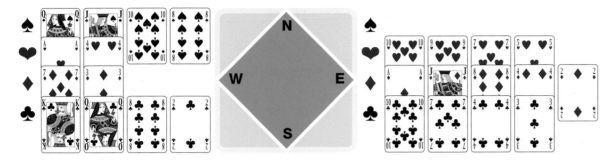

With the trumps breaking badly, the North–South spade game is destined for defeat. Diagnosing this outcome, West inflicts a penalty double.

Note that it is not a good idea to double freely bid games just because you hold a lot of points. The opponents knew they were missing these points when they decided to bid the game. They presumably have considerable distributional values to compensate for the lack of points. The time to double is when the opponents' auction is limited and you know that the cards are lying badly for them.

West	North	East	South
	1♠	Pass	2♠
Pass	3♦	Pass	4♠
Dble	Pass	Pass	Pass

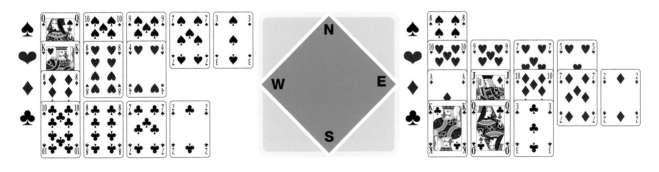

West	North	East	South
	1♦	Pass	1♠
Pass	2♦	Pass	2NT
Pass	3NT	Dble	End

North has shown a minimum-range opening with his 2♦ rebid and South's 2NT indicated around 11 points. North–South have no values to spare and East knows the diamond suit is lying very badly for them and will be impossible to establish. Also, his singleton spade suggests that the spade suit may lie poorly for them. The odds are good that 3NT will go down, possibly two down. East is therefore happy to end the auction with a penalty double.

TAKING OUT A DOUBLE
♠ ♥ ♦ ♣

When partner makes a penalty double, it will normally be right for you to pass. This is known as "leaving in the penalty double". The alternative action, to make a new bid, is known as "taking out partner's penalty double". It can be right only if you have a very shapely hand where you are confident that it will be better to play the contract your way.

CHAPTER 5

BASIC CARD PLAY

Bidding is easily learnt from a book. To play the cards really well, it is sometimes said that you need some innate ability. While that may be true at international level, it is entirely possible to become a good card player simply by acquiring the techniques that are explained in this book. In this section you will see the various types of "finesse", why it is often right to hold up an ace, and how you should decide whether to draw trumps immediately. You will learn why you should plan a contract right at the beginning, even before you play the first card from dummy. You will see how to take ruffs in the dummy, deciding whether or not to ruff with a high trump, also how to establish a suit, both at no-trumps and in a suit contract.

Right: Holding two ace–queen combinations, the player can visualize the possibility of finessing even before seeing his partner's hand.

THE FINESSE

Suppose you hold the ♦A and the ♦Q, with one of the defenders holding the ♦K. To score a trick with the queen, you will need to lead towards it, hoping that the defender in the second seat holds the king. You will then be able to score the queen at some stage, whether or not the defender chooses to play the king in front of the queen. The play is known as a "finesse" and the deal below shows three different types of finessing position:

Right: Declarer can avoid a trump loser by finessing against East's king. He has further potential finesses in both the red suits.

West leads the ♣J and you win with dummy's ♣K. In trumps you have the opportunity to "finesse against the king". You lead the ♠J from dummy and East follows with the ♠5. You play low from the South hand ("running the jack", as it is called). Because East holds the ♠K, your finesse wins. You lead a second round of trumps to the queen and cash the ace, drawing all the trumps.

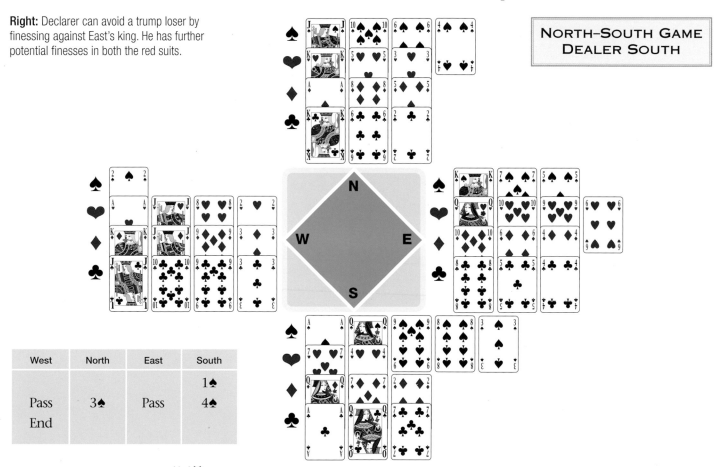

	NORTH–SOUTH GAME
	DEALER SOUTH

West	North	East	South
			1♠
Pass	3♠	Pass	4♠
End			

card led ▼

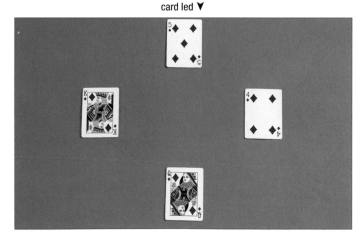

Above: A failed finesse. The attempt to score the ♦Q fails because the West holds the ♦K.

Both red suits offer you a further chance to finesse. You cross to the ♦A and lead a diamond towards the queen. If East held the ♦K you would score a trick with the ♦Q, whether or not East decided to rise with the king on the second round. As it happens, West holds the ♦K and the diamond finesse loses. West cashes another diamond winner and exits with a club, which you win in your hand. You have lost two diamond tricks and can afford to lose only one heart trick. You now take your third finesse, leading towards dummy's ♥K. Luck is with you on this occasion. West holds the ♥A and you will lose only one heart trick, whether or not West chooses to rise with the ♥A.

These were all examples of the "simple finesse", where only one relevant high card was missing in the suit. Next we will see some more complicated finesses, where two or more honours are missing.

The double finesse

When two high cards are missing, you may need to finesse twice in the same suit.

Right: A double finesse. Declarer hopes for three tricks.

You begin by leading a low diamond to dummy's ten. If West had held both the ◆K and the ◆J this first finesse would have won. You could subsequently return to your hand and finesse the ◆Q, scoring three tricks from the suit. As the cards lie, the first finesse loses and East wins with the ◆J. When you regain the lead, you play a second round of diamonds to the queen. This time you are lucky and the finesse wins. You score two diamond tricks.

Right: A combination finesse. Declarer hopes for two tricks.

Here you have no chance of making three tricks, but you can make two tricks unless East holds both of the missing honours. A finesse of the ♥J loses to the ♥K but a subsequent finesse of the ♥10 is successful.

This is a similar position:

Right: A deep finesse. Declarer finesses the ♠9 on the first round.

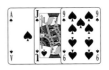

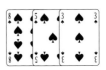

You lead low towards dummy and play the ♠9. This forces the ♠Q from East and you can then finesse against the jack successfully. You will score two tricks from the suit when West holds the king–ten or the queen–ten. The alternative play of finessing the jack on the first round is only half as good, since it will win only against the king–queen with West.

Above: Declarer's deep finesse of the ♠9 loses to the ♠Q. A subsequent finesse of the ♠J may succeed.

The two-way finesse

When you are missing a queen, you sometimes have to guess which defender holds the card.

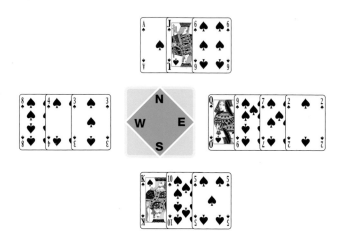

Above: A two-way finesse against a queen.

If you think that West holds the ♠Q you will play the ♠K and then lead a low spade to dummy's jack. If instead you think that East has the missing queen, you will play the ♠A and finesse the ♠10.

Before making such a guess, it is usually best to play the other suits. If you can obtain a count on the hand (determine the shapes of the defenders' hands), you can then play for the queen to be in the longer

Above: Another two-way finesse. To score two diamond tricks, declarer must guess which defender holds the ♦J.

holding. Suppose, for example, that you discover that East holds four spades to West's three, as in the diagram on the left. The odds will then be 4 to 3 in favour of East holding the missing queen.

The guess finesse

On some deals the success of the contract will depend on you guessing which finesse to take. Look at this deal, where you must score a club trick to bring your total to 12 tricks.

Right: A guess finesse. By leading a club early in the play, declarer can apply pressure on the defender in the West seat.

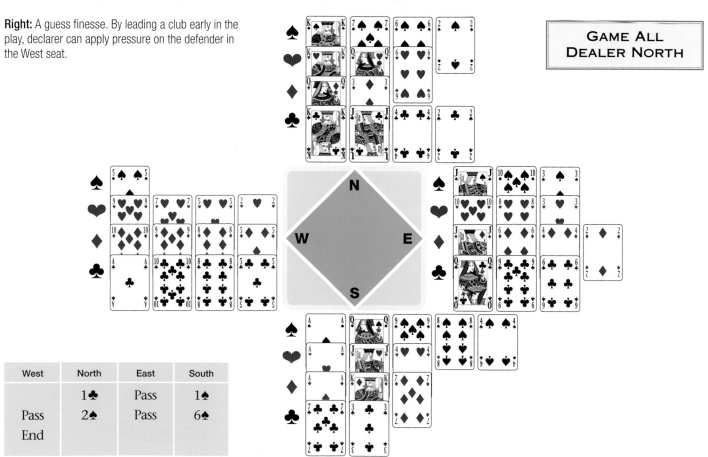

| GAME ALL |
| DEALER NORTH |

West	North	East	South
	1♣	Pass	1♠
Pass	2♠	Pass	6♠
End			

West leads the ◆10 against your small slam. All the suits are solid except the club suit. To make the slam, you will eventually have to lead a club towards dummy. When the defenders hold one honour each, you will need to guess which card to play from dummy. When West holds the ♣Q, you will make the slam by playing the ♣J. When West instead holds the ♣A, you will have to rise with dummy's ♣K. This is a "guess finesse" position.

The best way to play such contracts is to put the defenders under stress. Win the diamond lead with the ◆A and immediately lead the ♣3. It will be a difficult moment for West. For all he knows, you may hold a singleton club (and a possible loser in some other suit). In that case it would be correct for him to rise with the ♣A. Of course, if West does play the ♣A he will save you a guess. The same will be the case if he even pauses for a moment, wondering whether to play the ace. Should West produce a smooth low card, you will be inclined to place the ace with East. In that case your best chance is to finesse the jack of clubs, hoping that West holds the queen.

Suppose instead that you draw trumps and play your winners in the red suits, finally gathering up courage to lead a club. It will then be entirely clear to West that the defenders need two club tricks to beat the contract. It will be much easier for him to produce a smooth low card when he holds the ace.

The ruffing finesse

Suppose you are playing in a spade game with this side suit:

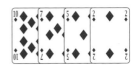

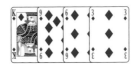

Right: A ruffing finesse. Declarer hopes that East holds the ◆K.

You can play a diamond to the ace and then lead the diamond queen, planning to run the card. East's king is caught in a "ruffing finesse". If he plays it on dummy's queen, you will ruff in your hand, setting up dummy's jack and ten. If instead East plays low, the queen of diamonds will score a trick directly. You can then continue with the jack of diamonds, scoring a third diamond trick whether or not East plays the king.

Suppose you held a side suit of ♣K–Q–J–4 opposite a void club in dummy. You could then take a ruffing finesse against the ♣A. You would lead the ♣K, hoping that the defender in second seat held the ♣A. When West chose to cover with the ace, you would ruff in the dummy, setting up two club tricks for yourself.

Right: Declarer takes a ruffing finesse on the second round of diamonds. When East covers the ◆Q with the ◆K, declarer ruffs in his hand.

THE HOLD-UP PLAY

It often happens in a no-trump contract that a defender leads from a five-card suit, finding his partner with three cards there. When declarer holds A–x–x in the suit, he should usually hold up the ace (in other words, refuse to play it) until the third round. One defender will then have no cards in the suit and it will be safe to allow him on lead later in the play. Let's see an example of this important technique:

**NORTH–SOUTH GAME
DEALER SOUTH**

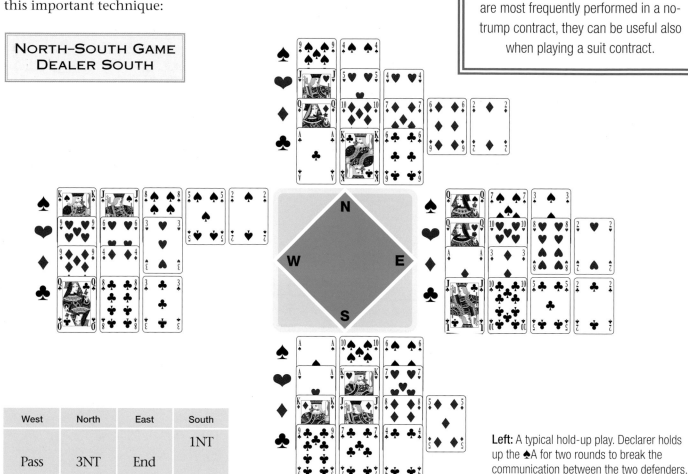

West	North	East	South
			1NT
Pass	3NT	End	

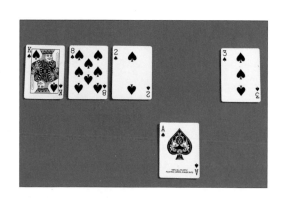

Left: A typical hold-up play. Declarer holds up the ♠A for two rounds to break the communication between the two defenders.

West leads the ♠5 against your contract of 3NT and East plays the ♠Q. You can see what will happen if you win the first (or second) round of spades. You will need to establish the diamond suit to bring your total to nine tricks. When you play a diamond, East will win with the ace and return a spade. The defenders will then score four spade tricks and the ♦A. They will reach the finishing tape before you. They will score five tricks before you have scored nine.

Instead, you should hold up the ♠A until the third round of the suit. East is now a "safe hand" and you will not mind him gaining the lead. When you play a diamond at Trick 4, good news arrives – it is East who produces the ♦A. Thanks to your hold-up, East has no spade to play. (If he did have a spade left, the suit would have broken 4–4 and would not cause any problem.) You can win whatever other suit East returns and score nine tricks to make the game: four

Above: Spade position after the hold-up. You will win the third round of spades, leaving East with no spade to play.

diamonds and five top winners in the other suits. If instead West had held the ♦A, the contract would have gone down however you played.

You should usually hold up an ace for two rounds, unless a switch to some other suit may beat the contract. Even if your stopper is a doubleton ace, it may be worth holding it up until the second round. Suppose West has led the ♥7 against 3NT and you have ♥ 10 8 3 in the dummy opposite ♥ A 4 in your hand. It is still worth holding up the ♥A until the second round. You will then break the defenders' communications when West holds six hearts and East has two. There are three missing spot cards lower than West's ♥7 (the 6, 5 and 2). If West has two of them, he will hold six hearts.

On the next deal, your stopper in the suit that has been led is a king. Once again, you need to hold it up until one of the defenders has no cards left in the suit.

West leads the ♥6 against your contract of 3NT and East wins with the ♥A. When he returns the ♥7, you should hold up the ♥K in order to break the link between the two defenders. You win the third round of hearts and run the ♣Q. The finesse loses, as it happens, but the contract will still be made. Because you held up your ♥K until the third round, East now has no heart to play. If he switches to a diamond, you will rise with the ace and score nine tricks for the contract: four clubs, three spades, one diamond trick and one heart trick.

Right: Holding up a king. Declarer holds up the ♥K on the second round of the suit, to break the communication between the two defenders.

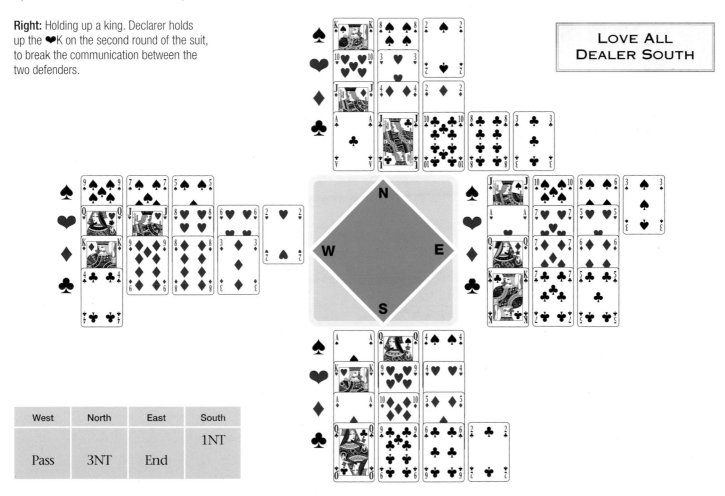

LOVE ALL
DEALER SOUTH

West	North	East	South
			1NT
Pass	3NT	End	

ESTABLISHING A SUIT AT NO-TRUMPS

You bid to 3NT, the opening lead is made and down goes the dummy. You will rarely have nine tricks readily available and may need to establish one or more suits in order to pass the finishing line. Sometimes this involves knocking out high cards. On other occasions you may need to duck a round of suit, thereby absorbing a defensive stopper.

Let's see a couple of deals that involve setting up a long suit in dummy:

Right: Ducking to retain the entry. Declarer ducks a round of diamonds to establish the suit and preserve the entry to dummy.

West leads the ♥Q and you duck the first round, since you are not afraid of a switch to another suit. You win the second round of hearts and see that you have seven tricks on top. If you can score four diamond tricks, this will bring your total to nine. How can you establish the diamond suit? Suppose you play ace, king and another diamond, finding that the suit breaks 3–2. You will establish two extra diamond winners in the dummy but there will be no entry to reach them.

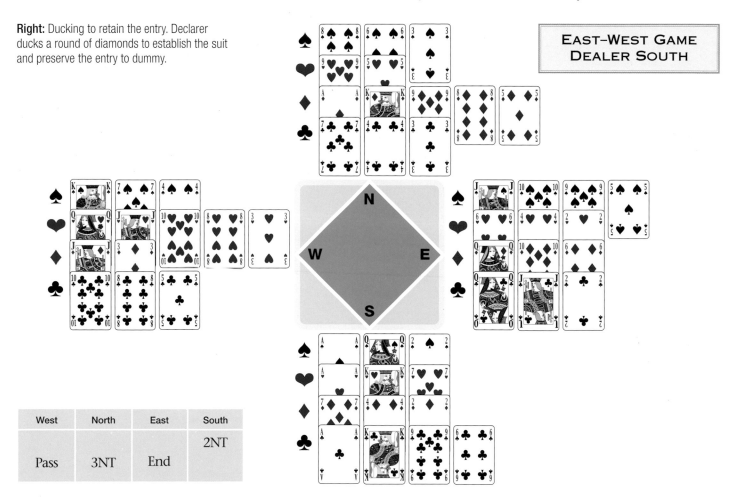

EAST–WEST GAME
DEALER SOUTH

West	North	East	South
			2NT
Pass	3NT	End	

ESTABLISHING A SUIT
♠ ♥ ♦ ♣

To establish, or set up, a suit means to play it until the remaining cards are all good and will each take a trick. For example, if you hold ♦K–Q–J–5 opposite ♦10 9–6–2, you can establish the diamond suit by knocking out the defenders' ♦A. If instead you hold ♣9–5–3 opposite ♣A–8–7–6–2, you can establish the suit by ducking two rounds of clubs, provided the defenders' clubs break 3–2.

Instead, you should duck the first round of diamonds. The defenders are certain to score a diamond trick, so let them win it at a time that is convenient for you. Let's say that East wins the first round of diamonds and clears the heart suit. You lead a diamond to the ace and both defenders follow suit. Because the defenders' diamonds divided 3–2, dummy's diamonds (the king, nine and eight) are good. You will play with the ♦K, followed by the two remaining cards in the diamond suit. Nine tricks and the contract are yours.

Sometimes you duck a round of dummy's long suit as a safety play to guard against a bad break. That's what happens on the next deal:

Right: Ducking as a safety play. Declarer ducks a round of clubs as a safety play against a 4–1 break in the suit.

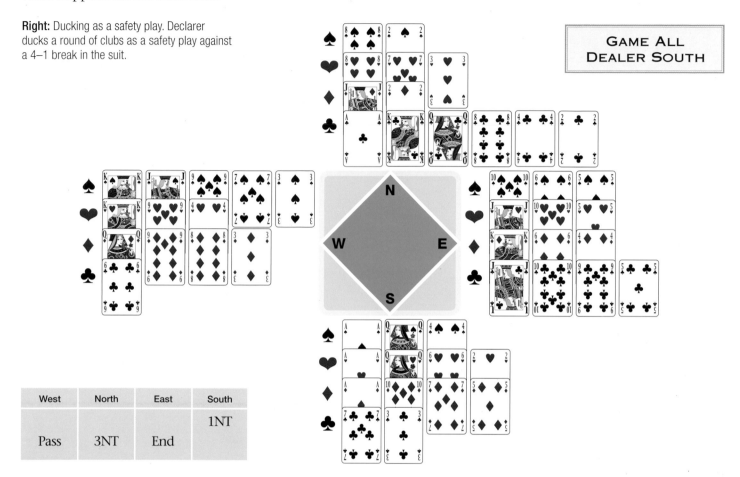

GAME ALL
DEALER SOUTH

West	North	East	South
			1NT
Pass	3NT	End	

West leads the ♠7 against 3NT and you win East's ♠10 with the ♠Q. You have four top tricks outside clubs, so five club tricks would give you the contract. If the defenders' clubs break 3–2, you can play the club suit from the top (beginning with the ace and king) and will score six club tricks. As the cards lie, however, you would go down in your contract. When the 4–1 club break came to light, you would score only three club tricks. No rescue operation would be available in the other suits.

To guard against a 4–1 club break, which happens more than one time in four, you should duck the very first round of clubs. You lead the ♣3 and play the ♣8 from dummy. East wins the trick but the contract is now certain to make. You win East's spade return and cross to dummy's ♣A to run the rest of dummy's club suit. You make five clubs, two spades and the two red aces, bringing your total to nine.

Right: Club position after the duck. Dummy's remaining clubs are ready to run.

This is an example of a "safety play". You give up a potential overtrick when the clubs break 3–2. In exchange for that, you make the game when clubs are 4–1. This is good business because an overtrick is worth only 30 while the game is worth 400 or 600 (depending on whether you are vulnerable).

PLANNING A NO-TRUMP CONTRACT

The first step in planning a no-trump contract is to count the top tricks at your disposal. Suppose you are in 3NT and there are seven top tricks. You will then need to plan the safest way to score two more tricks to bring the total to nine. Look at the typical 3NT deal below.

West leads the ♠5 against your game in no-trumps. You have seven top tricks and will therefore need two more tricks to make the game. Since your longest combined suit is clubs, it is natural to look in that direction first. You can create three extra club tricks by knocking out the ace and king of the suit. Next you must check whether it is safe to play on clubs. The defenders will win with their first club honour and clear the spade suit. When you knock out the other club honour, they will score at least three spades. You will lose a minimum of five tricks in the black suits and go down.

Next you see if there is any other possibility of making two extra tricks. You can do so in diamonds, if the suit breaks 3–3 and West holds the ♦Q. It's not a big chance but it is better than the certain defeat

awaiting you if you play on clubs. You win the first spade, in one hand or the other, cash the ♦K and finesse the ♦J. The finesse wins and when you cash the ♦A, both defenders follow. You have nine tricks and your game.

Above: Realizing there is insufficient time to set up the club suit, declarer finesses the ♦J instead.

Right: Attacking the right suit. After a spade lead against 3NT, declarer must decide whether to play on diamonds or clubs.

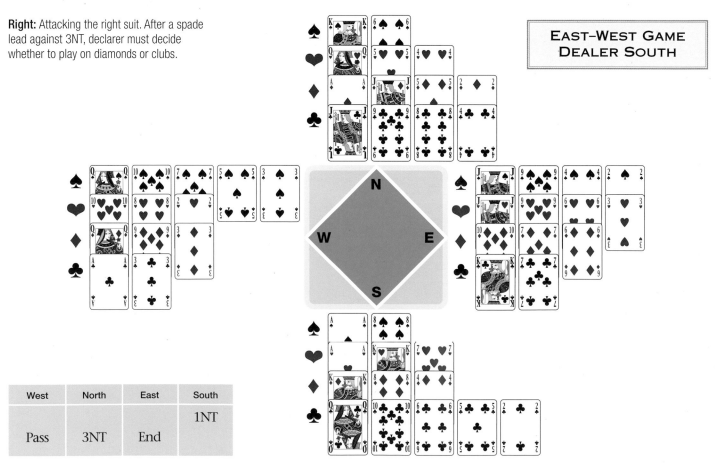

EAST–WEST GAME
DEALER SOUTH

West	North	East	South
			1NT
Pass	3NT	End	

The best plan will often depend on your reading of the opening lead and whether it is from a five-card suit or a four-card suit. Look at the 3NT contract below.

West leads the ♠2 against 3NT and you pause to make a plan. You have six tricks on top and therefore need three more tricks from somewhere. The diamond suit will provide three tricks, once the ace has been knocked out. You must ask yourself whether it is safe to play on diamonds. It is safe provided the spades are breaking 4–4, because the defenders will be able to score only one diamond and three spades. The fourth-best lead of the ♠2 tells you that West does hold only four spades (if the 2 is his fourth best card in the suit, he cannot have a fifth best card!). You therefore win the first trick with the ♠A and play on diamonds. The cards lie as you read them and the game is made.

Suppose that you were playing the same North–South cards and West had led the ♠5 instead of the ♠2. It would then be much more likely that he held five spades, a holding such as ♠Q–J–8–5–3. Fearing that you would lose four spades and the ◆A if you played on diamonds, it would be a more promising line of play to take the heart finesse. When East held the ♥K, you would make the game, scoring the three extra tricks that you needed from the heart suit.

Right: Reading the opening lead. Declarer deduces that the opening lead is from a four-card suit and plays accordingly.

Taking a heart finesse when spades are 4–4, as in the diagram, might lead to defeat. You could lose three spades, the ♥K and the ◆A.

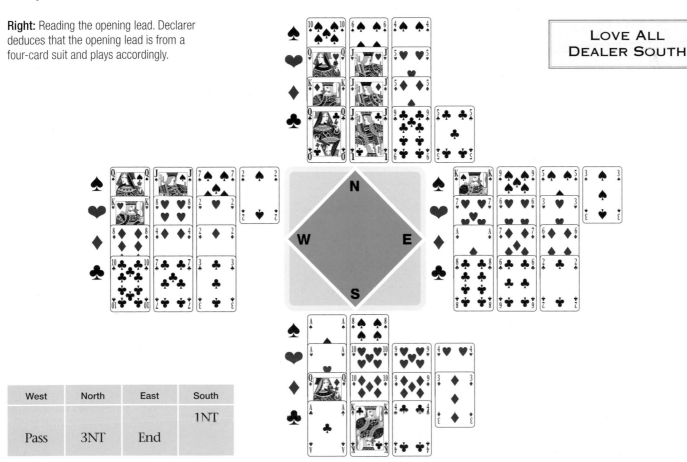

LOVE ALL
DEALER SOUTH

West	North	East	South
			1NT
Pass	3NT	End	

DRAWING TRUMPS

To "draw trumps" means to play sufficient rounds of the trump suit to remove all the trumps that the defenders hold. When you are playing in a suit contract, the general rule is that you should draw trumps immediately unless there is a good reason to do something else first. The reason to draw trumps is clear – you do not want the defenders to ruff any of your precious winners. If you play a few tricks in the side suits before drawing trumps, there is every chance that you will suffer a ruff.

We will start with a deal where an inexperienced declarer failed to draw trumps and it cost him the contract.

West led the ◆K and declarer won with the ◆A. Seeing a chance to dispose of the diamond loser in the South hand, his next move was to play on the club suit. Disaster! East ruffed the second club and returned a diamond. The defenders still had two aces to come and the contract went one down.

It was unlucky that the club suit broke so badly, yes, but declarer's duty was to ensure the safety of his contract. He should have played a trump at Trick 2,

allowing the defenders to win with the ace and cash a diamond trick. There would then have been only one further loser, a spade. Declarer's third spade could be discarded on dummy's club suit, after all the trumps had been drawn.

Above: After winning the diamond lead, declarer should draw trumps immediately to avoid suffering a ruff.

Right: Paying the price. Declarer fails to draw trumps and goes down in a contract that should have been made.

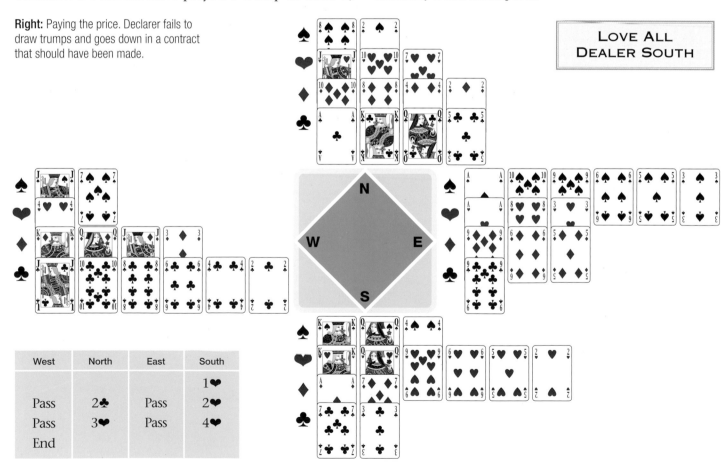

LOVE ALL
DEALER SOUTH

West	North	East	South
			1♥
Pass	2♣	Pass	2♥
Pass	3♥	Pass	4♥
End			

Right: A dangerous finesse. Declarer puts his contract at risk by taking an unnecessary finesse in diamonds.

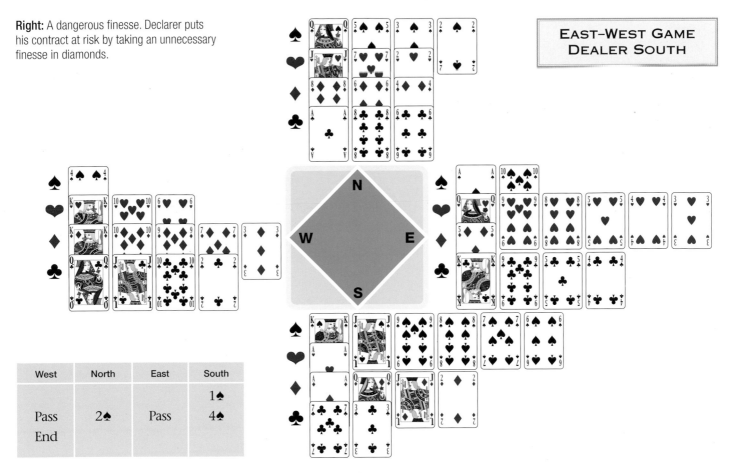

West	North	East	South
			1♠
Pass	2♠	Pass	4♠
End			

West led the ♣Q and declarer won with the ♣A in dummy. Since he had only one subsequent entry to dummy (the ♠Q) declarer "took advantage" of the chance to take a diamond finesse. His idea was to repeat a winning finesse later, after crossing to dummy with the ♠Q. It was not his lucky day. The diamond finesse lost to the king and West returned a diamond for his partner to ruff. The trump ace and a further loser in clubs then put the game one down.

Declarer could afford to lose a diamond trick, so there was no reason to avoid drawing trumps immediately and he should have played a trump at Trick 2, minimizing the chance of suffering an adverse ruff. If East rose with the ♠A and switched to the ♦5, declarer could win with the ace and draw the outstanding trump. Playing in this simple fashion, he would lose one trump, one diamond and one club. The game would be made.

EVERYONE SAT NORTH
♠ ♥ ♦ ♣

On the evening of 26 January 2006, a game of bridge was played at one of the most remote locations on the planet, the precise geographic South Pole: 90 degrees South. The weather was sunny, windy and… very cold. Rolf Peterson (USA) partnered Wendy Beeler (USA) representing the South Pole. Their opponents were Chris Dixon (a well-known England international) and Harry Otten (Netherlands). Naturally, because of the location, all four players sat North!

Right: Game at the South Pole. The temperature is -27 degrees C.

TAKING RUFFS IN THE DUMMY

One of the ways of creating extra tricks in a suit contract is to ruff a losing card in a side suit with a trump that would not otherwise have made a trick. Usually this means taking a ruff in the dummy. Suppose you have five solid trumps in your hand and three more trumps in the dummy. You begin with five trump tricks. If you can take one ruff in the dummy, you will score six trump tricks. Take two ruffs there and you will score a total of seven trump tricks. It is good business. Taking a ruff in your own hand, in the long-trump holding, will not bring you an extra trick. It may be useful in some tactical way (helping you to establish a suit in dummy, for example) but it will not create an extra trump trick.

When you need to score a ruff in dummy, it will often be wrong to draw trumps straight away because this would remove dummy's trumps. It is difficult to ruff something when you have no trumps left to ruff with! Look at the deal shown below.

West leads the ♠K and, looking at the South hand, you can see one spade loser, one diamond loser and a possible two losers in clubs. You need to reduce this total of four losers to three and the best idea is to ruff a club in dummy. You win the spade lead with the ace and must immediately play a club. (It would be foolish to draw trumps, of course, since you would then have no trumps in dummy and could not take a club ruff.) You lead the ♣Q and East wins with the ♣A. When he switches to a trump, you win with the ace, cash the ♣K and ruff a club with dummy's last trump. You then lead a diamond towards your hand, setting up an entry so that you can draw trumps. You will make seven trump tricks, including one ruff in dummy, and three side-suit winners for a total of ten. As it happens, a trump lead would have prevented a ruff and beaten your game.

Suppose next that you have a side suit of four cards in your hand and three cards in the dummy. If the defenders cards break 3–3, the 13th card in the suit will become good after three rounds. If instead the suit breaks 4–2 it may be possible to ruff the fourth round in dummy. Since one of the defenders will be out of the suit by then, you may need to ruff with a high trump.

> **GAME ALL**
> **DEALER SOUTH**

Right: Taking a ruff before drawing trumps. Declarer delays drawing trumps in order to ruff a club in dummy.

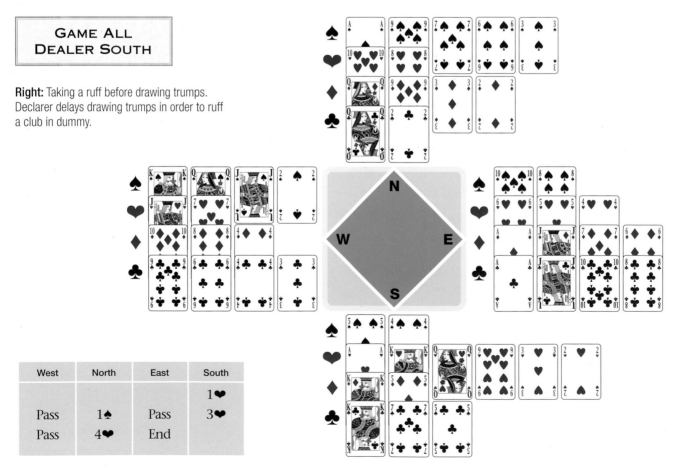

West	North	East	South
			1♥
Pass	1♠	Pass	3♥
Pass	4♥	End	

Right: Ruffing the fourth round. Declarer arranges to ruff the fourth round of a suit where he holds four cards opposite three.

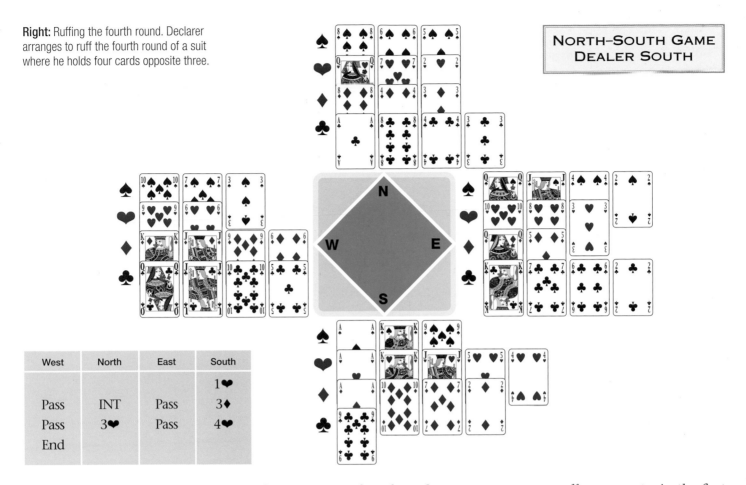

West	North	East	South
			1♥
Pass	INT	Pass	3♦
Pass	3♥	Pass	4♥
End			

West leads the ♣Q against your heart game and you win in the dummy. You have one losing spade in your hand and three potential losers in diamonds. All will be well if diamonds divide 3–3. If not, you may be able to ruff the fourth round of diamonds with dummy's ♥Q.

After winning the club lead, you continue with the ace and another diamond. East wins the second round with the ♦Q and switches to a trump. Since you may need to ruff the fourth round of diamonds with the ♥Q, to prevent an overruff, you must win the first round of trumps in your hand. You then concede a third round of diamonds. West wins and plays another trump. Again you win in your hand. You can then ruff the fourth round of diamonds with dummy's queen of trumps. You return to your hand with a spade honour and draw the last trump. The contract is yours. You made six trump tricks (five rounds of trumps and one ruff in the short-trump holding) and four winners in the side suits.

BLIND BRIDGE PLAYERS
♠ ♥ ♦ ♣

Even visually impaired players can play bridge. They use cards with Braille indentations, so that players can identify them by touch. The player on lead announces "I lead the queen of hearts" and the dummy then calls out all 13 of his cards. From then on, each card is named aloud as it is played by one of the four players. The procedure is the same whether only one player is blind, or all four players are blind.

Right: Braille cards. Look closely and you can see the raised dots.

105

ESTABLISHING A SUIT BY RUFFING

One of the advantages of playing in a suit contract is that you can use your trumps to establish a long suit. (Remember that "establish a suit" means to play that suit until the remaining cards are all winners.) By ruffing one or two rounds, until the defenders have no cards left in the suit, you can establish a winner or two. On the next deal it is dummy's club suit that needs to be established.

You reach a small slam in hearts and West leads the ♠Q. You have 7 trump tricks and 4 winners in the side suits – a total of 11. To bring the total to 12 you must establish dummy's club suit. Suppose you win the opening spade lead and draw trumps in three rounds. If clubs were 3–3, you could establish the suit with one ruff and reach the two winners by crossing to the ♦A. Since the clubs are 4–2, you would go down if you played this way.

To establish the clubs against a 4–2 break, you need to ruff two clubs in your hand. This can be done only if you make good use of the ♥Q as an entry to dummy. (An "entry" is a card that will allow you to cross to one hand or the other. An entry is usually an honour card.

However, you may also use a "ruffing entry". In other words, you cross to the other hand by ruffing a card.)

After winning the spade lead, you should cash the ace and king of clubs. You then ruff a club with the ♥9 (ruffing high to avoid an overruff by West) You continue with the ace and queen of trumps, East showing out on the second round, and ruff another club with the ♥10. You can then draw West's last trump with the ♥J, cross to dummy with the ♦A and play the established thirteenth card in clubs, discarding a spade or a diamond. Twelve tricks are yours.

PHYSICAL FITNESS REQUIRED
♠ ♥ ♦ ♣

Playing in major championships, which last for many days, can be an exhausting process. As well as being an expert bridge player, it is important to be physically fit. In the 1985 Venice Cup, Sandra Landy and Sally Horton of Great Britain played 656 hands, more than any open pair in that year's Bermuda Bowl.

Right: Using a trump entry. Declarer uses an entry in the trump suit to establish a side suit despite a 4–2 break.

LOVE ALL
DEALER SOUTH

Right: Ducking to preserve an entry. Declarer ducks the first round of the suit to be established, so he can use the ace as an entry on the second round.

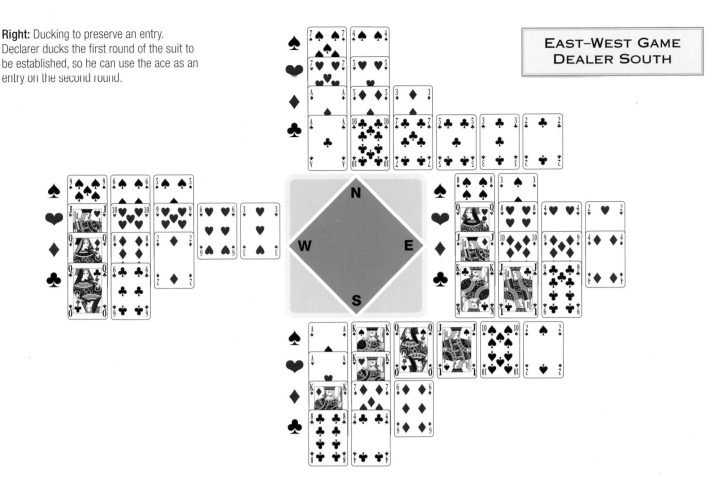

EAST–WEST GAME
DEALER SOUTH

When dummy's side suit is headed by the ace, it will often assist you to duck the first round of the suit. You can then use the ace as an entry on the second round. That's what happens on the deal shown above, where you again need to establish the club suit.

West leads the ♥J against six spades. You must aim to establish dummy's club suit, so that can discard the diamond loser. You win the heart lead and draw trumps in three rounds. If your next move is to play a club to the ace, you will go down. You will not have made full use of the ♣A. Instead you should duck the first round of clubs, playing a low club from both hands. In this way, you will preserve dummy's ♣A as an entry on the second round of clubs.

East wins the first round of clubs and switches to the ♦J. You win with the ♦K, saving dummy's ♦A as a later entry. You cross to the ♣A and ruff a club in your hand. The clubs break 3–2, you are pleased to see, and the club ruff establishes the suit. You can then cross to the ♦A to play one of the good clubs, throwing your diamond loser. The slam is yours.

Sometimes it is worth ducking a round of the suit that you are trying to establish, even when you do not have a certain loser there. By doing so, you can survive an adverse break in the suit.

Look at this diamond position:

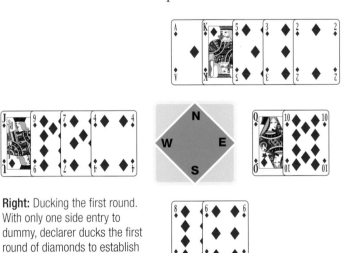

Right: Ducking the first round. With only one side entry to dummy, declarer ducks the first round of diamonds to establish the suit against a 4–2 break.

If you have only one entry to dummy in the other suits, it might well be worth ducking the first round of diamonds. You could then cross to the ♦A on the second round, cash the ♦K and ruff a diamond, establishing the suit even though the defenders' diamonds break 4–2. Suppose instead that you played the ace and king on the first two rounds, proceeding to ruff the third round. You would then need two further entries to the dummy – one to ruff the fourth round and another to reach the established diamond winner.

DISCARDING LOSERS

There are three main methods of disposing of a potential loser in your hand. You have already seen how you can take a finesse or ruff a loser in dummy. The third way to dispose of a loser is to discard it by leading a winner from the dummy. This is know as taking a discard.

Right: Taking a discard. Declarer has an easy discard on the third round of diamonds.

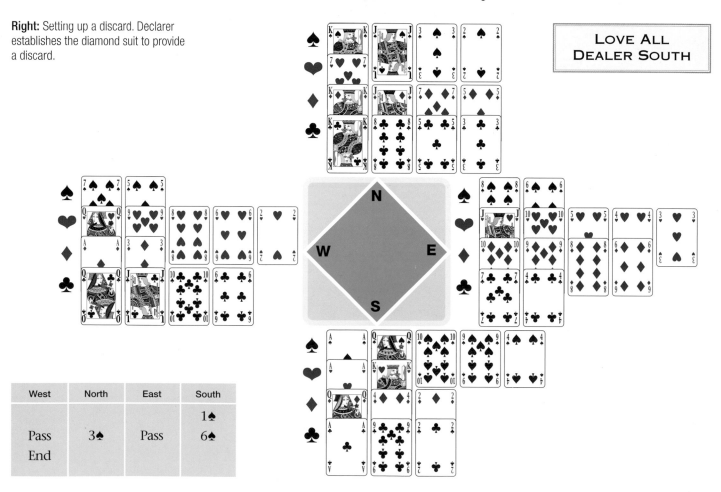

If you need to discard a loser, nothing could be simpler. You play the king, ace and queen of diamonds and throw a loser from your hand on the third round.

Right: Setting up a discard. Declarer establishes the diamond suit to provide a discard.

Sometimes life is more difficult and you must establish a suit before you can take a discard on it.

After a bold auction to a small slam on the deal below, West leads the ♣Q. There is a certain loser in diamonds and declarer must avoid losing a trick in clubs. This can be done only by establishing an extra winner in diamonds, on which the club loser can be discarded.

Declarer wins the club lead with the ace and draws trumps in two rounds with the ace and queen. He must now consider how to play the diamond suit. If the defenders' cards divide 3–3, it will be easy to set up the 13th diamond in dummy. Another possibility is that West holds a doubleton ♦A. By twice leading a low card towards the dummy, declarer can force West to play the ♦A without capturing an honour.

At Trick 4, declarer leads the ♦2 towards dummy. West plays low and the ♦K wins the trick. Declarer re-enters his hand with a heart and leads the ♦4 towards dummy. West has to play the bare ace and declarer is now assured of further tricks for the ♦Q and the ♦J. The last of these winners will provide a discard for his club loser.

| | LOVE ALL DEALER SOUTH |

West	North	East	South
			1♠
Pass	3♠	Pass	6♠
End			

Sometimes you must risk taking an otherwise unnecessary finesse, in order to set up a discard for one of your losers. That is the winning line on the deal shown below.

West leads the ♠J against your contract of six hearts. There are two potential losers in the South hand, one in diamonds, the other in clubs. The only real chance of avoiding the diamond loser is a successful finesse of the ♣10. If East holds the ♣J you score two club tricks, whoever is holding the ♣A.

You win the spade lead and draw trumps in two rounds, with the ace and queen. You then play a club to the ten. This forces the ♣A from West. You will win his return, cash the ♣K and re-enter dummy to discard your diamond loser on the ♣Q.

Right: Finessing to establish a discard. Declarer risks an otherwise unnecessary finesse in clubs to set up a diamond discard.

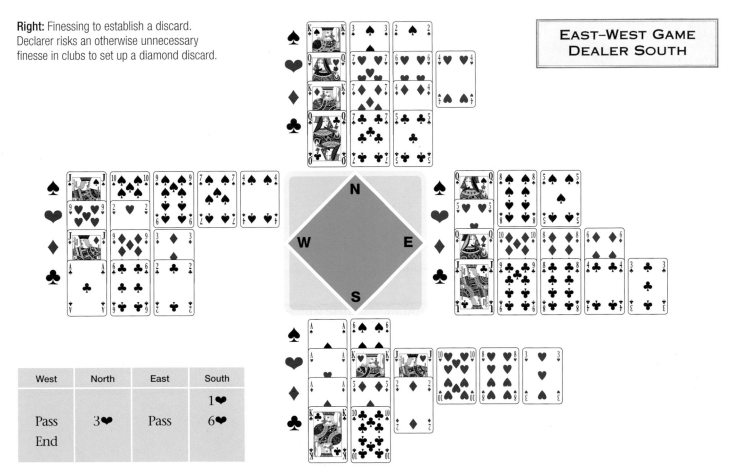

EAST–WEST GAME
DEALER SOUTH

West	North	East	South
			1♥
Pass	3♥	Pass	6♥
End			

THE POPULARITY OF BRIDGE
♠ ♥ ♦ ♣

By the 1950s bridge had become the most popular card game in the world. The USA's President Eisenhower was a regular player, facing expert opposition most Saturday nights. He also attended national tournaments, when possible. Alternative attractions such as television and computer games have caused a slight decline since then. Nevertheless, it is estimated that ten million Americans still play bridge.

Right: Dwight Eisenhower enjoyed bridge as much as golf and was considered an expert player.

PLANNING A SUIT CONTRACT

When you plan a no-trump contract, you count your top tricks and devise the safest plan to increase this to the number of tricks that you need. When you are planning a suit contract, it is usually easier to take a different approach. You consider the potential losers (losing tricks) in the hand with the longer trumps. Suppose you are in 4♠ and you can see five potential losers in your hand. You would then have to make a plan to reduce these five losers to just three. Look at the deal below.

Let's say that you have taken an optimistic view of your hand and bid a small slam in spades. West leads the ♥Q and you must make a plan for the contract. You look at the potential losers in the long-trump hand, South, taking each suit in turn. In spades you have no losers. Nor are there any losers in hearts, since the ace and king cover your two cards there. There are two potential losers in diamonds and one in clubs. You have a total of three potential losers and must reduce them to just one in order to make your ambitious slam.

In general, there are three basic ways in which you can save yourself a loser. You can ruff the loser, discard it, or take a successful finesse in the suit. Here you would plan to take a successful finesse in clubs, to remove the club loser, and to ruff one of the diamond losers. The next stage in making a plan is to decide the best order of play, in particular whether you should draw trumps straightaway. Here it would not be a good idea. Suppose you drew two rounds of trumps with the ace and king. When you subsequently conceded a diamond trick, to prepare for a diamond ruff in dummy, West would win and remove dummy's last trump. You would go down.

So, the plan would be to win the heart lead, in either hand, draw just one round of trumps and then play ace and another diamond. When you regained the lead, you would ruff your last diamond with dummy's ♠Q, draw trumps and eventually take a club finesse. Since West does hold the ♣K, you would make the slam. The contract was roughly a 50 per cent proposition – you would make it when West

Right: Counting the losers. Declarer sees three potential losers in 6♠ and plans to reduce these to just one.

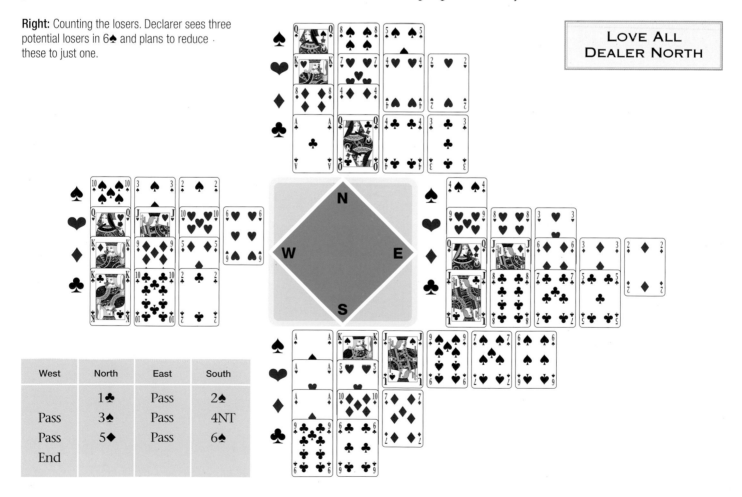

LOVE ALL
DEALER NORTH

West	North	East	South
	1♣	Pass	2♠
Pass	3♠	Pass	4NT
Pass	5♦	Pass	6♠
End			

held the ♣K and go down when East held that card. Let's see an example of planning a contract where a discard is necessary:

Right: Discarding losers. Declarer begins with three potential losers and plans to discard two of them on dummy's diamond suit.

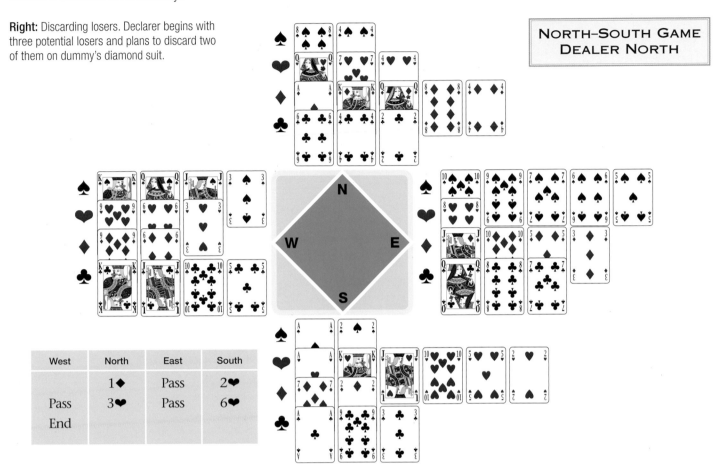

NORTH–SOUTH GAME
DEALER NORTH

West	North	East	South
	1♦	Pass	2♥
Pass	3♥	Pass	6♥
End			

A rough-and-ready auction carries you to six hearts and West leads the ♠K. As always, you look at the potential losers in the long-trump hand, South. You have one loser in spades and two further losers in clubs. There is no possibility of ruffing any of these losers, nor of taking a finesse in those suits. You must rely on discarding two of the three losers on dummy's diamonds.

If the defenders' diamonds break 3–3, you could take three discards on the diamonds and score an overtrick. Since you are only in a small slam, you should concentrate your efforts on planning the best way to score four diamond tricks, discarding two of your three losers. This can be done if the diamond suit breaks no worse than 4–2.

Next you must plan the order of play. The general idea will be to cash the ace and king of diamonds and to ruff a third round of the suit high. The remaining ◆Q–8 will then be good and you will need to reach them with the ♥Q. So, you draw two rounds of trumps with the ace and king. You cannot afford to draw the last trump at this stage, since you are relying on the ♥Q as a later entry to dummy. You cash the two top diamonds and ruff a diamond with the ♥J to avoid an overruff. You then enter dummy with the ♥Q, drawing West's last trump. Finally, you discard your two club losers on the queen and eight of diamonds. Count the tricks that you made: six trump tricks, four diamonds and two black-suit aces.

BRIDGE AIDS YOUR MEMORY
♠ ♥ ♦ ♣

The 2003 *New England Journal of Medicine* recommended bridge as a mentally challenging activity that could restrict memory loss in the aged and slow the onset of Alzheimer's disease. Just as physical exercise will keep your muscles in good shape, so does mental exercise keep the brain working well. "Using the mind actually causes rewiring of the brain, sprouting new synapses," said Professor Joseph Coyle.

CHAPTER 6

BASIC DEFENCE

Defence is generally reckoned to be the hardest part of the game. In the early stages of defending a contract, you may be operating partly in the dark. The declarer has the advantage of being able to see his partner's cards (the dummy). Meanwhile, as a defender, you can see only half of the cards that belong to your side.

In this section we will spend some time looking at opening leads – against no-trump contracts, against suit contracts and against slams. We will see also the basic rules for defending in both the second seat and the third seat. (The term "in the second seat" means that you are the second player to play a card to a particular trick.)

The defenders are allowed to pass information to each other, by signalling with the cards that they play. We will look here at "attitude signals", where you tell partner whether you like the suit that he has led and would welcome a continuation of that suit. We will see also how to maintain communication between the two defenders' hands.

Right: To some extent you can defend by following general guidelines, such as to lead your fourth-best card and to play high in the third seat. In addition, you must always try to calculate how to beat the opponents' contract.

OPENING LEAD AGAINST NO-TRUMPS

You have two options, when choosing an opening lead against a no-trump contract. You can make an attacking lead, from your own strongest suit, or you can make a passive lead – aiming to avoid giving a trick away. An attacking lead is appropriate on most deals.

To beat a contract of 3NT, you need to score five tricks before the declarer can score nine. The main advantage you have over the declarer is that you can make the first lead and perhaps establish some extra tricks for your side. In general, you should lead your longest and strongest suit. Even if you give away a trick by doing so, you may eventually establish, and then be able to cash, some long cards in the suit.

Suppose the bidding has been 1NT – 3NT and you are on lead with this hand:

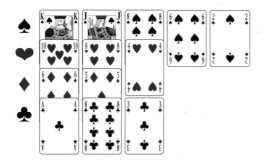

It is obvious to lead a spade. If you are lucky and find partner with the ace or queen of the suit, you will have an excellent chance of beating the contract. Even

if partner holds only the ♠10 and your lead allows declarer to score the queen and ace of the suit, all is not lost. You partner may gain the lead early in the play and be able to clear the spades before your entry card, the ♣A, has been removed.

Once you have decided which suit to lead, the choice of card is determined by the following table:

- From a suit headed by a "sequence" of three touching (i.e. adjacent) honours lead the top card: the ace from A–K–Q, the king from K–Q–J.

- From a suit headed by a "broken sequence" (such as A–K–J, K–Q–10 or Q–J–9) also lead the top card.

- From a suit headed by an "interior sequence" lead the middle honour: the jack from K–J–10, the 10 from K–10–9.

- From a three-card suit headed by touching honours, lead the top card: the queen from Q–J–8.

- Otherwise lead your fourth best card from a suit containing one or more honours. Lead the 3 from Q–10–7–3, the 5 from K–J–9–5–2.

- When your suit does not contain an honour, lead the second-best card: the 6 from 8–6–5–3, the 7 from 9–7–6–5–2.

Above: Interior sequence lead. From this hand you would lead the ♥10, the top of an interior sequence.

Above: Second-best from four small. From this hand you would lead the ♠7, the second-best card from a weak suit.

When the opponents have bid some suits

It is generally inadvisable to lead a suit that one of the opponents has bid. Suppose you are sitting West and this has been the auction:

West	North	East	South
			1♥
Pass	2♣	Pass	2NT
Pass	3NT	End	

You have to choose a lead from:

It would be a poor idea to lead a heart and you should choose either a spade or a diamond. It is usually better to lead a major suit rather than a minor. That is because the opponents are more likely to have bid any major suit that they hold (or perhaps sought a fit there with Stayman) than to have bid a minor suit. You should therefore prefer a spade lead to a diamond lead. This is particularly so because your spades here are stronger.

Above: Low from an honour holding. Suppose your partner opened 1♥ and you are now on lead against 3NT. You should lead the ♥4. The old-fashioned lead of the ♥K is too likely to give declarer an extra trick.

Leading partner's suit

When partner has bid a suit, particularly if he has overcalled, you should usually lead that suit even when you are short there. Indeed, his principal reason for making the bid may have been to suggest a good opening lead. Even when partner has not bid, it may be a good idea to lead a short suit when your own hand is very weak and you have little prospect of gaining the lead later. Suppose the bidding has been 1NT – 3NT and you are on lead with this hand:

There is not much prospect of a club lead succeeding. Even if you could establish the suit, you have no high card elsewhere with which to gain the lead. Partner may hold around 12 points, including an entry card or two, so you should try to find his long suit. A three-card holding is a better lead than a doubleton and here you should lead the ♥10.

Above: High from touching honours. After opponents' bidding of 1♥ – 3♥ – 4♥, it is natural to lead a spade. Lead the ♠Q against a suit contract, as someone will surely ruff the third round. (Against no-trumps, you would lead the ♠2 instead.)

DEFENCE IN THE SECOND SEAT

The general rule when defending in the second seat is: "Second hand plays low". The reason for this is that it will often cost you a trick to rise with an ace or a king when a low card is led. Look at this diamond position:

Right: Second hand plays low. When South leads the ◆3, West must play low in the second seat or declarer will score three diamond tricks.

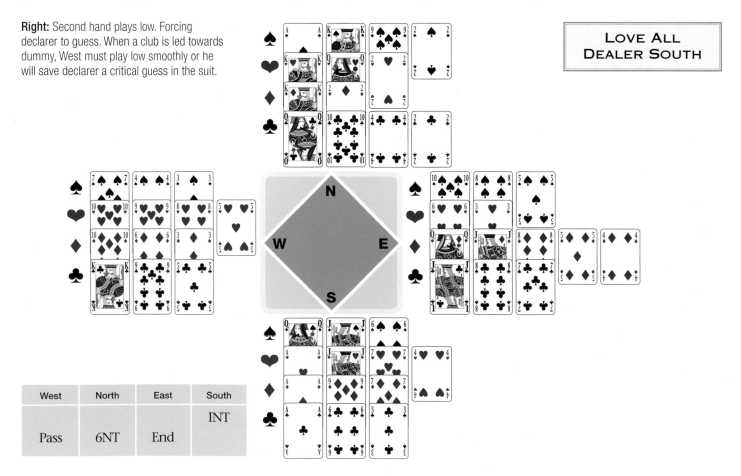

Declarer leads the ◆3 from the South hand. If West plays the ◆A "on air", as it is called, declarer will make three diamond tricks. If West instead follows the general rule and plays low in the second seat, dummy's

king or jack will win but the ace will capture South's queen on the second round. Declarer will score only two diamond tricks. Another reason to play low in that diamond position is that East might hold the ◆Q. By rising with the ◆A, you would save declarer a guess in the suit.

On the deal shown below, declarer can make his slam only by guessing correctly in clubs. West must be careful not to give the club position away.

Sitting West, you lead the ♥10 against 6NT. Declarer has 11 top tricks and needs to establish an extra trick from the club suit. Suppose he wins the heart lead with the ace and immediately leads the ♣3 from his hand. If you rise with the ♣K, or give the position away by thinking of playing it, you will save declarer a guess. If instead you follow smoothly with a low club, declarer will have a difficult guess to make. Because so many defenders would give away the position of the king if they held it, declarer is likely to play the ♣10 from dummy, hoping that you hold the ♣J. After misguessing the clubs, he will have no way to recover.

Right: Second hand plays low. Forcing declarer to guess. When a club is led towards dummy, West must play low smoothly or he will save declarer a critical guess in the suit.

LOVE ALL
DEALER SOUTH

West	North	East	South
			INT
Pass	6NT	End	

Here is another deal where a defender will benefit from following the "second hand low" rule:

Right: Second hand plays low. Playing low to prevent a ruffing finesse. When a heart is led towards dummy, West must play low or he will allow his partner's ace of hearts to be trapped in a ruffing finesse.

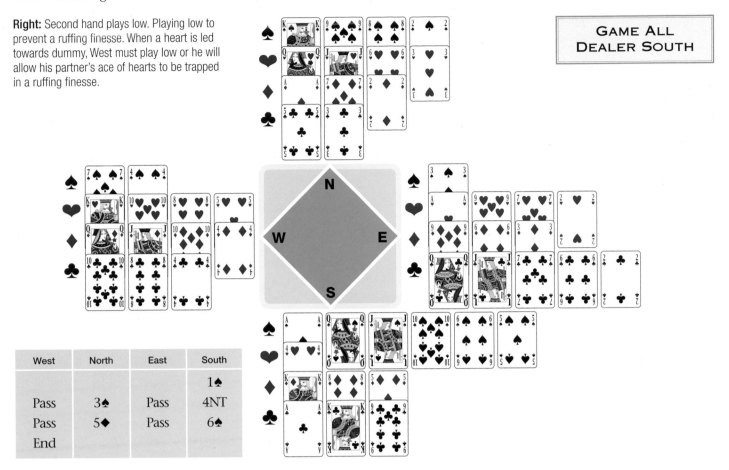

GAME ALL
DEALER SOUTH

West	North	East	South
			1♠
Pass	3♠	Pass	4NT
Pass	5♦	Pass	6♠
End			

Sitting West, you lead the ◆Q against South's small slam. He wins with dummy's ◆A and East signals with the ◆3, showing no interest in the suit. Declarer draws trumps with the ace and queen and then leads the ♥4 from his hand. If you mistakenly rise with the ♥K, the slam will be made. There are still two entries to dummy in the trump suit. Declarer will use one of these to run the ♥Q through East's ♥A (a play known as a "ruffing finesse"). If East plays low, declarer will throw his diamond loser. If instead East covers, declarer will ruff and use his remaining trump entry to reach the established ♥J.

When declarer leads the ♥4 from his hand, you should follow the general guideline "Second hand plays low", playing the ♥5. East will win dummy's ♥Q with the ♥A and declarer will have no way to avoid a further loser on the third round of diamonds. The slam will go one down and South's adventurous bidding will prove costly.

Right: West correctly plays low on the first round of hearts and prevents declarer from setting up a winner in the suit.

OPENING LEAD AGAINST SUIT CONTRACTS

Choosing an opening lead against a no-trump contract is relatively easy. As we saw in an earlier section, you normally lead from your own longest and strongest suit, hoping to set up some long cards. When the contract is in a trump suit, setting up long cards is not a relevant concept because declarer will usually be able to ruff the later rounds of a suit. These are the main types of lead to consider:

- Lead a strong side suit, such as Q–J–10–7 or K–J–8–3, with the aim of setting up some quick winners.

- Lead a short suit, such as 8 or 9–5, aiming to score a ruff.

- Lead a trump, hoping to reduce the number of ruffs that declarer can make.

- Lead a safe suit, such as 9–8–6–5 or 8–4–3, to avoid giving a trick away.

When you have decided to lead a strong side suit, the choice of card is generally dictated by the same table that we saw in the section on leading against no-trumps. You would lead the top honour from a sequence such as K–Q–J–7, fourth-best from K–10–8–5–2 and second-best from a suit with no honour card: 9–7–6–3.

There are two important exceptions, where you would lead differently against a suit contract, compared with no-trumps:

- Do not underlead an ace against a suit contract. To lead from a suit such as A–9–8–2, whether you lead the ace or the 2, is usually a very poor idea. The purpose of an ace is to capture a king or a queen.

- From a four-card or longer suit headed by two touching honours, such as K–Q–8–3 or Q–J–7–6–2, lead the top honour against a suit contract. The third round will normally be ruffed by someone, so make sure that your honours contribute to the first two rounds.

Suppose the bidding has been 1♠ – 4♠ and you have to choose a lead from one of these hands:

1

Lead the ♥5 from (1). You need to find four defensive tricks from somewhere. If you can find partner with the ♥Q or ♥A, you may be able to score some heart tricks.

2

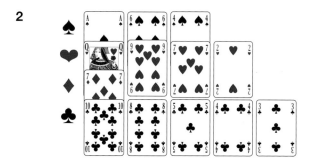

On (2) you should lead the singleton ♦7. When you hold the ace of trumps, there is an extra chance of scoring a ruff because declarer will not be able to draw trumps as soon as he gains the lead.

3

On hand (3) it is unattractive to lead from any of the side suits because your honours there are not accompanied by a high second-best card. It is better to lead from K–J–x–x than from K–10–x–x, better to lead from K–9–x–x than K–8–x–x. When the second-best card is no higher than a 9, there is more chance of giving away a trick by leading the suit than there is of establishing one. So, make the safe lead of a trump on (3).

Leading a trump

As we saw with hand (3) above, you sometimes lead a trump because you have no attractive side-suit lead. There are also a couple of situations where a trump lead stands a good chance of working well. The first is when responder has left the opener in his second suit. After an auction such as 1♠ – 1NT – 2♦, it is likely that responder will have one spade and three or four diamonds. By leading a trump, you may reduce the ruffs that declarer can take.

The other situation is when partner has left in your take-out double of a one-bid. Suppose you double 1♥ and everyone passes. Your partner has indicated long and strong hearts and you should lead a trump, even when you hold only a singleton, to allow him to begin to draw trumps. Except in the situation just mentioned, it is unwise to lead a singleton trump. By doing so, you may damage your partner's four-card holding (such as Q–J–x–x or A–J–x–x), reducing the number of trump tricks that he would otherwise score.

Active or passive?

You will often find yourself having to choose between an active lead (such as attacking in a side-suit of ♦K–J –8–2) and a passive lead such as a trump from ♥6–5–3. In general, you must risk an active lead, hoping to score or set up side-suit tricks, when declarer may otherwise be able to throw his losers away.

Suppose the opponents' bidding is: 1♠ – 2♣ – 2♠ – 4♠ and you are on lead with:

You can visualize a good club suit in the dummy, one that will supply discards once trumps are drawn and the clubs are established. You must make the active lead of the ♦2, hoping to find your partner with the ♦Q or the ♦A. In this way you may score whatever

diamond tricks are your due, before declarer has time to discard his diamond losers on dummy's club suit. When such a lead fails, because declarer holds the ace and queen of diamonds, you will usually find that your lead has given nothing away. Declarer could have discarded his diamond losers anyway.

Suppose next that the opponents' bidding is 1♥ – 2♥ – 4♥ and you are lead with:

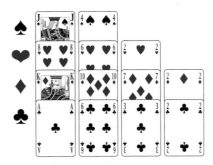

A diamond lead is now much less attractive. Your second card is the 10 rather than the jack. Also, there is less reason to think that declarer will be able to discard any diamond losers that he may hold. A diamond lead might be right but in the long run it will pay you to lead a passive trump, aiming not to give a trick away.

┌─────────────────────────────────────┐
LEAD AWAY FROM A KING
♠ ♥ ♦ ♣

Don't be afraid to "lead away from a king". If the bidding suggests you should be active, leading from such as ♦K–J–8–3 is a promising attack.
└─────────────────────────────────────┘

DEFENCE IN THE THIRD SEAT

The general rule when defending in the third seat is: "Third hand plays high". The reason for this is that you do not want the next player to win the trick cheaply. Even if your card does not win the trick, it will force out a higher one from the opponent on your left. This may promote a trick or two in the suit for the defenders.

Suppose your partner, West, has led the ♦2 in this lay-out:

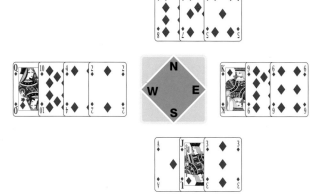

Above: West leads the ♦2 and East must play the ♦K (playing high in the third seat) to prevent declarer scoring a cheap trick with the ♦J.

You play "third hand high", rising with the ♦K. Declarer wins with the ♦A but will score only one trick in the suit. Your partner's ♦Q–10 are now worth two tricks, sitting over declarer's ♦J. If you had not followed the general guideline, playing a lower card, declarer would have won the first round with the ♦J and scored two tricks from the suit.

The situation is less clear-cut when dummy holds a high card, one that can beat your second-best card:

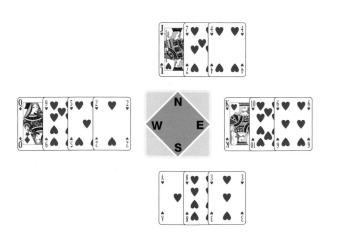

Above: Finessing against the dummy. West leads the ♥2 and East must play the ♥10 to restrict declarer to one trick in the suit.

Suppose West has led the ♥2 against a contract of 4♠. Since it is poor practice to underlead an ace against a suit contract, you can place the ♥A with South. You should therefore play the ♥10 on the first trick, retaining your ♥K to deal with dummy's ♥J later. The ten will force South's ace and he will make only one heart trick. If you play the ♥K instead, declarer will make tricks with both the ace and the jack.

Even if the contract was in no-trumps and West might therefore hold the ♥A, it would still be right to play the ♥10 at Trick 1. If South held ♥Q–8–3, he would be certain to make a trick from the suit anyway. Sometimes in these situations you do have to guess which card will work best. As a general rule, you should play your second-best card if it is the nine or higher.

Above: In the heart position shown on the left, East correctly plays the ♥10 to avoid giving declarer a second heart trick.

DALLAS ACES
♠ ♥ ♦ ♣

The world's first professional bridge team, known as the "Dallas Aces" and later simply as "The Aces", was formed in 1968 by financier Ira Corn. His objective was to win the world championship for the USA after a gap of many years. Six players were hired: James Jacoby, Robert Wolff, William Eisenberg, Robert Goldman, Michael Lawrence and Robert Hamman. They were paid a salary and expected to practise for up to 50 hours a week. They won the world championship in 1970 and successfully defended it in 1971.

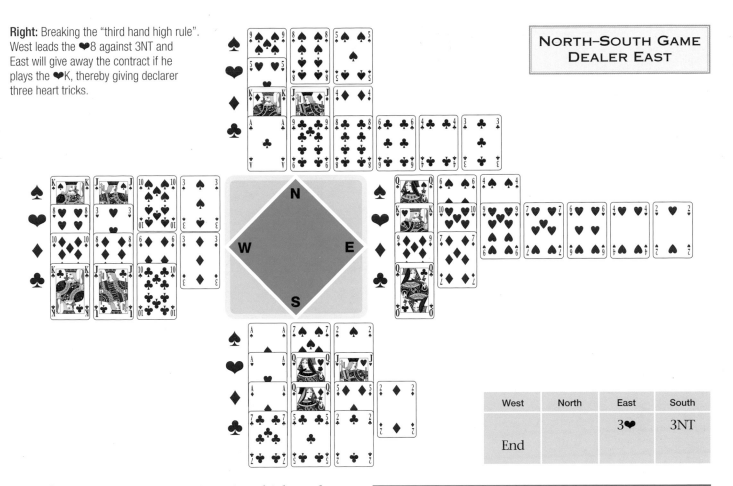

Right: Breaking the "third hand high rule". West leads the ♥8 against 3NT and East will give away the contract if he plays the ♥K, thereby giving declarer three heart tricks.

West	North	East	South
		3♥	3NT
End			

There are various situations in which a player should break the "third hand high" rule. One is when he cannot possibly promote a higher card by playing high, and may give declarer an extra trick by doing so. Look at the deal above.

Sitting East, you open with a pre-emptive three-bid in hearts. South overcalls 3NT and West leads the ♥8. It is clear from the high spot-card lead that declarer holds the ace, queen and jack of hearts. If you play "third hand high", contributing the ♥K to the first trick, declarer will score three heart tricks. He has six top winners immediately available in the other three suits and will therefore make his contract easily.

The singleton heart in dummy prevents declarer from making three heart tricks under his own steam and you should therefore play a discouraging ♥2 on the first trick. Declarer will win with the ♥Q and duck a club, hoping to establish that suit. You win with the ♣Q and must decide what to do next. Persevering with hearts is no good because declarer will score the nine tricks already mentioned. Instead you should switch to spades. Declarer will hold up the ace of spades until the third round and play ace and another club. West wins the third round of clubs and the 13th spade will then be the setting trick.

LOW SPOT-CARD FROM STRENGTH
♠ ♥ ♦ ♣

When your partner leads a low spot-card he is likely to hold an honour in the suit (unless he is leading a short suit). When he leads a high spot-card, he is denying an honour in the suit. This knowledge will often affect your play in the third suit.

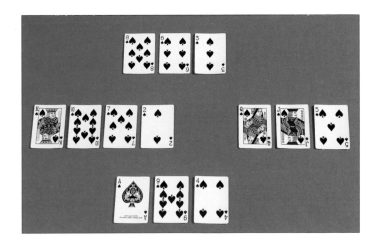

Above: Low from equals in third seat. West leads the ♠2 and dummy plays ♠3. East should play the ♠J (lowest from equals). When this forces South's ♠A, West deduces that East must hold the ♠Q or declarer would have won with that card.

ATTITUDE SIGNALS

When your partner leads a low spot-card to a trick, you will generally have to play "third hand high" in an attempt to win the trick or to force out a high card from the next hand. The situation is different when your partner leads an honour card, such as the ace or king, or when the trick has been won by the hand on your right. In those cases you can choose from your available spot-cards in the suit to pass a signal to your partner. The traditional method of signalling, when partner has led to the trick, is to play high when you would like a continuation of the suit, low when you would not.

Suppose the contract is 4♠ and your partner, West, has led the ♦A in this lay-out:

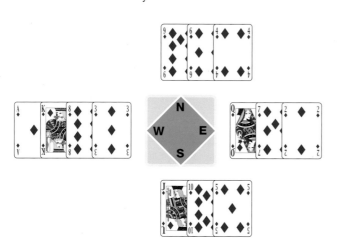

Above: Encouraging signal. West leads the ♦A and East gives an encouraging signal by following with the ♦7.

Sitting East, you play the ♦7 (your highest available spot-card) to show that you like diamonds and would be happy with a continuation of the suit. West will play the ♦K next and then a low diamond to your queen.

FOUR-COLOUR PACK

♠ ♥ ♦ ♣

Players sometimes revoke (fail to follow suit) because they confuse a club spot-card for one in spades, or a heart spot-card for one in diamonds. In an effort to help players to avoid revoking, a four-colour pack was invented. It had orange diamonds and red hearts, blue clubs and black spades.

You would give a "high to encourage" signal when you held a doubleton too:

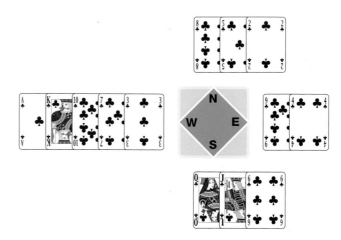

Above: Encouraging from a doubleton. West leads the ♣A and East gives an encouraging signal by following with the ♣9.

West leads the ♣A against a suit contract and you encourage with the ♣9. He cashes the ♣K at Trick 2 and then leads a third round, which you ruff.

SIGNALLING WITH A HIGH CARD

♠ ♥ ♦ ♣

When you decide to signal with a high card, be as clear as possible. To signal encouragement from ♥K–8–6–2, play the ♥8 rather than the ♥6.

Above: A special signal. West leads the ♠A and dummy plays the ♠3. East should play the ♠Q. This special signal tells partner that both the ♠Q and the ♠J are held. Knowing this, West may decide to lead a low spade to the jack on the second round.

When you do not want a continuation, you signal with your lowest spot-card:

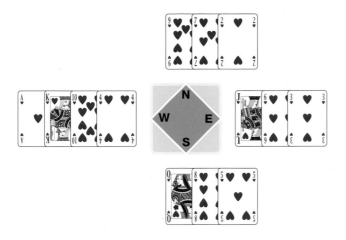

Above: Discouraging signal. West leads the ♥A and East gives a discouraging signal by following with the ♥3.

West leads the ♥A. If he continues with a second round of hearts, he will set up South's ♥Q. You warn him that you do not want a heart continuation by signalling with the ♥3 on the first round. West will then switch to a different suit and declarer will not be given an undeserved heart trick.

Reading an attitude signal

You can only signal with the cards that you have been dealt! If you want to discourage from ♠J–8–7, you will have to play the ♠7 and hope that partner can read that as a low card. Suppose this is the spade lay-out:

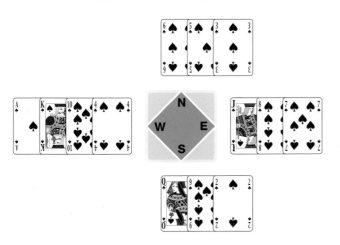

Above: Reading the ♠7. West leads the ♠A and must decide whether his partner's ♠7 is an encouraging or discouraging card.

West leads the ♠A and you signal with the ♠7. If South follows with the ♠2, West should realize that he can see the ♠4 in his own hand, the ♠6–5–3 in dummy and the ♠2 from declarer. So, even though the ♠7 may

seem like a fairly high spot-card, it is in fact the lowest spot-card out and is therefore a discouraging signal. (A cunning declarer might drop the ♠9 on the first round, hiding the ♠2 in the hope that West would read the ♠7 as an encouraging card.)

Similarly, when you want to encourage from ♣K–3–2 you will have to play the ♣3 and hope that partner notices that the ♣2 is missing and that you may therefore be playing your highest spot-card. This may be the club position:

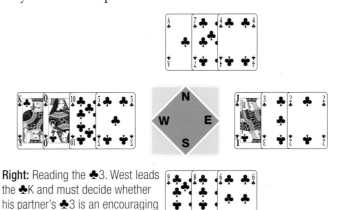

Right: Reading the ♣3. West leads the ♣K and must decide whether his partner's ♣3 is an encouraging or discouraging card.

West leads the club king and dummy wins with the ace. You signal encouragement with the ♣3 and South plays the ♣6. West should take account of the fact that the ♣2 has not yet appeared and you may therefore be signalling encouragement from ♣J–3–2. (It is possible that South is playing deceptively, by hiding the ♣2 from such as ♣J–6–2, but not many players are up to such trickery.)

Above: An encouraging signal. West leads a speculative ♦K against a contract of 4♠ and South wins with the ♦A. East should play an encouraging ♦8, to show that he holds the ♦Q. If West can gain the lead with a high trump, he may then cross to the ♦Q for a diamond ruff.

GIVING PARTNER A RUFF

Near the start of a hand, before declarer has had the chance to draw trumps, the defenders may be able to score a ruff or two. This happens most often when the player on lead holds a side-suit singleton. Look at the deal below.

Sitting East, you see partner lead the ♦4. Declarer plays low from dummy and you win with the ♦A, South playing the ♦5. It is fairly obvious that the opening lead is a singleton. First of all, it would not be attractive for West to lead from ♦Q–6–4. Secondly, if declarer held a singleton ♦5, he would probably have played the ♦J from dummy. So, you are going to return a diamond at Trick 2, to give partner a ruff.

Which diamond should you lead? It is a common agreement among good players everywhere that when you give partner a ruff, you should tell him which suit you would like to be returned on the next trick. Here you hold the ♣A and would very much like a club return. You indicate this by leading the ♦2 for the ruff – your lowest diamond asks for a return in the lower remaining side suit, clubs. West ruffs and duly returns a club. You win with the ♣A and give partner a second

diamond ruff to defeat the contract. Suppose you had held the ♥A instead of the ♣A. You would then have led the ♦10 to give partner his ruff. Leading your highest diamond would ask for a return in the higher of the remaining side suits. This is known as "giving a suit preference signal".

If you have no particular preference between the other two side suits, you would indicate this by leading a middle card to give partner his ruff.

HOLDING THE ACE IN THIRD SEAT
♠ ♥ ♦ ♣

Suppose partner leads the ♥9 against a spade game and you hold ♥A–10–8–6–2. If the lead is a singleton, it will be right to win immediately and give partner a ruff. If the lead is from a doubleton and partner holds the ace of trumps, it may be better to duck, retaining the ♥A to give partner a ruff later. In general, you should assume a singleton lead, since it is a more attractive proposition for your partner.

Right: Giving a suit preference signal. East wins his partner's singleton diamond lead and must suggest the best return with his choice of card to deliver the ruff.

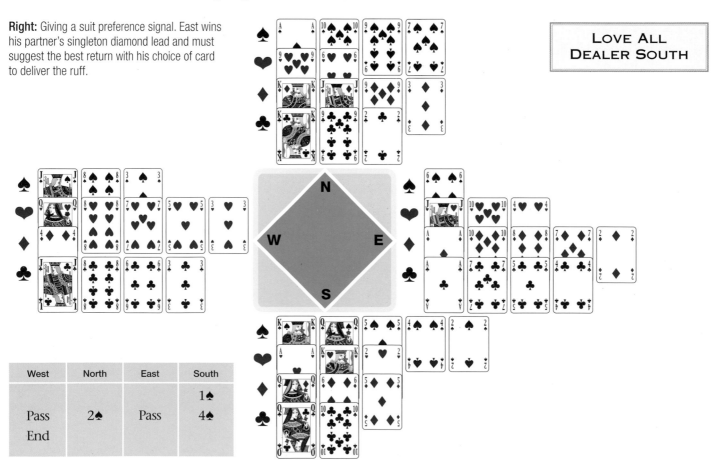

LOVE ALL
DEALER SOUTH

West	North	East	South
			1♠
Pass	2♠	Pass	4♠
End			

On the next deal, West must be alert to the possibility of a ruff and must not allow declarer to draw trumps.

Sitting West, you lead the ♦10. East wins with the ♦A and switches to the ♣9. Declarer plays the ♣J and you win with the ♣K. When you return a club, declarer wins in his hand with the ♣A and leads the ♥3 towards dummy. You must think carefully before playing to this trick.

Since East would not have led the ♣9 from ♣10–9–7, you know that your partner began with a doubleton club. If you play low on the first round of trumps, dummy will win with the ♥10 and a second round of trumps will remove partner's last trump. Instead you must leap in with the ♥A. You can then return a third round of clubs while your partner still has a trump. He ruffs with the ♥5 and the contract goes one down.

Right: Winning the trump ace immediately. When the defenders have the chance of scoring a ruff, they must not allow declarer to slip through a round of trumps.

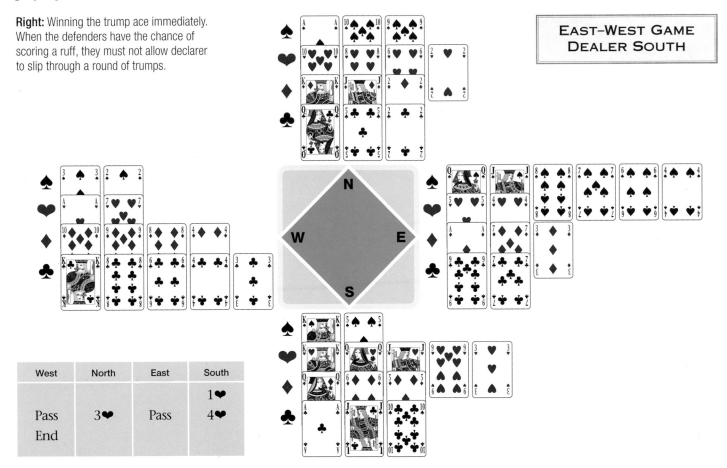

EAST–WEST GAME
DEALER SOUTH

West	North	East	South
			1♥
Pass	3♥	Pass	4♥
End			

PRECISION CLUB SYSTEM
♠ ♥ ♦ ♣

The Precision Club system was invented by C.C.Wei, a ship owner who was born in Shanghai. The system was successfully employed by the Taiwan team in the 1969 and 1970 world championships, also by the Italian team when they won the 1972 Olympiad and the 1973 and 1974 world championships. In Precision, nearly all hands of 16 points or more are opened 1♣. Opening bids of 1♥ and 1♠ promise at least a five-card suit and a response of 1NT is forcing. An opening bid of 2♣ shows 11–15 points and an unbalanced hand containing at least five clubs.

Above: Playing Precision, with 16 points, you would open 1♣.

OPENING LEAD AGAINST A SLAM

A sound general rule is to look for an aggressive lead against a suit slam, and a passive lead against 6NT. Against a grand slam, there is no point in trying to establish a trick with your opening lead. If you were to gain the lead, to cash the established winner, the grand slam would be down anyway! So, always look for a safe lead against a grand slam.

Leading against a small slam in a suit

When declarer is in a contract such as 6♠, he will usually have to lose the lead once during the play. To beat the slam, it will often be vital that you have established a second trick to cash by the time the defenders gain the lead. Look at this typical slam deal.

You are sitting West and must choose a lead. Declarer is likely to have plenty of tricks in spades and diamonds. You must hope that your partner has one high card in these suits and must aim to set up a second winner elsewhere. A club lead is a much better prospect than a heart lead. You hold the king of the suit, so you will only need to find partner with the queen to set up a potential trick there. If you lead a

heart instead, you will need to find partner with the king of the suit. But even if partner does hold the ♥K, it may not make a trick if declarer has the ♥A sitting over it. You lead the ♣3, and the slam is doomed. Declarer wins East's queen with the ace, draws trumps and runs the ◆J. When your partner wins with the ◆K, he returns a club and the slam is one down.

One hand proves nothing, you may think, and declarer might easily have held the ace and queen of clubs. It is true, but in that case it is unlikely the slam could be beaten. In the long run it will pay you handsomely to make attacking leads against a small slam in a suit.

CHOOSING A LEAD
♠ ♥ ◆ ♣

Sound advice is to choose an aggressive lead against a small slam in a suit. When leading against 6NT, do the opposite – choosing a safe lead that will give nothing away.

Right: Leading aggressively against a suit slam. West leads the ♣3 against South's suit slam, since this represents the best chance of setting up a defensive trick.

NORTH-SOUTH GAME
DEALER NORTH

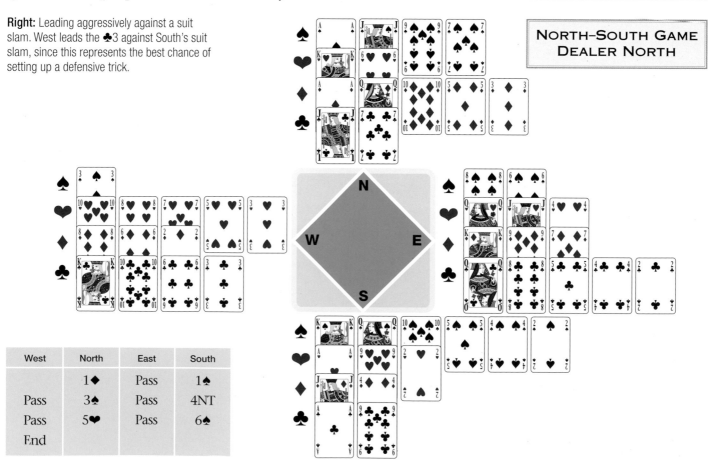

West	North	East	South
	1◆	Pass	1♠
Pass	3♠	Pass	4NT
Pass	5♥	Pass	6♠
End			

Leading against 6NT

In a typical 6NT contract, declarer will have 10 or 11 top tricks at his disposal and will have to seek an extra trick or two to reach his target. You should not make life easy for him by giving away a trick on the opening lead. Leading from something like ♠K–J–8–7–2 is a great idea against 3NT, because you hope to establish several tricks in the suit. It would be a very poor idea against 6NT because declarer is likely to have multiple honours in every suit and would then be certain to score the ♠Q as well as the ♠A. You are West on this typical 6NT contract and must choose a lead:

Right: Choosing a safe lead against 6NT. West leads the ◆7 against 6NT, since leading any other suit would be more likely to give away a trick.

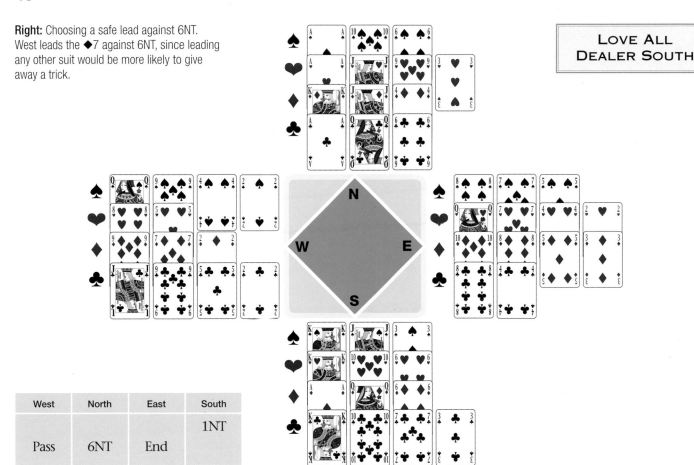

		LOVE ALL **DEALER SOUTH**

West	North	East	South
			1NT
Pass	6NT	End	

It would be incredibly dangerous to lead a spade or a club. There is every chance that leading from an honour will give away a trick, or save declarer a guess. So, you must choose between ♥8–5 and ◆9–7–3. It is slightly safer to lead from the tripleton. When you have a doubleton, there is more chance that your partner will hold four cards to the queen or jack and you might give away the position. You should lead the ◆7 (second best from a poor suit). Declarer may still make the contract – he may not. At least you will not have handed it to him on a plate.

MAINTAINING COMMUNICATIONS

It is often important for the two defenders to keep in touch with each other during the play. In other words, they must take steps to ensure that a defender can reach the hand of his partner, particularly when that player has some winners to cash. To maintain communications effectively, it is necessary that the defenders can read the lie of the suit involved. This can be done by following a standard method when choosing the card to return on the second round.

Look at this typical 3NT deal:

Right: West maintains communications. Defending 3NT, West must decide whether or not to win with his ♠K on the second round of the suit.

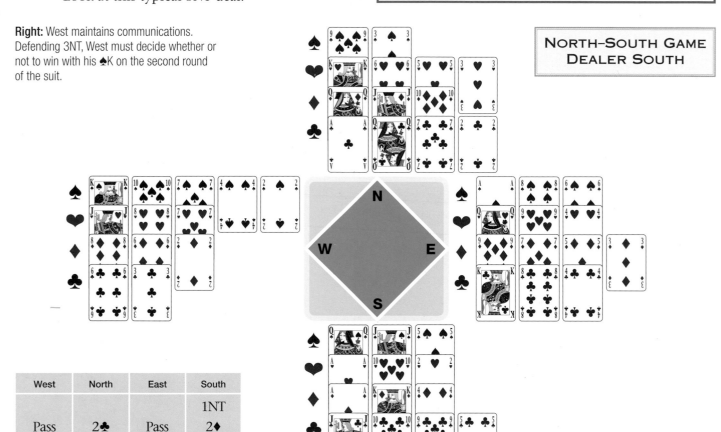

**NORTH–SOUTH GAME
DEALER SOUTH**

West	North	East	South
			1NT
Pass	2♣	Pass	2♦
Pass	3NT	End	

Sitting West, you lead the ♠4. East wins with the ace and returns the ♠8, South playing the queen. Suppose you make the mistake of winning with the king. The contract will then be made, whatever you do next. If you clear the spade suit, declarer will win with the jack and run the ♣J. When your partner wins with the ♣K he will have no spade to return.

With the spades lying as in the diagram, you must hold up the ♠K on the second round, allowing South's ♠Q to win. By doing so, you leave the defenders'

communications intact. When declarer takes a losing club finesse, East can return a third round of spades to your king. You will then cash two more spade winners to defeat the game.

It would not be a good move to duck the second round of spades if South begun with ♠Q–5, so you need to know declarer's spade holding. Your partner will assist you in this regard by following this rule with his return on the second round of the suit you have led:

- with two cards remaining, return the top card
- with three or more cards remaining, return the original fourth-best card.

On the deal we have just seen, East returned the ♠8. This could not possibly be his original fourth-best card, so his holding had to be ♠A–8–6. (South had denied four spades with his Stayman response, so East could not hold a doubleton ♠A–8. Even if the bidding had been 1NT – 3NT, you would have to hope that East had started with three spades.) The right defence was therefore for West to hold up the ♠K on the second round.

Let's see a deal where West should not hold up his honour on the second round:

Right: West reads declarer for a doubleton in the suit led. West needs to know the lie of the heart suit before deciding whether to win the second round of hearts.

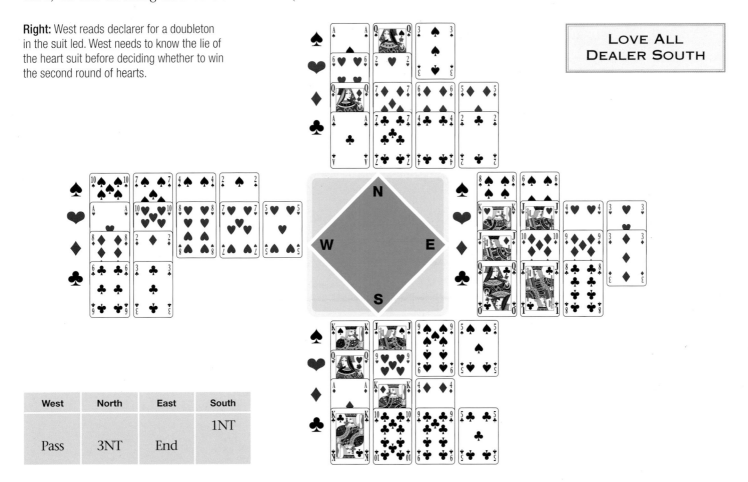

LOVE ALL
DEALER SOUTH

West	North	East	South
			1NT
Pass	3NT	End	

PLAYING IN A 1–1 FIT
♠ ♥ ♦ ♣

In the semi-final of the 1998 Spingold, played in Chicago, Bobby Levin and Steve Weinstein played in a contract of four spades with a trump holding of a singleton ♠7 in declarer's hand and a singleton ♠J in the dummy. Weinstein opened 3♦ and Levin responded with a psychic 3♠ on a hand with five-card diamond support and only one spade. Weinstein raised to 4♠ and the contract went eight down vulnerable for the loss of 800. Had their team-mates also played in 4♠, scoring +650, the loss would have been only 4 IMPs. They actually went one down in 6♠, for an adverse swing of 15 IMPs.

You lead the ♥7 against 3NT and East wins with the ♥K. He returns the ♥3 and declarer plays the ♥Q. You must now decide whether to win with the ♥A or to hold up.

If South started with ♥Q–J–9, you would have to hold up, to preserve communications as on the previous deal. In that case, however, your partner would have started with ♥K–4–3 and would have returned the ♥4. Partner's return of the ♥3 tells you that declarer began with either ♥Q–9 or ♥Q–J–9–4. In neither case can there be any reason to hold up the ♥A. You win with the ♥A, therefore, and continue with the ♥5. South did indeed start with a doubleton heart and the defenders score five heart tricks to beat the game. A misguided hold-up at Trick 2 would have allowed declarer to make the contract.

CHAPTER 7

INTERMEDIATE BIDDING

You should always be reluctant to allow the opponents to choose trumps at a low level, particularly if they have found a trump fit. The first topic in this section on intermediate bidding will be "balancing", where the player in the pass-out seat bids without the normal values, to prevent the opponents from winning the auction too cheaply. The universally popular transfer responses to 1NT will be described, where you respond in one suit to show length in the next higher suit. Next the important topic of bidding slams is covered, in particular "control-showing cue-bids", where you bid a suit in which you hold an ace or a king rather than one where you have some length. After a discussion of three types of conventional double – negative, responsive and competitive doubles – the section ends with a discussion on sacrificing, where you bid a contract that you expect to fail. Your aim is to lose fewer points than you would if the opponents were allowed to make their contract instead.

Right: The right-hand opponent opened 1♥. To express this minor two-suiter, overcall 2NT (the Unusual No-trump convention).

BALANCING

When the strength between the two sides is evenly divided, or nearly so, you should be very reluctant to let the opponents choose trumps at a low level. This is particularly the case if they have found a trump fit. When you are in the pass-out seat, you should consider making a call of some sort, even when your own hand is quite weak. The fact that the opponents have stopped low implies that your partner is likely to hold reasonable values. Making such a call, in the pass-out seat, is known as "balancing" or "protecting".

Balancing against a one-bid

Suppose the bidding starts in this fashion

West	North	East	South
1♥	Pass	Pass	?

and you hold one of these hands in the South seat:

1

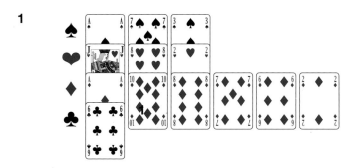

East did not have enough to respond, so your partner may well hold 10 points or so. Rather than allow West to choose trumps, you should overcall 2♦ on (1). You would not be strong enough to overcall 2♦ in the second seat. In the protective seat, however, you are entitled to bid with around a king less than normal. It's the same on (2). An overcall of 1NT would

2

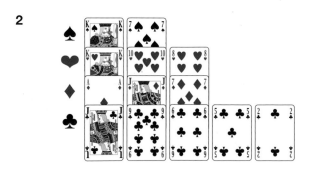

normally show a stronger hand but, in the protective seat, you may bid 1NT on around 11–14 points. If your partner happens to hold 12 points himself, you may be able to make game.

3

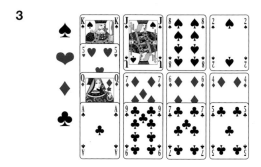

Hand (3) is worth a double. You would be reluctant to double in the second seat, with only 10 points. In the protective seat you can be bolder. Since you may be three points lighter than normal for any action taken in the protective seat, your partner should bid cautiously when advancing towards a possible game.

Balancing against a two-level fit

When the opponents have found a trump fit but stopped at the two-level, the odds are very favourable for balancing. Your side must hold something approaching half the strength in the pack. Since you are both relatively short in the opponents' suit, there is a good chance that you will have a playable fit yourselves somewhere. Suppose the bidding starts

West	North	East	South
1♦	Pass	2♦	Pass
Pass	?		

and you hold one of these hands in the North seat:

1

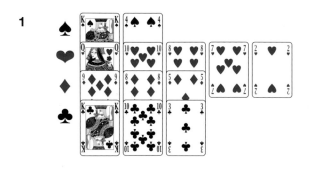

Compete with 2♥ on (1), rather than let the opponents choose trumps at the two-level. Do not worry that your partner, who is likely to hold around 10 points, will carry you too high. Remembering that you did not overcall 1♥ on the first round, he will realize that you are bidding the combined values of your own hand and his.

2

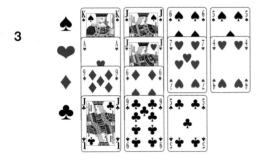

Similarly, you should bid 3♣ on (2). The opponents will often then bid 3♦, which may go down. On hand (3) you should double for take-out.

3

When you hold the minor suits and the opponents have found a fit in a major, you can use 2NT (the Unusual No-trump) to ask partner to choose one of the minor suits.

West	North	East	South
1♥	Pass	2♥	Pass
Pass	?		

Sitting North, you hold one of these hands:

1

2

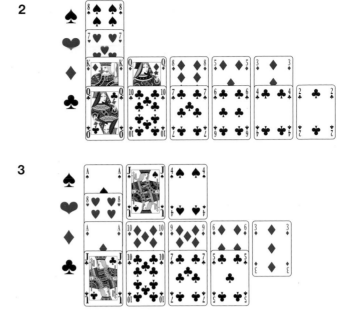

3

On hands (1) and (2) you would bid 2NT, asking partner to choose a minor. On hand (3) you would prefer to double, despite holding only three cards in the other major, spades.

Above: Dangerous to protect. Suppose you hold this hand and the opening 1♦ is followed by two passes. Ask yourself "Where are the spades?" Your partner did not overcall 1♠ and there is a risk that the opponents may find a spade fit if you bid. It is safer to pass.

HESITATIONS
♠ ♥ ♦ ♣

Many disputes that arise during tournament play involve hesitations. It is perfectly acceptable to think for a while before making a bid or playing a card. You often give away information by doing so, however, particularly if you think for a while and then pass. Your partner must be particularly careful not to take advantage of the information gained.

TRANSFER RESPONSES

Many social players, and nearly all tournament players, use "transfer responses" when partner has opened 1NT. A response of 2♦ shows at least five hearts and asks the opener to rebid 2♥. A response of 2♥ shows at least five spades and asks the opener to rebid 2♠. There are two big advantages of this method. The first is that the 1NT opener will play any contract in responder's five-card major. His hand will be hidden from view and his honour holdings will be protected from the opening lead. The second advantage is that after a start of 1NT – 2♦ – 2♥, the responder has a second chance to bid. He can continue with a further bid, such as 2NT, 3♦ or 3NT, having already shown five hearts.

Responder may use a transfer response to sign off in his long major. A transfer response does not promise any values at all. You may be very weak, intending to play in your long suit at the two-level. Or you may have a slam in mind. Here the responder has no ambitions:

Above: Oswald Jacoby, who originally conceived the idea of transfer responses in bridge.

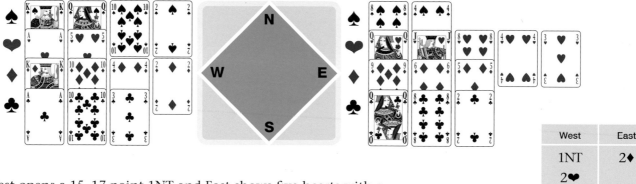

West	East
1NT	2♦
2♥	

West opens a 15–17 point 1NT and East shows five hearts with a transfer response. Since he has no game ambitions, he passes the requested 2♥ rebid.

Because bidding 2♦ forces the opener to rebid 2♥, the responder has a chance to describe his hand further. If he continues with 2NT this will show the values to invite game:

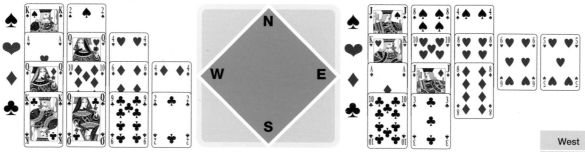

West	East
1NT	2♦
2♥	2NT
4♥	

With a minimum hand in the 15–17 point range West would pass 2NT, or correct to 3♥ with three-card heart support. Since West has 16 points, heart support and a possible ruffing value, he is happy to bid 4♥, accepting the game invitation.

The responder has these options after a start of 1NT – 2♦ – 2♥:

Pass	no game ambitions
2♠	natural and forcing
2NT	inviting a game
3♣/3♦	natural and game-forcing
3♥	inviting a game, at least six hearts
3NT	asking opener to choose between 3NT and 4♥
4♥	to play.

Breaking the transfer

When the opener has four-card trump support and an upper-range hand, he should bid one level higher than normal. This is known as "breaking the transfer". Game may now be reached when responder was not quite strong enough to make a try himself:

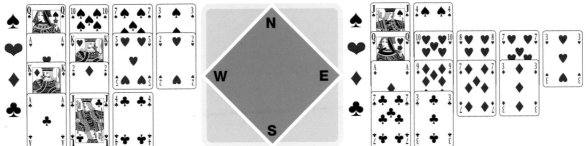

West	East
1NT	2♦
3♥	4♥

With just 7 points and a five-card suit, East would have passed a rebid of 2♥. When partner shows four-card heart support and an upper-range opening, East raises to game.

Transfers opposite a 1NT overcall

When partner has overcalled 1NT, it is a good idea for the responder to use Stayman and transfer bids.

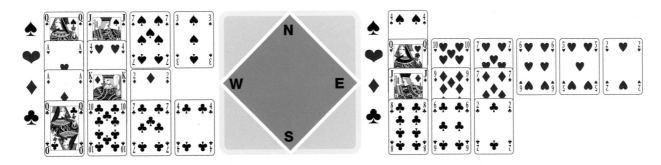

East has a weak hand and seeks sanctuary in his long heart suit.

West	North	East	South
			1♦
1NT	Pass	2♦	Pass
2♥	End		

Transfers opposite a 2NT opening

A similar method is used opposite an opening bid of 2NT. A 3♦ response shows at least five hearts and asks opener to rebid 3♥. A response of 3♥ shows at least five spades and asks opener to rebid 3♠.

CONTROL-SHOWING CUE-BIDS

S uppose you have found a trump fit and have values to spare, so far as a game contract is concerned. You want to tell partner that a slam may be possible and to ask his view on the matter. It is not much use bidding some form of Blackwood. The meaning of a Blackwood bid is: "I know we have the values for a slam and I just need to check that there are not two aces missing." No, the only way to invite a slam, without going past the game-level, is to make a control-showing cue-bid. In other words, you bid a new suit (usually at the four-level or higher) after the trump suit has been agreed. This bid shows a control – an ace, king, singleton or void – in the suit that you have bid.

Making a cue-bid with trumps agreed

Suppose the bidding has started like this:

West	North	East	South
1♠	Pass	3♠	Pass
?			

You are sitting West. Partner has agreed spades as trumps and you have to assess slam prospects on the three hands shown below:

1

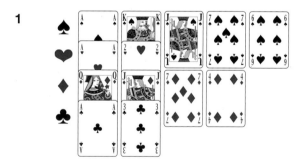

On (1) you can visualize a slam if partner has a diamond control. You make a control-showing cue-bid of 4♣. This passes the message: "I am strong enough to consider a slam and I have a control in the club suit." Your partner may now make a cue-bid himself, or perhaps sign off in 4♠. If he were to cue-bid 4♥, that would show a heart control. It would also deny a diamond control, since you show your cheapest control first. You would then sign off in 4♠, knowing that there were two top diamond losers.

2

On (2) you would cue-bid 4♦, meaning: "I am strong enough to consider a slam and I have a control in diamonds but no control in clubs." If partner were to cue-bid 4♥, that would show a heart control and also a club control. Without a club control, he would have signed off in 4♠, knowing that there were two top losers in clubs.

3

Hand (3) is not strong enough to suggest a slam, opposite partner's limit raise of 3♠, and you would bid 4♠.

Note that after a start of 1♠ – 2♠, a rebid of 3♣ by the opener would not be a cue-bid. Because the bidding has not yet been forced to game, a bid in a new suit is a game try. A bid in a new suit is a cue-bid only when the auction is already game-forcing.

AVOID THE FIVE-LEVEL
♠ ♥ ♦ ♣

The secret of good slam bidding is to investigate a possible slam while the bidding is still below the game level. When the bidding starts 1♠ – 3♠ – 4♣ (where 4♣ is a control-showing cue-bid), a slam is suggested but the bidding can still stop in 4♠. Ideally, you should play in 4♠ or 6♠. To investigate a slam and then stop in 5♠ is to take an unnecessary risk of going down.

Cue-bidding only with first-round control

The advantage of cue-bidding on both aces and kings, as just described, is that you can diagnose when you have two top losers in a suit. It is a method that was popularized by the great Italian teams of the 1970s. It does mean that you cannot be sure how many aces are held but, of course, you can usually bid Blackwood after making a cue-bid or two, thereby discovering whether there are two aces missing. Nevertheless, some partnerships prefer to make a cue-bid only when they hold a first-round control (the ace or a void). It is something that you must discuss with your partner.

Agreeing a suit by making a cue-bid

On some auctions there is not enough space to explicitly agree partner's suit before making a cue-bid. When a bid at the four-level cannot logically be natural, it will be a cue-bid that agrees the suit last bid by partner. Let's see an example of this:

BLACKWOOD CONVENTION

During a slam auction a bid of 4NT is the Blackwood convention, conceived by Easley Blackwood. It asks your partner how many aces he holds and the traditional responses are:

5♣ with none or four aces
5♦ with one ace
5♥ with two aces
5♠ with three aces

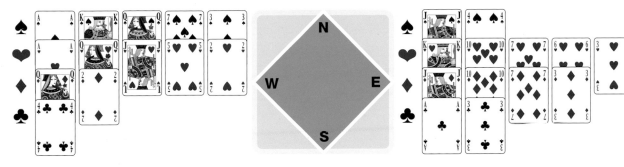

East has a super fit for hearts and indicates this by cue-bidding 4♣ instead of merely raising to 4♥. West has no diamond control, so he signs off in 4♥. Suppose West had held one diamond and two clubs instead. With the diamond suit controlled in his own hand, he would then have been much more interested in a slam. The bidding would have continued to the six-level:

West	East
1♠	1NT
3♥	4♣
4♥	

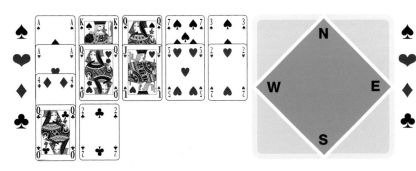

West uses the Blackwood 4NT convention, discovering that partner has one ace. He then bids a small slam in hearts, which is easily made.

You can see from this example how important it can be to show where you hold a control, rather than merely stating how many controls you have. Swap East's minors and he would have cue-bid 4♦ instead of 4♣. West would then know that there were two top losers in clubs and would sign off in game.

West	East
1♠	1NT
3♥	4♣
4NT	5♦
6♥	

BIDDING SLAMS

The foundation of a successful slam auction has nothing to do with Blackwood or control-showing cue-bids. Both players must use the early rounds of the bidding to convey their general playing strength and to look for a trump fit. Only when both these tasks have been completed, and the playing strength for a slam has been confirmed, is it appropriate to check on controls.

The requirements for a slam

Two elements are necessary to make a small slam. You must have the playing strength to make 12 tricks. You also need the controls to prevent the defenders from scoring two tricks.

Look at these two hands:

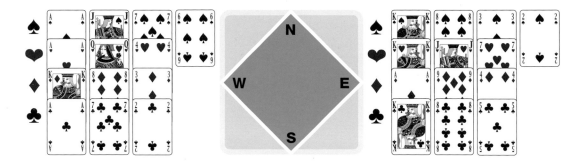

All the aces and all the kings are held, but there is insufficient playing strength for a slam. There are only 10 tricks on top and some luck will be required in the spade suit, even to score 11 tricks.

The next pair of hands contain playing strength in abundance but there is a flaw in the control situation:

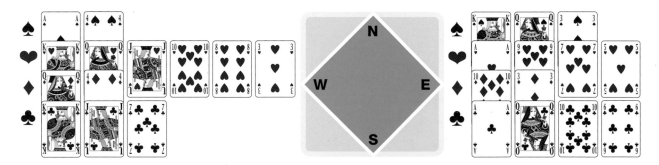

An excellent heart fit, with 13 top tricks. Unfortunately no diamond control is held and the defenders will be able to score the first two tricks.

Assessing whether the power for 6NT is present

We will look first at how to assess whether the playing strength for a slam is present. To make 6NT when two balanced hands face each other, you will need 33 points or more. This is comparatively easy to judge. Once your partner has shown his own point-count, you simply add your own to assess the total. Let's see two typical slam auctions in no-trumps.

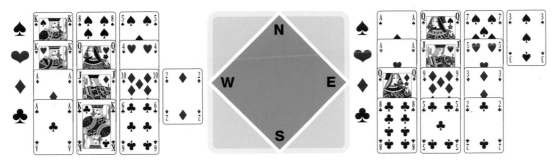

With 13 points opposite 20–22, East can be sure that the combined point total will be at least 33 points. He therefore leaps to 6NT. There are nine top tricks and the slam will be made if South holds the ◆K or the spades split 3–3.

West	East
2NT	6NT

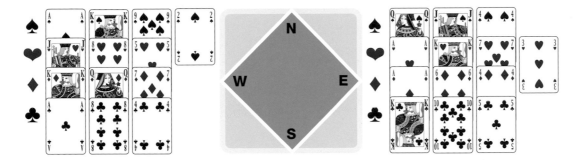

With 17 points facing a partner holding 15–17 points, East is not quite strong enough to jump to 6NT. He invites a slam by raising to 4NT. With a minimum hand for his strong no-trump, West would pass. Here he holds a maximum 17 points and therefore accepts the invitation, bidding 6NT. There are 11 tricks on top and you would seek a 12th by leading towards the ♥J, succeeding when South held the ♥Q or when hearts broke 3–3 (plus some other small chances).

West	East
1NT	4NT
6NT	

Assessing whether the power for a suit slam is present

It is somewhat more difficult to assess whether you have sufficient power to make a slam with a trump suit. High-card points are not so important as playing strength and the quality of the trump suit. In general, you should consider a slam when you have considerably more strength than you would need to raise to game.

There are several situations where the playing strength should be present for a slam, provided you can find a sound trump suit. Suppose the opener has a medium strength hand (16–18 points) and the responder has an opening bid himself. Provided a good trump fit can be found, the values for a slam should be there. The same is true when the responder has made a jump shift (for example 1◆ – 2♠) or when a positive response has been given to a 2♣ opening.

Remember that when partner opens 2♣ and rebids in a suit, he is showing that he has enough strength for a game in his own hand. If you hold an ace in your hand, or a king and a queen, this will often be enough to produce a slam.

Above: Lorenzo Lauria, senior member of the Italian team and winner of five world championships.

Here are some typical auctions investigating a slam contract:

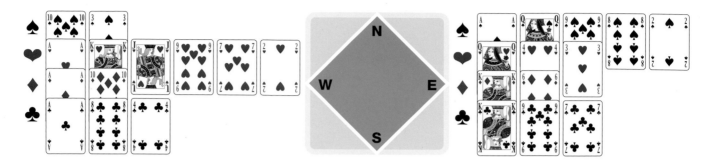

East has considerably more strength than would be needed to raise to 4♥ on the second round. Since he has a control in both the minor suits, he is happy to bid Blackwood. Partner shows three aces and the excellent small slam is reached. (In the later section on Advanced Bidding, we will look at Roman Key-card Blackwood, widely popular in tournament play, where the responses to 4NT identify not only the four aces but also the king and queen of trumps.) Even when a player has made a very strong bid, he may decide to sign off at the game-level when he is minimum for his call.

West	East
1♥	1♠
3♥	4NT
5♠	6♥

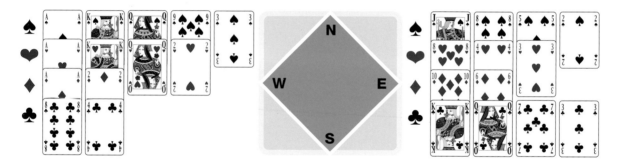

West bids just 4♠ to inform his partner that he has nothing to spare for a 2♣ opening. West has three losers in the minor suits and is confident that East will advance over 4♠ anyway, if he holds something like ♦K and the ♣A.

Let's make the West hand somewhat stronger by adding the ♦K:

West	East
2♣	2♦
2♠	3♠
4♠	

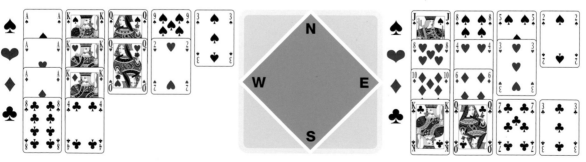

Now West suggests a slam by cue-bidding his diamond control. East is impressed by the fact that West has visualized a slam, despite holding no control in the club suit. He therefore shows his club control, bypassing the 4♠ safety level. This encourages West to jump to a small slam in spades.

West	East
2♣	2♦
2♠	3♠
4♦	5♣
6♠	

You can see that control-showing cue-bids have two purposes. Their main mission is to show a control in one of the side suits. They are used also to indicate a strong hand that is interested in a slam:

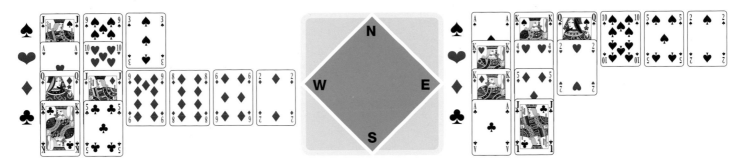

West	East
1♦	2♠
3♠	4♣
4♥	6♠

West has a minimum opening and no top honour in spades, the agreed trump suit. Nevertheless, he should be willing to cue-bid his ♥A because it does not carry the bidding past the next level of the trump suit (here 4♠). As it happens, this information is enough to persuade East to bid a slam. East knows that there cannot be a grand slam available, of course, because West's cue-bid in hearts denies the ♦A.

Play in 6NT when the values are present

When you assess the combined point-count at 33 or more, it is usually wise to play in 6NT rather than in six of a suit. By doing so, you may avoid defeat when the suit that you would otherwise have chosen as trumps happens to break badly:

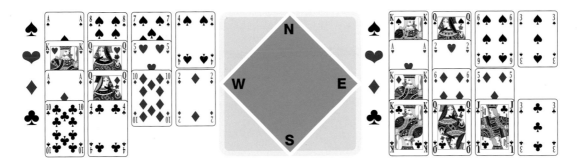

West	East
1NT	6NT

It is not a good idea to seek a spade fit by bidding Stayman on the East hand. The resultant contract of 6♠ will then go down when the spade suit breaks 4–1. Since East knows that 33–35 points are present, he should bid the slam in no-trumps. By doing so, he will also avoid the small chance of an adverse club ruff.

Bidding a grand slam

The general advice about bidding grand slams is that you should do so only when you are confident that 13 tricks are present. Remember that if you fail in a grand slam you lose both the small slam bonus and the game bonus that you would otherwise have accrued. When playing duplicate it is particularly expensive to bid a grand slam and go one down, only to discover that your opponents stopped at the game-level on the same cards. You could then have obtained a big swing by bidding and making a small slam.

NEGATIVE DOUBLES

In rubber bridge, where few conventions are played, the most common type of penalty double is that of an overcall, in an auction such as 1♠ – 2♦ – Dble. In tournament bridge, such doubles are almost universally played for take-out nowadays and are known as "negative doubles". The time has come to take a look at this method.

The negative double

When you open with one of a suit and partner doubles an overcall up to the level of 3♠, this is for take-out. Such a double is known as a "negative double". (It was originally known as a Sputnik double, since it was conceived around the time of the Russian space satellite of that name.) It suggests that you have no accurate natural bid to make and that you hold one or both of the unbid suits.

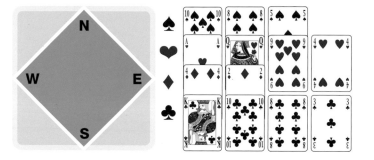

West	North	East	South
1♦	1♠	Dble	

East is strong enough to bid at this level but has no satisfactory natural bid to make. A response of 2♣ would overstate his values. He solves the problem by making a negative double. He strongly suggests four cards in the unbid major and may well have a club suit too. If partner rebids 2♣, 2♦ or 2♥, East will pass on this occasion. If instead he held 11 points or more he would show the additional strength by bidding again.

The higher the auction is, the more values a negative double will show. When the overcall is at the three-level, responder will need almost the values for making game:

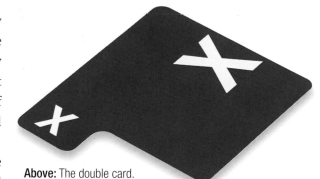

Above: The double card.
Nowadays a double card is used many more times for take-out than for penalties.

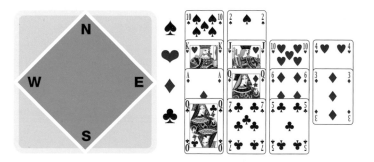

West	North	East	South
1♣	3♠	Dble	

At this level West will quite often pass the double for penalties. That is because it may be easier to score five or six tricks in defence, rather than make a contract at the four-level with no particularly good fit.

Responder has a long suit

When you play negative doubles, the responder has two ways of bidding a new suit. Look at these two sequences, where East holds length in hearts:

1

West	North	East	South
1♠	2♣	Dble	Pass
2♦	Pass	2♥	

2

West	North	East	South
1♠	2♣	2♥	

In sequence (1) responder begins with a negative double and then introduces his long suit on the next round. In (2) he bids his long suit directly instead. It makes good sense to differentiate between these sequences in terms of strength. Most players treat sequence (2) as forcing, showing a strong hand with responder, and sequence (1) as non-forcing. Some players use the sequences the other way round, however, and it is something you should discuss with your partner.

Above: Weak with hearts. On this type of hand you will use sequence (1) or (2), according to the methods you have agreed with your partner.

The opener re-opens with a double

When the double of an overcall is played for take-out, responder has to pass when he has a strong holding in the opponent's suit and would like to have doubled for penalties. The penalty will often return to the fold because his partner will re-open with a take-out double most of the time:

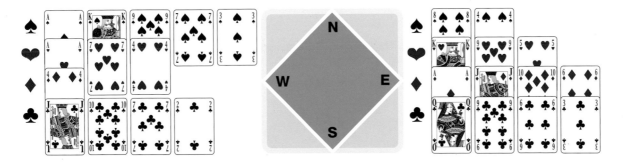

The opponents have stopped at the two-level, so the odds are good from West's point of view that his partner has several points and had to pass because he held length in diamonds. West doubles for take-out, mainly in the hope that partner can pass for penalties. As you see from this example, such a double does not promise any extra values with the opening bidder.

West	North	East	South
1♠	2♦	Pass	Pass
Dble	End		

RESPONSIVE AND COMPETITIVE DOUBLES

It is rarely advantageous to double the opponents at a low level when they have found a trump fit. In this section we will look at two situations in which the other side has found a fit and it is therefore best to play a double for take-out instead of for penalties.

The responsive double

When an opening bid has been doubled for take-out and the next player raises to the two- or three-level, a double by the fourth player is also for take-out. It is known as a responsive double.

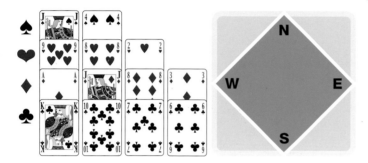

West	North	East	South
	1♥	Dble	2♥
Dble			

West can tell that his side holds at least half the points in the pack and therefore has no wish to allow the opponents to choose trumps at the two-level. Rather than guess which minor suit to bid, and perhaps end in a 4–3 fit, he makes a responsive double. Since East will almost always hold four spades for his take-out double of 1♥, West would tend to respond in spades if he held four of them. The responsive double on this auction is therefore likely to be based on a hand with the minor suits. Unless East has values to spare, he will rebid 3♣ or 3♦ at his next turn.

Many pairs play responsive doubles up to the level of 3♠ but it is something that you should agree with your partner. As we saw with the negative double, your partner is more likely to pass a double for penalties when the level of bidding is already quite high.

West	North	East	South
			1♠
Dble	3♠	Dble	Pass
Pass	Pass		

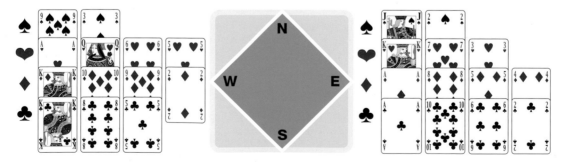

East's responsive double is for take-out but West cannot visualize a game their way, on his minimum double including a doubleton spade. He passes the double for penalties.

The competitive double

Similarly, you can double for take-out when your partner has overcalled and the opponents have found a trump fit:

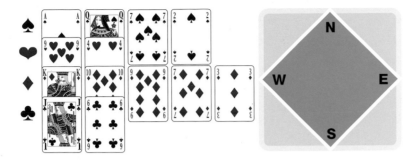

West	North	East	South
	1♥	2♣	2♥
Dble			

West's double is for take-out and is known as a competitive double. It suggests length in the unbid suits, spades and diamonds here, and a tolerance for partner's clubs, probably a doubleton. As before it would rarely be profitable to double for penalties at such a low level, once the opponents have found a trump fit.

Competitive doubles apply up to the level of 3♠, although you must agree this with your partner. As with the responsive double, partner will be more inclined to pass the double, the higher the level of the auction:

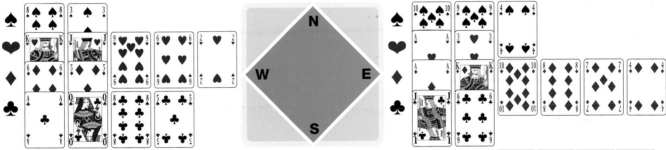

West	North	East	South
	1♠	2♦	3♠
Dble	Pass	Pass	Pass

West's double is for take-out, a competitive double that shows values in hearts and clubs. East has no fit for either of these suits and decides that the best idea is to pass the double for penalties.

THE VALUE OF CONVENTIONS

Three famous Scientists vs Traditionalists matches have been played. One team was allowed to play unlimited conventions while the other could make only natural bids. In 1965, in New York, the Scientists (Roth/Stone, Mitchell/Stayman, Jordan/Robinson) beat the Traditionalists (Murray/Kehela, Becker/Hayden, Mathe/Schleifer) by 53 IMPs over 180 deals. In 1990, in London, the Scientists (Soloway/Goldman, Garozzo/Eisenberg) beat the Traditionalists (Zia/Chagas, Wolff/Forrester) by two sessions to one. In 1992, again in London, the Scientists (Hamman/Wolff, Rodwell/Meckstroth) beat Traditionalists (Chagas/Branco, Forrester/Robson) by 70 IMPs over 128 deals, winning a prize of $50,000.

Above: Jeff Meckstroth of the USA, a multiple world champion.

SACRIFICING

Suppose your opponents bid to 4♥, a contract that is destined to succeed. If they are vulnerable, they will pick up a score of +620. When you and your partner hold a spade fit, it may be worthwhile for you to contest with 4♠. Even if you go two down, this will cost you only 300 when non-vulnerable, or 500 when vulnerable. That is good business already. In addition, the opponents may see fit to bid 5♥. If that contract goes one down, you will have done very well. Bidding a contract that you expect to fail, in the hope that it will cost you less than the opponents' contract, is known as sacrificing.

Sacrificing at the game-level

The most common arena for sacrificing is the game-level. Here is a typical sacrifice deal:

Right: East–West can make 4♥ so it is profitable for North–South to sacrifice in 4♠, where the penalty will be less than the value of a game by the opponents.

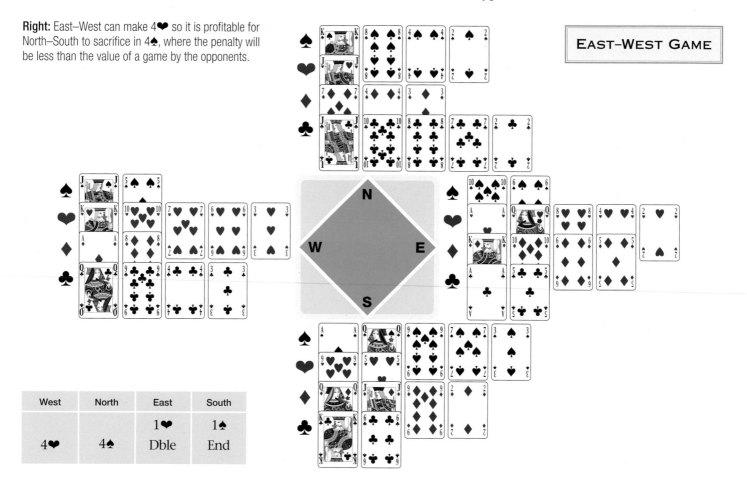

EAST–WEST GAME

West	North	East	South
		1♥	1♠
4♥	4♠	Dble	End

TRUMP ECHO
♠ ♥ ♦ ♣

When defending at no-trumps, or following to a side suit in a suit contract, it is normal to play high–low to show an even number of cards. This is known as a "count signal". Somewhat strangely, it is widely agreed that a high–low signal in the trump suit has a quite different meaning. It shows precisely three trumps. Some players have the agreement that such a peter (or echo) also shows that you have the desire to score a ruff somewhere.

East–West bid to a game in hearts, a contract that will easily be made. Non-vulnerable against vulnerable, North decides to sacrifice in 4♠. He does not expect the contract to be made, but there is every chance that the cost will be less than that of the opponents' heart game.

So it proves. East–West are almost certain to find their diamond ruff but the penalty will still be only 300, much less than the 620 that the heart game would have provided. If either East or West had decided to bid 5♥, rather than accept a perhaps inadequate penalty from the spade game, this contract would have been defeated. With two spades in each hand, East-West were deterred from attempting a five-level contract.

The five-level belongs to the opponents

A well-known guideline on sacrificing is that the five-level belongs to the opponents. In other words, if you have pushed the opponents to the five-level, it is rarely advantageous for you to bid five of a higher suit. Take your chance of beating their contract instead. For example, suppose that on the deal we have just seen East–West decided to advance to 5♥. It would be poor tactics for North–South to sacrifice again in 5♠. They should be content to have pushed their opponents to a possibly dangerous level.

Here is another typical sacrifice situation:

Right: When South sacrifices in 5♣, East-West should be wary of advancing to 5♥ and should therefore double.

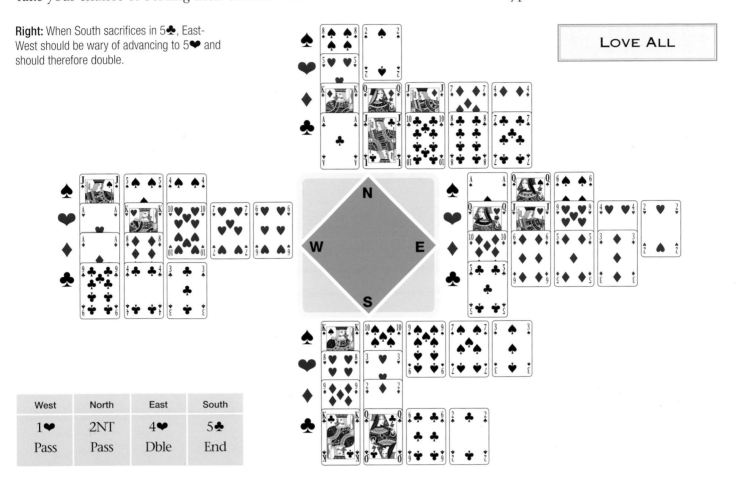

LOVE ALL

West	North	East	South
1♥	2NT	4♥	5♣
Pass	Pass	Dble	End

With the score at Love All, North enters the auction with an Unusual No-trump call to show length in both minor suits. South judges that the heart game is likely to succeed and sacrifices in 5♣. This runs to East, who takes note of the guideline "the five-level belongs to the opponents". Since the opponents have chosen to play in clubs, there is no reason for East to place his partner with a singleton diamond. There will be a loser or two in those suits. If the ♠K is missing, it is more likely that South will hold it than North (who has his length in the minor suits). So, East judges well to double. The cards lie well for North–South and the sacrifice goes only one down. Had East–West taken the push to 5♥, they would have gone down instead.

Left: South does not expect to make 5♣ but he expects it to cost less than a heart game made by the opponents.

CHAPTER 8

INTERMEDIATE CARD PLAY

It is time to see some important areas of card play that mainly involve looking at a contract as a whole, rather than considering only one particular suit. First you will see how to maintain communications between declarer's hand and the dummy – when one defender is "safe" and the other is "dangerous", you must plan to finesse or duck tricks into the safe hand. The important techniques of reversing the dummy and crossruffing are described next. Then you will see the various ways in which you can prevent the defenders from taking a ruff, also when you should delay drawing trumps because some other task is of higher priority. The idea of safety play is discussed and how you should calculate the best play with an unfamiliar card combination. Finally, you will see how a hold-up play can be useful in a suit contract as well as in no-trumps.

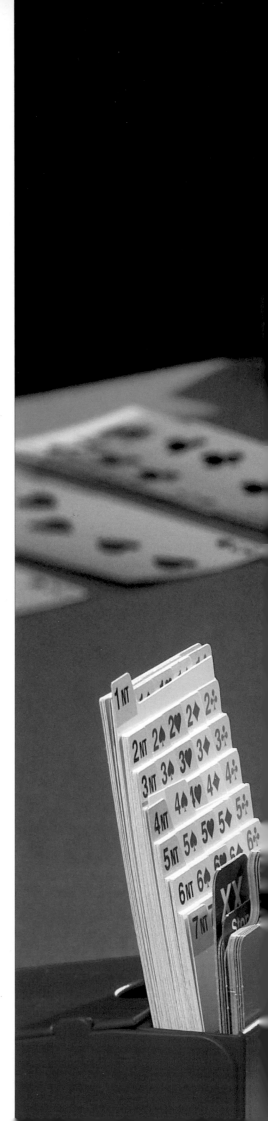

Right: Declarer has won the opening lead and is considering the best line of play. In a suit contract, the presence of a trump suit will offer you more options than in a no-trump contract.

MAINTAINING COMMUNICATIONS

There is little point in creating an extra winner or two in the dummy if you have no entry with which to reach the dummy. An important part of planning a contract is to preserve the entries that you will need to get backwards and forwards between the two hands. The first deal involves two important techniques in this area:

Right: Declarer maintains communication to his diamond winners. Playing in 3NT, South has to employ two different techniques to set up and enjoy the diamond suit.

Hoping that your diamond suit will prove useful, you leap to 3NT on the South cards. The ♣Q is led and you must take some care with the entries to the South hand. The first step (often important) is to win the opening lead in the right hand. Here you must win with dummy's ace of clubs, preserving the club king as a later entry to your hand.

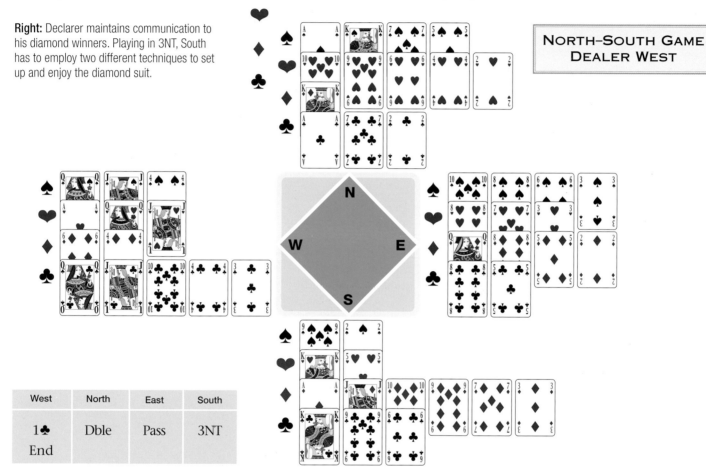

**NORTH–SOUTH GAME
DEALER WEST**

West	North	East	South
1♣	Dble	Pass	3NT
End			

HESITATING WITH A SINGLETON
♠ ♥ ♦ ♣

It is illegal to give false information to the opponents deliberately. For example, suppose you have only one card in the suit that has just been led. It would be illegal to hesitate before playing it, thereby creating the impression that you had a choice of more than one card to play. A similar situation arises when the declarer leads a queen (or jack) from hand and the ace is in dummy. It would be unacceptable to hesitate in second seat when you did not hold a high honour.

Suppose your next move is to cash the king of diamonds. You are most unlikely to make the contract. The only entry to your hand will be the king of clubs. If you cross to that card and play the ace of diamonds, you will make the contract only when the diamond queen happens to fall doubleton.

Instead, you should overtake the king of diamonds with the ace, thereby gaining an entry to the South hand. You then lead the jack of diamonds, forcing out East's queen. The game cannot then be defeated. The defenders can take at most one diamond and three hearts. When you regain the lead, you will have five diamonds and the two ace–kings in the black suits, giving you a total of nine.

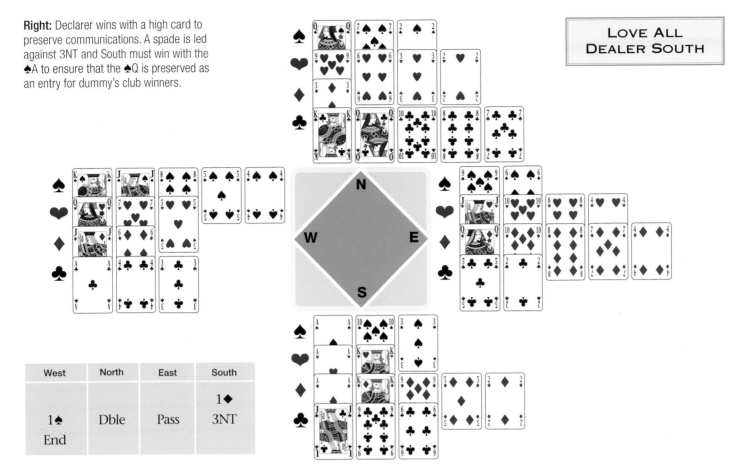

Right: Declarer wins with a high card to preserve communications. A spade is led against 3NT and South must win with the ♠A to ensure that the ♠Q is preserved as an entry for dummy's club winners.

LOVE ALL
DEALER SOUTH

West	North	East	South
			1♦
1♠	Dble	Pass	3NT
End			

North's double on the first round is a "negative double", suggesting length in the unbid suits, hearts and clubs. West leads the ♠5 against the eventual contract of 3NT and, sitting South, you must consider the play carefully. You play low from dummy and East produces the ♠9. It may seem natural to win with the ♠10 but you will go down if you do so. When you play on clubs, West will hold up the ace until the third round. With ♠Q–7 facing ♠A–3 you will not have a spade entry to dummy. You will score only two club tricks and fall one trick short of your target.

To make the contract you must win the first trick with a higher card than is necessary. You capture East's ♠9 with the ace, even though your ♠10 would have been good enough to win the trick. When you play on clubs, West again holds up his ace until the third round. It will do him no good. Whatever suit he chooses to play next, you will be able to win and lead towards the ♠Q, establishing it as an entry for the two good clubs in the dummy. By disposing of the ♠A on the first round, you promote the ♠Q into a potential entry card.

Left: Helen Sobel and Charles Goren of the USA: one of the game's most famous partnerships.

SAFETY PLAYS IN A SINGLE SUIT

The best way to play a suit often depends on how many tricks you need from it. Suppose you have to play this diamond suit:

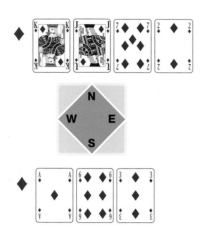

Above: The best play in this diamond suit depends on whether you need four diamond tricks or just three.

If you needed all four tricks from the suit, in order to make the contract, West would have to hold ♦Q–x–x. You would cash the ♦A and finesse the ♦J.

Now suppose that you need only three diamond tricks to make the contract. If you play the suit in the same way (♦A first, then finesse the ♦J), you will make the required three tricks when West holds the ♦Q, when diamonds break 3–3 and when East has a singleton ♦Q. You will fail in your objective when East holds ♦Q–x. When you need only three tricks, you should make the "safety play" of cashing the king and ace, then leading towards the jack on the third round. You will still make the required three tricks in the three situations just noted. You will succeed also when East holds ♦Q–x.

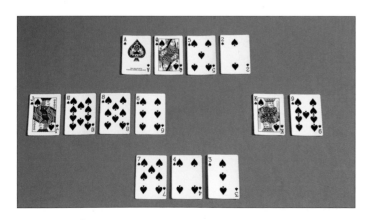

Above: Safety play. Needing only two tricks from the suit, you should duck a round, play the ♠A and then lead towards the ♠Q on the third round.

That's the idea of a safety play, then. You give yourself the maximum possible chance of making the number of tricks that you need. Suppose you are in 6♥ with this trump suit:

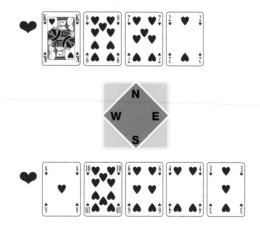

Above: If you can afford one loser in this suit, you must search for a safety play to avoid losing two tricks.

Let's say that there are no losers in the side suits. You are therefore looking for a safety play in the trump suit that will guard against two losers. If you play the ♥A first, you will lose two tricks when East began with ♥Q–J–x–x. Similarly, it is not safe to cash the ♥K first, in case West has all four missing trumps. The safe play is to lead towards dummy and play the ♥9. If West follows and East wins with the queen or jack, the suit must be breaking 3–1 at worst and you will lose only one trump trick. If West shows out on the first trump lead, your finesse of the ♥9 loses to one of East's honours, but you will later finesse the ♥10 to escape for one loser. (It would be just as good to lead towards the South hand on the first round, intending to finesse the ♥10.)

This is another combination that arises frequently:

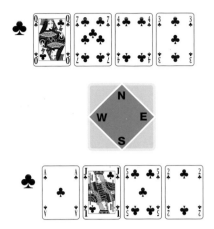

Above: If you need only three club tricks from this combination, you must seek a safety play that gives you the best chance of success.

When you need four club tricks, you play low to the jack in the hope that East holds a doubleton king. The king will then fall under the ace on the second round and dummy's ♣Q–7 will then score the remaining two tricks in the suit.

Suppose instead that you need only three club tricks. The safety play in that case is to cash the ♣A on the first round, thereby avoiding defeat when West holds a singleton ♣K.

Right: A safety play in the trump suit. To avoid losing two trump tricks to a bad break, declarer must play the suit in a special way.

We will look at one more suit combination, this time in the context of a complete deal.

West leads the ♥Q against 6♠ and your sole concern is to avoid two trump losers. If you were in the poor contract of 7♠, you would play the ace and king of trumps, hoping that the ♠Q fell. In the more sensible contract of 6♠ you can afford one trump loser. After winning the heart lead, you should cash the ♠A. You then cross to the South hand with a diamond and lead a low trump towards dummy on the second round.

When West follows with a low card, you will finesse dummy's ♠9. If the finesse loses to the ♠10, the suit will be breaking 3–2 and you are home. If instead East shows out, you will lose only one trump trick to West's remaining ♠Q–10.

When West holds ♠Q–10–8–2, as in the diagram, it will do him no good to "split his honours", playing the ♠10 on the second round. Your ♠9 and ♠J would then be equals against his ♠Q.

Suppose instead that West shows out on the second round of trumps. You then rise with dummy's king and lead towards the jack of trumps. This safety play guards against ♠Q–10–x–x in either defender's hand.

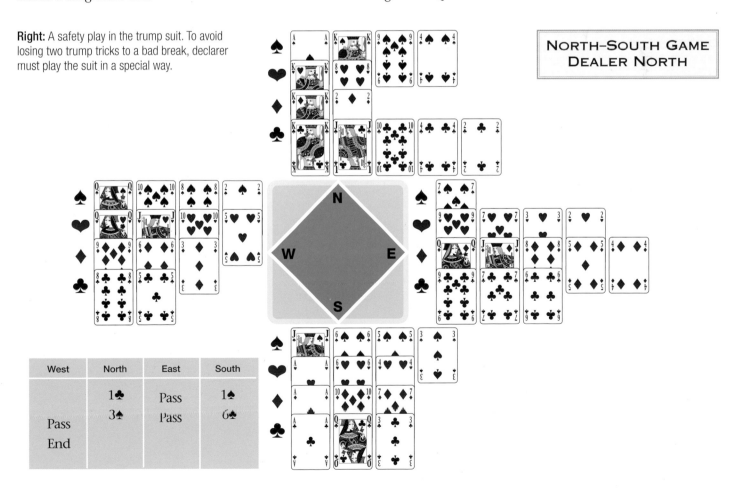

NORTH–SOUTH GAME
DEALER NORTH

West	North	East	South
	1♣	Pass	1♠
Pass	3♠	Pass	6♠
End			

153

FINESSING INTO THE SAFE HAND

It often happens that one defender's hand is "safe" and the other is "dangerous". For example, a defender may be dangerous because he has some winners to cash or can lead through an unprotected king. When you have a choice of finesses to take, you should usually finesse into the safe hand. Even if the finesse happens to fail, it will be the safe defender who gains the lead. The 3NT contract, shown below, is an example of that:

Right: Taking the right finesse first. When you may have to take two finesses (in clubs and diamonds here), it is usually best to finesse first into the safe hand.

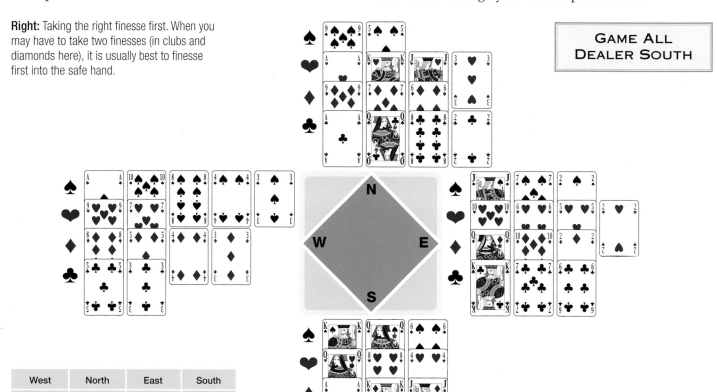

GAME ALL
DEALER SOUTH

West leads the ♠4 and you win East's ♠J with the ♠K. You have eight top tricks and must decide which minor-suit finesse to take.

Suppose you run the ♣J at Trick 2. East will win with the ♣K and return a spade. The defenders will score four spades and one club, putting you one down. It was not a good way to play the contract because the club finesse was "into the dangerous hand". If it lost, East would damage you with a spade return.

West	North	East	South
			1NT
Pass	2♣	Pass	2♦
Pass	3NT	End	

MOST COMMON HAND SHAPE

♠ ♥ ♦ ♣

Although 4–3–3–3 is the flattest possible shape for a bridge hand, it is only the fifth most common shape. Its frequency is 10.5 per cent. The most common shape is 4–4–3–2, which has a frequency of 21.5 per cent. It is followed by hands of 5–3–3–2 shape (15.5 per cent), 5–4–3–1 shape (12.9 per cent) and 5–4–2–2 shape (10.6 per cent).

A better idea is to cross to the ♥J and lead a diamond to the jack. This finesse is "into the safe hand". As it happens, the finesse succeeds and the contract is yours.

Suppose the diamond finesse were to lose, though. West could not profitably continue spades from his side of the table. (If he did play a spade, hoping that his partner held the ♠Q, he would give you your ninth trick.) If West played any suit other than a spade, you would win the trick and still be able to take the club finesse. By finessing into the safe hand you give yourself two chances instead of one.

Sometimes you have a two-way finesse for a missing queen. When you can afford to lose a trick in the suit and still emerge with enough tricks for your contract, it makes good sense to finesse into the safe hand. Look at the deal shown below.

West leads the ♥4 against 3NT and East plays the ♥Q. You hold up the ♥A until the third round, aiming to exhaust East of his cards in the suit. There are eight tricks on top and a ninth trick must come from the diamond suit. You can finesse either defender for the missing ♦Q and must decide which way to take the finesse.

You will score an extra trick from the diamond suit, even if the finesse fails. So you can afford the finesse to fail, provided the defenders do not cash enough tricks to beat you.

Right: Finessing into the safe hand. When you have a two-way finesse in a suit (diamonds, here) and can afford to lose a trick, finesse into the safe hand.

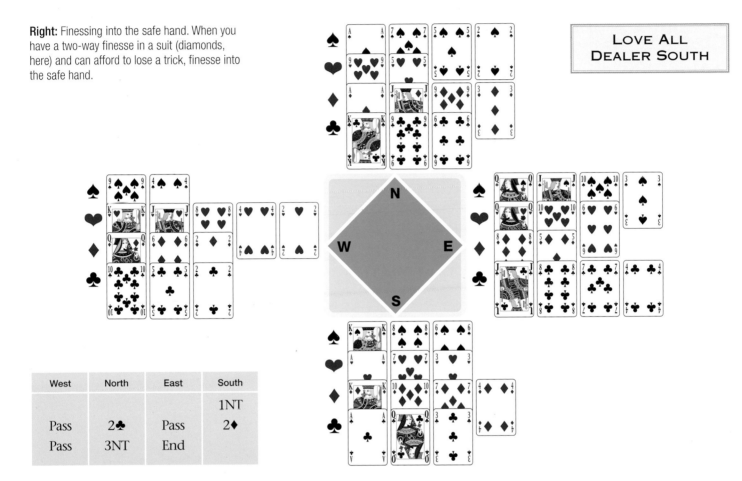

LOVE ALL
DEALER SOUTH

West	North	East	South
			1NT
Pass	2♣	Pass	2♦
Pass	3NT	End	

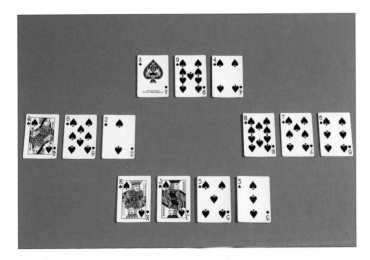

Above: Finessing into the safe hand. Suppose you only need three spade tricks. When West is the danger hand, it makes sense to lead low to the 9, losing a trick to the safe East hand.

Suppose you cross to the ♦A and run the ♦J on the way back, finessing East for the missing queen. This finesse is into the danger hand. If it loses, West will cash two hearts to beat the contract. Instead you should cash the ♦K and lead a low diamond towards dummy, intending to finesse West for the missing ♦Q. If the finesse loses to East, you will still make the contract. East has no hearts left and can do you no damage. (If he did have another heart, the suit would have broken 4–4 and would pose no problem.) As the cards lie in the diagram, the diamond finesse through West will succeed and you will end with an overtrick. The point to remember, though, is that by finessing into the safe hand you would make the contract whether the finesse succeeded or not.

REVERSING THE DUMMY

Suppose you are playing in a spade contract with this trump holding:

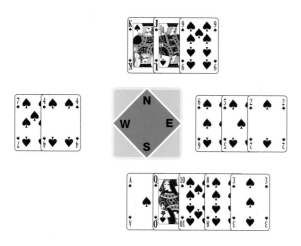

Above: If this is your trump suit, a ruff in the short-trump hand will give you an extra trick and a ruff in the long-trump hand will not.

You begin with five trump tricks and that will be the final number if you draw trumps near the start of the hand. Suppose instead that you take one ruff in the short-trump holding (the dummy). You will then make six trump tricks – five in your hand and one extra trick

Right: A typical dummy reversal. South increases the total number of trump tricks by ruffing three diamonds in the South hand.

from the ruff. If instead you ruffed something in the long trump hand, it would not give you an extra trick. You would still make just five trump tricks.

So, ruffing in the short trump hand gives you an extra trick; ruffing in the long trump hand does not. This is true in general, but if you take so many ruffs in the long trump hand that it becomes the short trump hand you can gain a trump trick. Look back at the spade position above. Take three ruffs in the South hand and you would score six trump tricks – three rounds of trumps in the North hand and three ruffs in the South hand. This is known as "reversing the dummy". Let's see an example featuring that very spade holding:

**NORTH–SOUTH GAME
DEALER SOUTH**

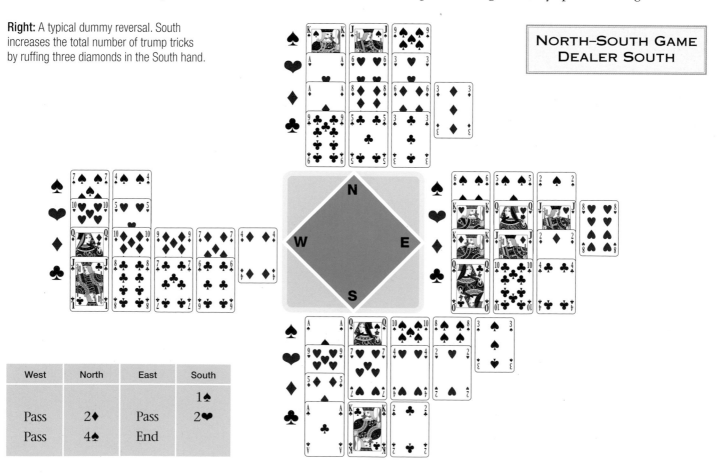

West	North	East	South
			1♠
Pass	2♦	Pass	2♥
Pass	4♠	End	

West leads the ♠4 and you see that you have nine tricks on top. Without a trump lead, you could simply have given up two rounds of hearts and played to ruff the fourth round in dummy, if necessary. If you play that way now, though, the defenders will be able to remove dummy's trumps before you can take your heart ruff. A better idea is to reverse the dummy, aiming to ruff all three of dummy's diamond losers in the South hand.

You win the trump lead with the ♠9, cash the ♦A and ruff a diamond. You then play the ace and king of clubs, just in case a defender could discard his clubs as you ruff the diamonds. Returning to dummy with the ♥A, you ruff another diamond with the ♠A. You ruff with such a high trump because you want to lead the ♠10 next to dummy's ♠K. A third diamond ruff with the bare ♠Q gives you the first nine tricks and the ♠J is in the dummy, ready to give you a tenth trick.

It can also be worthwhile ruffing in your hand if this enables you to score the low trumps there. Had you attempted to draw trumps instead, these cards might have been losers.

Let's see a deal that illustrates this technique. Look at the 4♥ contract shown below, where the ace and king of trumps are accompanied by three low trumps.

West leads the ♦Q against your heart game and you win with dummy's ace. Even if trumps are breaking 3–2, you would still need some luck to avoid losing three clubs in addition to one trump. The best way to play the hand is to aim to make all five trumps in your hand (by ruffing three diamonds). Add in the five side-suit winners and that will come to ten. What is more, this line may well succeed when the trumps break 4–1.

Since entries to dummy are not plentiful, you should ruff a diamond at Trick 2. You then cash the ace–king of trumps, revealing that West began with four trumps. You continue with the king, queen and ace of spades, followed by a second diamond ruff. A club to the ace returns the lead to dummy and you ruff dummy's last diamond, both defenders following. Ten tricks are now before you. As you foresaw when you made your plan, you scored five side-suit winners and all five trumps in the South hand.

MAKE A PLAN AT THE START
♠ ♥ ♦ ♣

It is not always right to draw trumps straight away.
Always make a plan before starting to play the contract.

Right: Scoring the low trumps. Declarer reverses the dummy in order to make tricks with the low trumps in his hand.

LOVE ALL
DEALER SOUTH

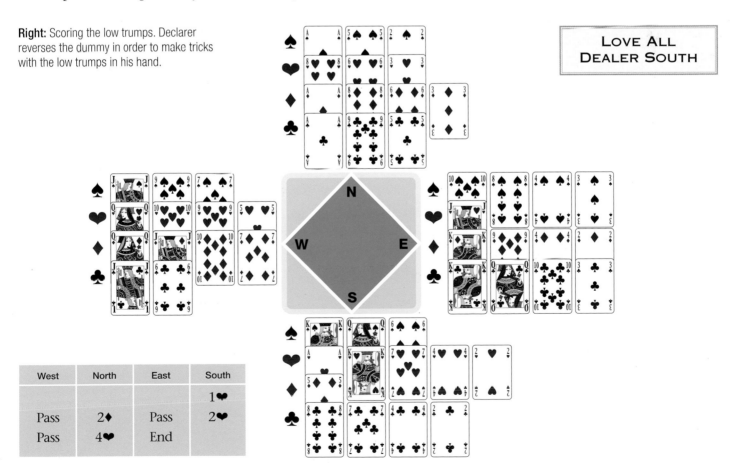

West	North	East	South
			1♥
Pass	2♦	Pass	2♥
Pass	4♥	End	

THE CROSSRUFF

Sometimes you are in a suit contract and both hands contain a singleton or void. In that case the best line of play may be to take several ruffs in each hand, never actually drawing trumps. The 4♠ contract shown below is a good example of this technique, which is known as the "crossruff":

Right: A typical crossruff. Declarer scores eight trump tricks by ruffing diamonds in dummy and hearts in his hand.

West leads the ♦K against your game in spades. If you begin by drawing trumps, you will be well short of your target. Instead you should aim to make the two side-suit aces along with eight trump tricks. You must score all eight of your trumps separately, by taking ruffs in both hands.

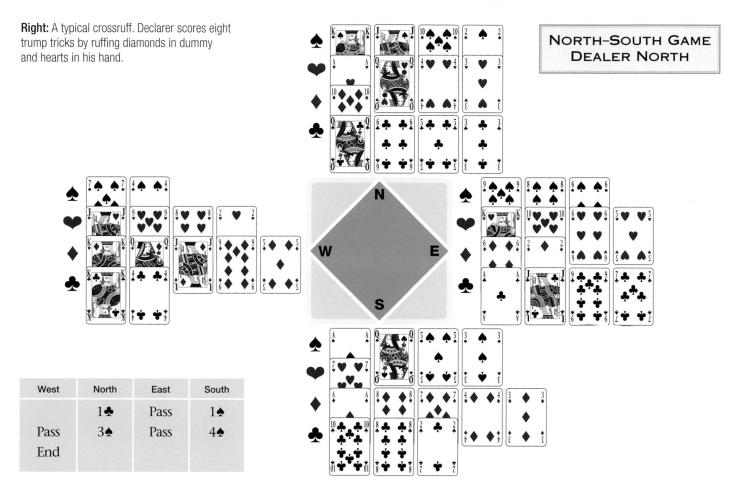

NORTH–SOUTH GAME
DEALER NORTH

West	North	East	South
	1♣	Pass	1♠
Pass	3♠	Pass	4♠
End			

QUALITIES NEEDED
♠ ♥ ♦ ♣

Many personal qualities bring a reward when it comes to playing bridge – patience, concentration and logical thought among them. Marshall Smith of the USA was once asked what qualities were required of a champion bridge player. Smith replied: "He needs the conceit of a peacock, the night habits of an owl, the rapacity of a crocodile, the sly inscrutability of a snake, the memory of an elephant, the boldness of a lion, the endurance of a bulldog and the killer instinct of a wolf."

You win the diamond lead with the ace and ruff a diamond with the ♠2. You cash dummy's ♥A and ruff a heart in the South hand, again with a low trump. When you ruff a second diamond East shows out. Since this ruff is with a high trump, East cannot overruff. You ruff a heart with the last low trump in the South hand and the contract is then safe. A diamond ruff, a heart ruff and a fourth diamond ruff, all with high trumps, bring your total to nine tricks and the ace of trumps will make it ten.

The important point to remember is that you take the early ruffs with low trumps, when the risk of an overruff is minimal. Later, you can ruff with high trumps and the defenders are powerless.

On many hands you draw trumps first and then cash your side-suit winners. Since you never draw trumps when playing a crossruff, you should cash your side-suit winners at the beginning of the hand. If you fail to do this, the defenders may discard from those suits while you are crossruffing. They may then be able to ruff your winners. Look at this deal:

Right: Cashing the side-suit winners first. Declarer cashes the two winners in spades before embarking on the crossruff.

North's 4♦ rebid is a splinter bid, showing a sound raise to game in hearts with at most one diamond. South advances to a small slam, via Roman Key-card Blackwood and West leads the ♣5. As declarer, you can count four winners in the side suits. If you can add eight trump tricks, scored on a crossruff, this will bring the total to 12.

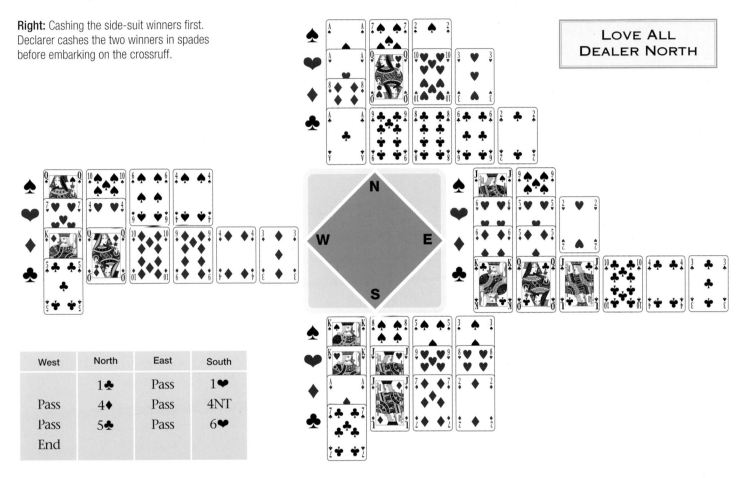

LOVE ALL
DEALER NORTH

West	North	East	South
	1♣	Pass	1♥
Pass	4♦	Pass	4NT
Pass	5♣	Pass	6♥
End			

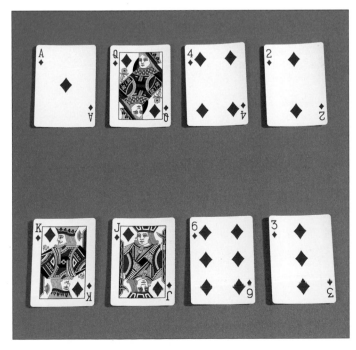

Suppose you embark on the crossruff immediately, ruffing clubs in your hand and diamonds in the dummy. When you take a second diamond ruff in dummy, East will discard one of his spades. It will no longer be possible for you to score two spade tricks, because East can now ruff the second round of the suit. The slam will go down.

To make the contract you must cash the ace and king of spades at the start, before the defenders have had an opportunity to discard any spades. Only then do you start the crossruff. Eight trump tricks will indeed come your way and the slam is made. In addition to the trump tricks, you will score two top spades and the minor-suit aces.

Left: Ruff low first. Suppose this is your trump suit and you need eight trump tricks on a crossruff. You would take the first four ruffs with low trumps. You would then continue with a "high crossruff", ruffing with the four honours.

AVOIDING A RUFF

The most straightforward way to prevent the defenders from taking a ruff is to draw trumps. When you are missing the king or queen of trumps, you must be wary of taking an unnecessary trump finesse. If the finesse fails, the defender who wins the trick may be able to give his partner a ruff. You will often encounter deals like this:

Right: Avoiding a ruff by refusing a trump finesse. West leads his singleton diamond and declarer will go down if he takes a trump finesse.

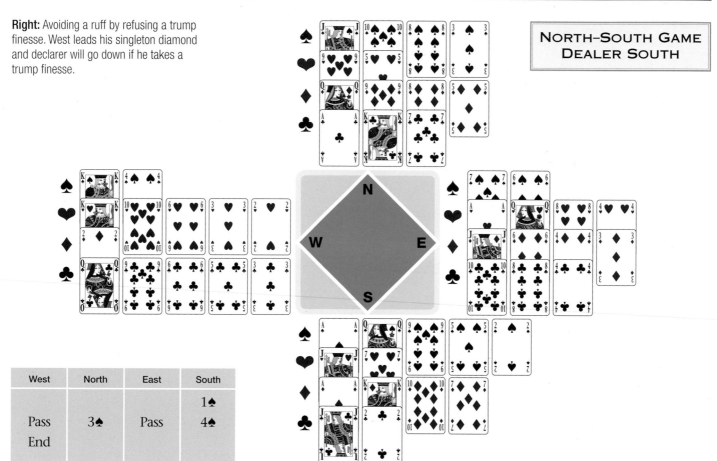

**NORTH–SOUTH GAME
DEALER SOUTH**

West	North	East	South
			1♠
Pass	3♠	Pass	4♠
End			

West leads the ♦2. You play low from dummy and East plays the ♦J, won with your ace. It could hardly be more obvious that the opening lead is a singleton. Suppose you cross to dummy in clubs and run the ♠J. If the finesse loses, West can cross to his partner's hand with a heart and the ensuing diamond ruff will put the contract one down.

Since you have only two losers in the side suits, you can afford to lose a trump trick. You should therefore play ace and another trump. West wins the second round of trumps with the king and can no longer score a diamond ruff, because he has no trumps left. You will make the contract easily. This is another example of a safety play. You give up your best prospect

of picking up the trumps for no loser in exchange for maximizing your chance of making the contract.

You would make the same sort of play if dummy's trumps were ♠K–8–7–2 and your own trumps were ♠A–J–5–4. Suppose you took your best chance of playing the trumps for no loser, playing the ♠K and then finessing the ♠J. You would run the risk that West could win the second round from ♠Q–9–3 and cross to partner's hand with a heart to receive a diamond ruff.

To avoid such a fate, you would make the safety play of cashing the ace and king of trumps instead. You do not mind losing a trick to the queen of trumps. What you cannot afford is to lose two trump tricks – one to the queen, one to a ruff.

Similarly, when a ruff is threatened you may decide to forego a finesse in a side suit:

Right: Drawing trumps to avoid an adverse ruff. West leads ace and another heart against 4♠ and declarer must calculate whether to finesse the ♥J.

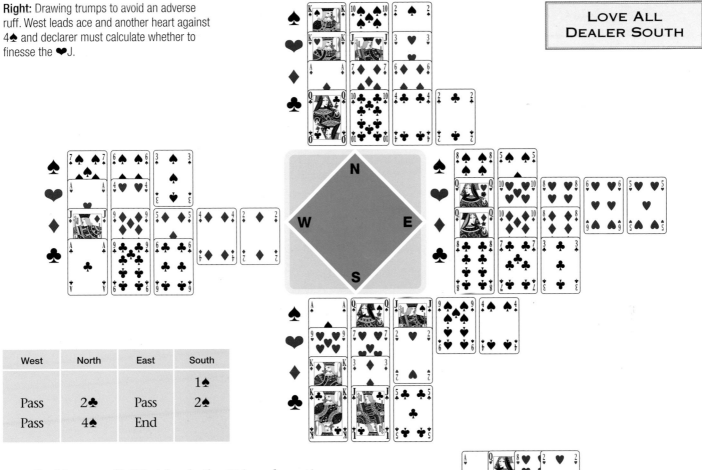

LOVE ALL
DEALER SOUTH

West	North	East	South
			1♠
Pass	2♣	Pass	2♠
Pass	4♠	End	

Seeking a ruff, West leads the ♥A and continues with a second round of the suit. Suppose you see no harm in playing dummy's ♥J. East will win with the ♥Q and give West a heart ruff. You will go one down. Instead you should rise with dummy's ♥K. You can then draw trumps and will make the contract easily, losing just two hearts and one club.

There were two main reasons to play the ♥K at Trick 2. One is that players rarely lead from an ace–queen combination but often try their luck from a doubleton ace. The more compelling reason was that you would risk the contract by finessing the ♥J.

There are many similar positions. Suppose you reach a small slam in clubs, with a heart side suit as shown on the right.

West leads the ♥4 and you have no potential losers outside the heart suit. If you play a low card from dummy, you are running the risk that the opening lead is a singleton. In that case East will win with the ♥K and give partner a ruff. You should play safe for your slam. You rise with the ♥A, draw trumps and give the defenders a heart trick.

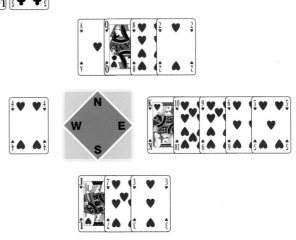

Above: When West leads the ♥4 against your small slam in clubs, you must be wary that the lead is a singleton.

A LIKELY SINGLETON
♠ ♥ ♦ ♣

If a player opens with a pre-emptive bid of 3♠ and later leads a spot-card in a different suit, this is very likely to be a singleton, led in the hope of receiving a ruff. Unless his shape is precisely 7–2–2–2, a pre-empter will hold a singleton in his hand.

THE HOLD-UP IN A SUIT CONTRACT

In an earlier section we looked at the very common play of holding up an ace in a no-trump contract. The purpose was to exhaust the holding of one defender. He then became "safe" and you could afford to lose the lead to him. Exactly the same play – holding up a stopper – can be effective in a suit contract too. Look at the deal shown below.

West leads the ♥K against 4♠. Even if trumps break 3–2, there are four potential losers: one spade, two hearts and one diamond. As declarer, you must seek to discard one of your heart losers on dummy's diamond suit.

Suppose you win the first trick with the ♥A and draw two rounds of trumps. You are over the first hurdle when the trump suit breaks 3–2. You will not make the contract, however. When you play a diamond, East will win with the ◆A and return his remaining heart, allowing West to score two heart tricks and beat the game.

The best chance of making the contract is to duck the first round of hearts. When West continues with a second round of the suit, you win with the ♥A and lead the ◆K. You are now favoured with two strokes of luck. Firstly, it is East who holds the ◆A (if West held the card, he would be able to cash a heart winner). Secondly, East has no heart to play. Your hold-up on the first round of hearts did indeed exhaust his heart holding.

Let's say that East returns a club. You win the trick and play the queen and jack of diamonds, discarding your last heart. You will lose just one trump, one heart and one diamond. The game is yours.

As you may have noted, it would be a mistake to draw two rounds of trumps before leading the ◆K. East could then defeat you with a hold-up play of his own! By ducking the first round of diamonds and winning the second, he would leave you with no entry to reach the established ◆J in the dummy.

On the deal shown at the top of the next page you can diagnose that a hold-up at Trick 1 will work well. The opening lead marks East with the ♥K, so he will not be able to be able to continue the suit without allowing you to score both the the queen and ace.

Right: Holding up an ace in a suit contract. West leads the ♥K against the spade game and declarer must hold up for one round, to break the link between the defenders' hands.

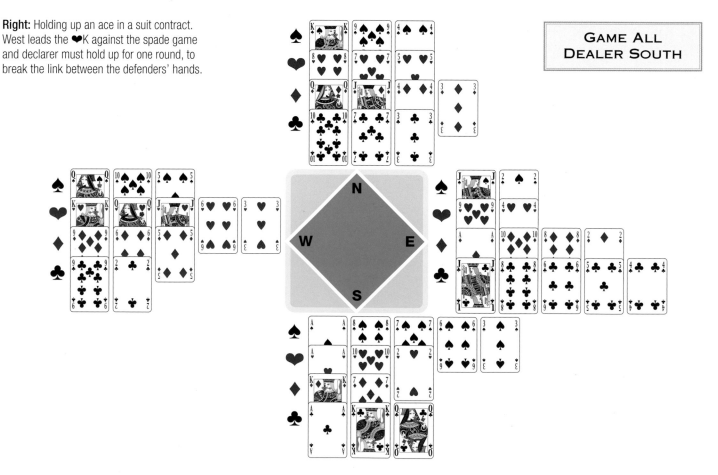

GAME ALL
DEALER SOUTH

Right: Retaining a guard in the suit led. West leads the ♥8 against 4♠ and declarer allows East to win the first trick, diagnosing that he holds the ♥K.

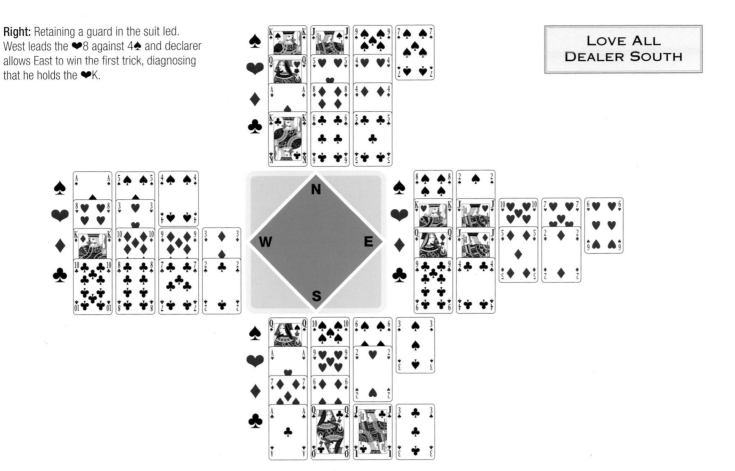

West leads the ♥8 against 4♠. You play low from dummy and East plays the ♥10. You can see four potential losers: one trump, two hearts and one diamond. A heart can be discarded from dummy on the fourth club but the risk is that the defenders will claim their four tricks before you can take a discard.

The first task is to read the likely lie of the heart suit. West would not have led the ♥8 from ♥K–J–10–8, so the lead must be from spot cards, leaving East with the ♥K–J–10. The winning play is therefore to duck the first trick, allowing East's ♥10 to win. He cannot continue the suit safely because you would run a heart return to dummy's queen. (You would then make the contract because, by good fortune, the ace of trumps lies with West, the defender who cannot deliver a heart ruff.)

Let's say that East senses this and switches to a diamond instead. You win with the ace and play a trump. When West takes the ace of trumps and plays another heart, you win with the ace, draw trumps and play four rounds of clubs, discarding dummy's last heart. You will then lose one trump, one heart and one diamond, making your game. Had you won the first round of hearts, the defenders would have scored two tricks in the suit when West won with the ♠A.

PLAYING SPEED
♠ ♥ ♦ ♣

The normal rate of play in duplicate bridge events is eight hands per hour. Some hands take longer to bid and play than others, of course, and the players are expected to make up time by playing more quickly when they get behind on the clock. Fines can be administered for slow play, but it is often difficult to ascertain which pair was to blame.

Right: The 1973 Las Vegas Falls Nationals.

WHEN TO DELAY DRAWING TRUMPS

When you are playing in a suit contract, the general rule is that you should draw trumps immediately unless there is a good reason to do something else first. The most common reason for playing a side suit instead is that you need to take a quick discard, or perhaps establish a discard. Look at this deal:

Right: Setting up a discard before drawing trumps. If declarer draws trumps immediately, rather than setting up a discard on the clubs, his 4♠ contract will go down.

West leads the ◆Q against your spade game. There are three aces to be lost, so you cannot afford a further loser in the diamond suit. Suppose you win the opening lead and play a trump immediately. East will win with the ace of trumps and clear the diamond suit. With no way to avoid a diamond loser, you will go one down.

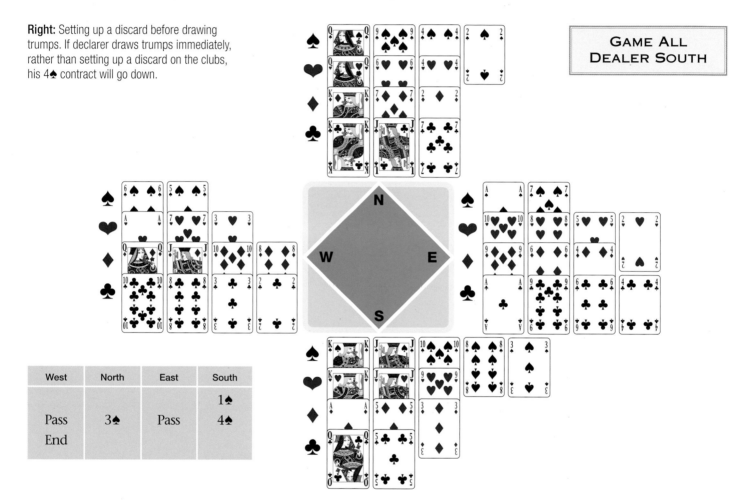

GAME ALL
DEALER SOUTH

West	North	East	South
			1♠
Pass	3♠	Pass	4♠
End			

SOMERSET MAUGHAM
♠ ♥ ◆ ♣

Somerset Maugham said, "If I had my way, I would have children taught bridge as a matter of course, just as they are taught dancing. In the end it will be more useful to them. You can play bridge as long as you can sit up at a table and tell one card from another. In fact, when all else fails – sports, love, ambition – bridge remains a solace and an entertainment."

To make the contract you must delay drawing trumps, setting up a discard on the club suit instead. You win the diamond lead with the ◆A, preserving the ◆K as a later entry to dummy and lead the ♣Q. Let's say that East holds up the ♣A for one round. When you continue with a club to the king, East wins with the ace and returns a diamond. Now you reap the benefit of winning the first round of diamonds in your hand. You win with the ◆K and discard your diamond loser on the established ♣J. You can then play trumps safely and will make the game for the loss of just three aces.

Another reason to delay drawing trumps is when you need to make good use of the trump entries to dummy. This is most often the case when dummy contains a long side suit that you need to establish. That is the situation on the next deal:

Right: Establishing a side suit before drawing trumps. Declarer delays drawing trumps, so he can use the trump ace as an entry to establish dummy's diamond suit.

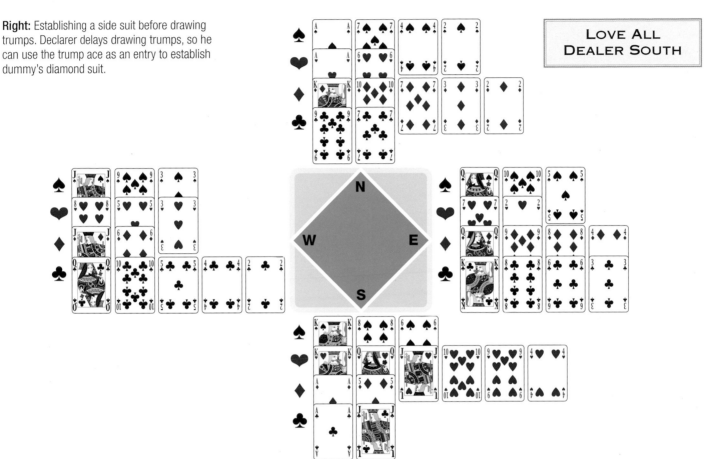

LOVE ALL
DEALER SOUTH

West leads the ♣4 against 6♥ and you win East's ♣K with the ♣A. You have 11 top tricks and must seek to establish at least one extra trick from dummy's diamond suit. Suppose your first move is to draw trumps. You continue with the ace and king of

Above: Declarer sees that he cannot afford to draw trumps straightaway.

diamonds and then ruff a third round of diamonds. All would be well if diamonds divided 3–3. When they break 4–2, as in the diagram, you will go down. You have only one entry left to the dummy (the ♠A) and the diamonds are not yet established.

You need to use the ♥A as an extra entry to the dummy. After winning the club lead, you play the ace and king of diamonds. You ruff a third round of diamonds with the ♥K (to avoid a possible overruff). Next you cross to the ♥A and ruff a diamond with the ♥Q. You can then draw the outstanding trumps and cross to the ♠A to score the established ♦10.

To make such a contract, you must form a plan right at the start. If you make the mistake of drawing trumps first, it will be too late for any planning. You need to establish the diamonds. This will require two ruffs when the defenders' cards divide 4–2, in which case you will need to use the ♥A as an entry to take the second ruff.

DUCKING INTO THE SAFE HAND

To establish a suit, it is often necessary to duck a round – in other words to let the defenders win an early trick in the suit. When one of the defenders is "safe" and the other is "dangerous", you must try to duck a trick into the safe hand. Here is a straightforward example of the play:

Right: Establishing a suit by ducking into the safe hand. Declarer holds up the ♠A twice and then sets up the diamond suit by ducking a round into the safe East hand.

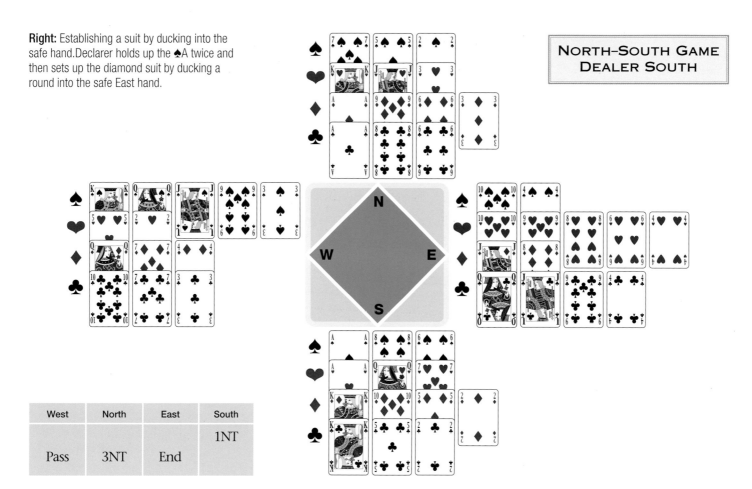

**NORTH–SOUTH GAME
DEALER SOUTH**

West	North	East	South
			1NT
Pass	3NT	End	

West leads the ♠K against 3NT. Since you are well protected in the other three suits, nothing can be lost by holding up the ♠A until the third round. East discards a heart on the third round of spades. You have eight tricks on top and must try to develop a ninth trick from the diamond suit. This must be done without allowing West to gain the lead.

Suppose you play the ace and king of diamonds and concede a third round of the suit. All would be well if East began with three diamonds. He would win the third round and would have no spade to play. If the cards lie as in the diagram, however, you will go down. West will win the third diamond and cash two spades to put you one down.

You should lead the ◆2 from the South hand and play the ◆9 from dummy. You are ducking the trick into the safe hand. East wins with ◆J and has no spade to play. You win his return in some other suit and cash a total of nine tricks to make the game. Had you played ace, king, and another diamond instead, West would have won the third round of the suit and beaten the contract by cashing two more spade tricks.

Sometimes you duck a round of a suit as a safety play, to guard against a bad break. By ducking into the safe hand, you avoid the risk that the suit will break badly and you would otherwise have to lose a trick to the danger hand. That is the situation on the deal shown opposite.

West leads the ♥4 against 3NT and you win East's ♥Q with the ♥K. (If instead you were to allow the ♥Q to win, East would continue with a second heart and West would hold up his ♥A to maintain communication between the defenders.) You have eight tricks on top and need to develop a ninth trick from the diamonds. If the suit divided 3–3, you would have two extra diamond tricks ready to take, simply by playing the suit from the top. If you play that way here, East will win the fourth diamond and beat you by returning a heart through your ♥J–7. To make the contract even when East holds four diamonds, you need to duck a diamond trick into the safe (West) hand.

At Trick 2 you cross to the ♠A. You then lead the ♦5. When East follows with a low spot-card you cover with the ♦8, ducking a diamond trick into the safe hand. West wins with the ♦10 but cannot continue hearts successfully from his side of the table. If he switches to a club, you will rise with dummy's ♣A. You then play a diamond to the queen and return to dummy with the ♠K to score three more diamond tricks for the contract.

By making this safety play, ducking a round of diamonds, you would score only four diamond tricks instead of five when the suit divided 3–3. The potential loss of an overtrick is a small premium to pay for making the game when diamonds break 4–2.

If East began with ♦J–10–4–2 he would (if awake) play one of his honours on the first round, to prevent you ducking the trick into the safe hand. The contract could not then be made when the heart suit lies as in the diagram.

Right: Ducking into the safe hand in case a suit breaks badly. Declarer ducks a diamond into the safe (West) hand, so that he can establish the suit when the defenders' cards break 4–2.

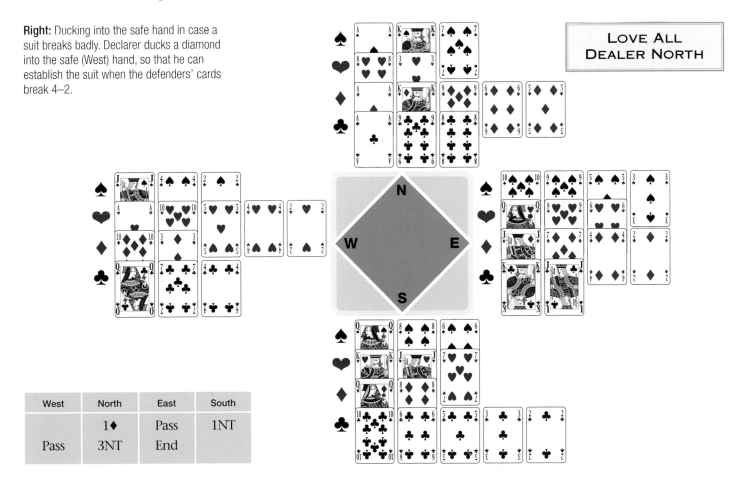

LOVE ALL
DEALER NORTH

West	North	East	South
	1♦	Pass	1NT
Pass	3NT	End	

PUT THE SAFE HAND ON LEAD
♠ ♥ ♦ ♣

Suppose you are in a suit contract, with a side suit of ♦K–8–2 in dummy and a singleton ♦5 in your hand. When West leads the ♦Q, it is obvious that East holds the ♦A. If you think that West could make a damaging play at Trick 2, you should cover with the ♦K, to make sure that East wins the first trick. Otherwise you should duck.

CHAPTER 9

INTERMEDIATE DEFENCE

It is a familiar concept to plan the play of a hand when you are the declarer. It can be just as important to plan the defence of a contract and here you will see how you can do this, both in a suit contract and in no-trumps. You will see also how dangerous it can be to defend too actively by attacking new suits. This is all too likely to give away an unnecessary trick. You need to study all the available evidence before deciding whether to be active or passive with your defence. One of the most difficult areas of defence, contrary to what some players will tell you, is whether to cover an honour card that has been led. You need to make such decisions in advance, so that you do not give information away by thinking about your play when a particular card is led. Finally the important topic of retaining the right cards in defence will be addressed.

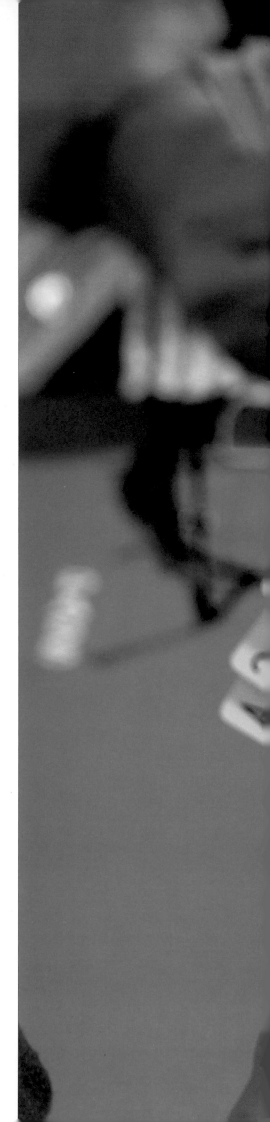

Right: The opponents' bidding will often give you a good idea what the general line of defence should be. The opening lead represents an important part of the defence.

PLANNING THE DEFENCE IN A SUIT CONTRACT

To defend accurately is not easy. You must think clearly and, above all, you must count. You count the tricks available to the defenders and to declarer. You count the points shown by declarer and by your partner. You also count the distribution of the suits, hoping to end with a complete count of the hand. If you think this sounds rather like hard work, you are right. It is the price that has to be paid in order to become a top-class defender.

Counting tricks for the defence

On the following deal, East's defence is dictated by counting the tricks that he can see for the defenders.

Sitting East, you see partner lead the ♣2. You win with the ♣A and pause to plan the defence. It is unlikely that the defence will score any tricks from the major suits. You must therefore hope for four tricks from the minors. You can score three club tricks only if West has led specifically from ♣K–J–2, which is not a big chance. It is more likely that you can score two

club tricks and two diamond tricks. So, you should switch to the ♦2 at Trick 2. As the cards lie, declarer will rise with the ♦K and West will score tricks with the ace and jack of diamonds. The ♣K will then be the setting trick. As you see, a wooden club return at Trick 2 would have allowed the contract to make. West would win with the club king but could not attack diamonds effectively from his side of the table.

The recommended defence might succeed also when declarer held ♦K–J–x. He would then have to guess which diamond honour to play. If he decided to rise with the ♦K, he would again lose four tricks in the minors and go one down.

Right: Counting the defensive tricks. By counting the tricks available to the defence, East makes the right play on the second trick.

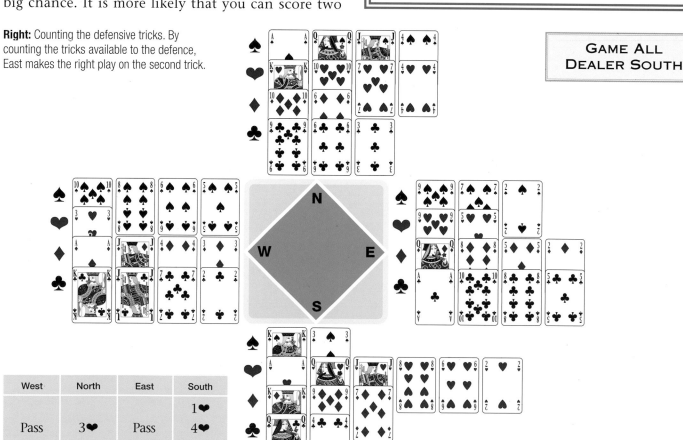

GAME ALL
DEALER SOUTH

West	North	East	South
			1♥
Pass	3♥	Pass	4♥
End			

On the next deal, counting defensive tricks allows East to judge that he should delay giving partner a ruff.

Right: Delaying a defensive ruff. West leads his singleton club against 4♠. By counting the defensive tricks, East calculates that it is not right to give partner a ruff at the second trick.

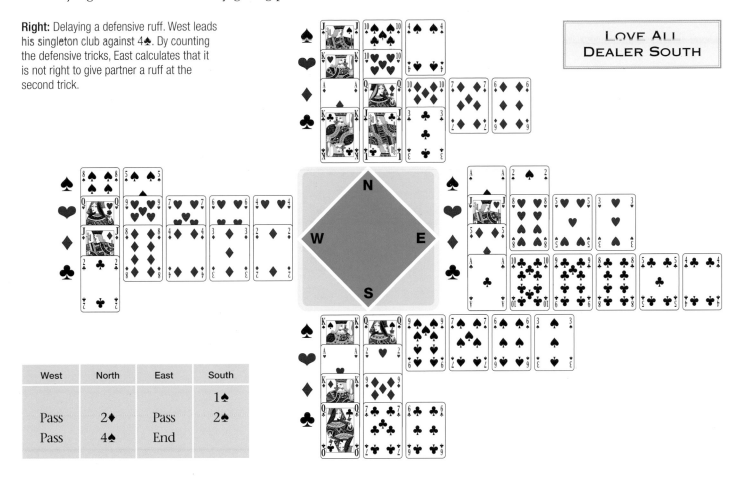

LOVE ALL
DEALER SOUTH

West	North	East	South
			1♠
Pass	2♦	Pass	2♠
Pass	4♠	End	

You hold the East cards. Your partner leads the ♣2 and you win with the ♣A. The odds are high that the opening lead is a singleton. Suppose you return a club immediately, however, giving partner a ruff. You must ask yourself how many tricks the defenders will score. Ace of clubs, a club ruff and the ace of trumps. That is three tricks. If partner started with three trumps, you will be able to give him a second club ruff but that is no certainty. As the cards lie, West will not be able to score a second club ruff and the game will be made.

Instead of returning a club without thought, you should pause to make a plan for the defence. You know that you can give partner the lead with a club ruff. Since you hold the ace of trumps, there is no need to deliver the ruff immediately. To ensure that you score a ruff too, you must switch to your singleton diamond at Trick 2. Declarer wins the trick in the dummy and leads a trump. You rise with the ace of trumps and only now give your partner a club ruff. He returns a diamond, allowing you to ruff, and the game goes one down.

GRAND MASTER
♠ ♥ ♦ ♣

Rixi Markus (1910–92) was the first woman to become a Grand Master under the World Bridge Federation ranking scheme. Rixi was a tigress at the table but very charming once the game was over. Her most famous partnership was with Fritzi Gordon (1916–92). Together they won two World Pairs Olympiads, a World Teams Olympiad, and eight European championships.

Above: Rixi Markus

Above: Fritzi Gordon

Counting tricks for the declarer

On many deals you can reach the right decision in defence by counting the tricks that are available for declarer. Take the East cards on the deal below.

West leads the ◆Q, which marks declarer with the ◆K. If he holds six solid trumps, he will make the game easily because there is no way that you can score three quick heart tricks, however the cards lie. You must therefore assume that West holds a trump trick.

Suppose you return the ◆7 at Trick 2, aiming to knock out South's ◆K and establish a diamond trick for the defence. It is quite likely then that declarer will score five trump tricks, four clubs and the ◆K.

Right: Diagnosing a switch by counting declarer's tricks. West leads the ◆Q against the spade game. By counting the number of tricks available to declarer, East sees the need to switch to hearts.

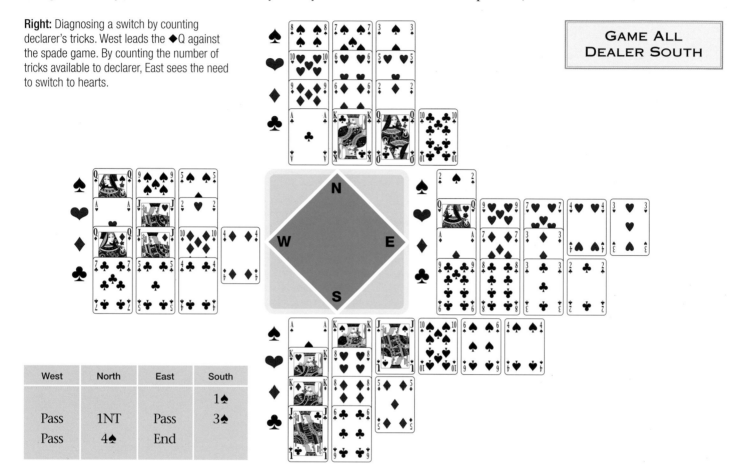

GAME ALL
DEALER SOUTH

West	North	East	South
			1♠
Pass	1NT	Pass	3♠
Pass	4♠	End	

With discards threatened on dummy's clubs, you should switch to the ♥4 at Trick 2, claiming whatever tricks may be available there. As the cards lie, your partner will score two heart tricks and his eventual trump trick will put the game one down.

As you see, a diamond return would have allowed the game to make. Declarer would win with the ◆K, draw two rounds of trumps and turn to the club suit. The diamond loser would be thrown on the third club and one of the heart losers on the fourth club. It would make no difference whether or not West chose to ruff this trick with the ♠Q. Declarer would lose only one trump, one diamond and one heart.

When you can see that declarer has quick discards available, you must switch immediately to the side suit where you may have some quick winners to take.

Here is another deal where you can benefit from counting declarer's tricks. Again you are in the East seat.

West leads the ♣J and declarer plays low from dummy. You must now decide whether to play your ♣A. It may seem attractive to play low, in order to avoid giving declarer two club tricks when he began with ♣Q–x–x. Before doing so, you should check how many tricks declarer will have after such a start to the defence. He will almost certainly have six trump tricks. To this you must add two diamond tricks, once the ◆A is dislodged, one club trick with the queen and one heart trick. That is a total of ten, so you can expect the contract to succeed if you play low at Trick 1.

To beat the contract you need to score the minor-suit aces and two heart tricks. To allow this to happen, you must rise with the ♣A at Trick 1 and then switch

to the ♥J, knocking out one of the dummy's heart stoppers. Declarer has no way to counter such a lively defence. No doubt he will draw trumps and play a diamond towards the dummy. Your partner will rise with the ◆A and play a second round of hearts, giving you two tricks in the suit. The game then goes one down.

You might achieve the same result by counting the possible tricks for the defence. Since there is only one likely trick in the black suits (the ♣A), you will need the ◆A and two heart tricks to beat the contract.

If you watched such a defence in a major championship, you might gasp in amazement. As you see, you can calculate quite logically that it is the only real chance to beat the contract. You must attack the heart suit before the ◆A is removed.

Right: Visualizing the defensive tricks. West leads the ♣J against the spade game and East must count declarer's tricks to diagnose the winning defence.

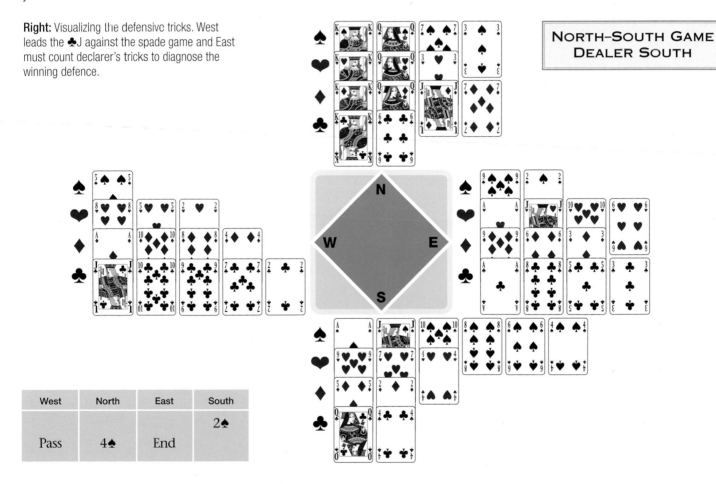

NORTH–SOUTH GAME
DEALER SOUTH

West	North	East	South
			2♠
Pass	4♠	End	

THE QUESTION TO ASK
♠ ♥ ◆ ♣

When defending, do not restrict yourself to automatic plays such as "leading up to weakness" and "returning partner's suit". Instead, ask yourself the question: "How can this contract be defeated?" If you need partner to hold a particular card, such as an ace, continue the defence on the assumption that he holds this card.

PLANNING THE DEFENCE IN NO-TRUMPS

Defending at no-trumps tends to be easier than in a suit contract. With the elements of ruffing and trump control not present, you can concentrate on communications and on setting up the tricks that you need to beat the contract. When you are sitting over the dummy, the most important decision is often whether to continue partner's suit or to switch elsewhere. By counting declarer's potential tricks, you may find a clear indication of the best chance.

Counting tricks for the declarer

Take the East cards on this deal and see if you would have come to the right "continue or switch?" decision.

West leads the ♥5 against 3NT and your jack is won by South's ace. Declarer leads the ♣Q at Trick 2, West following with the ♣7. You win with the king and pause for a moment to decide what to do next. Is it possible that your partner led from ♥K–Q–x–x–x and that the heart suit is now ready to run? No, because if declarer had started with ♥A–x–x, he would have held up the ace

for two rounds to exhaust you of your holding in the suit. So, declarer began with ♥A–K–x. (He should have won the first trick with the ♥K, to make this less obvious to you, but not all declarers know that.)

It may seem natural to knock out declarer's last heart stopper, nevertheless. Before doing this, you should count the tricks that would then be at declarer's disposal. He would have three club tricks, two hearts and almost certainly four diamond tricks. That is a total of nine. So, you cannot afford to continue with partner's suit. You must hope to score four quick tricks elsewhere and this can be achieved only in the spade suit. Switch to the ♠Q in the hope that partner holds ♠A–10–x–x. When the cards lie as in the diagram you will beat the contract.

Defenders who follow simple rules such as "Always return partner's suit" would allow this contract to be made. Good bridge is rarely a question of following this or that rule. In defence, you must think clearly whether a particular defence has a chance of beating the contract.

Right: Counting declarer's tricks. By counting the tricks available to declarer, East diagnoses the right switch when he gains the lead.

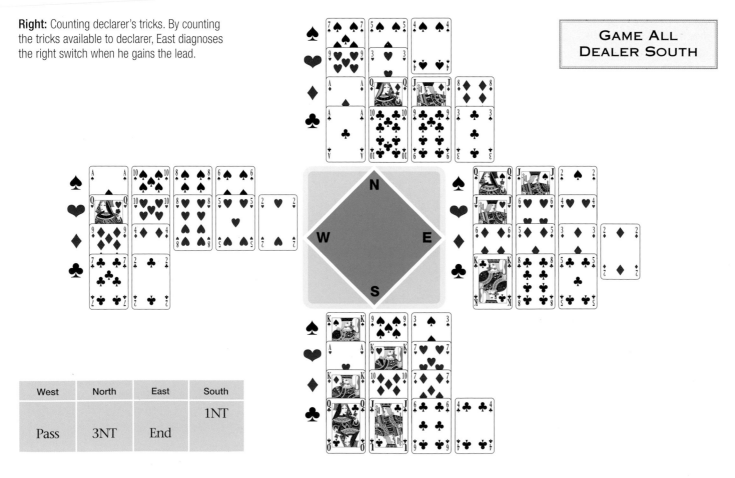

GAME ALL
DEALER SOUTH

West	North	East	South
			1NT
Pass	3NT	End	

Above: When the ♥J is won with the ♥A, the defender places declarer with ♥A–K.

Reading the opening lead

A clever gadget known as "The Rule of Eleven" will often assist you in reading the lie of the suit that partner has chosen to lead. When partner has made a fourth-best lead from a suit headed by an honour, you subtract the spot-card that he has led from 11. The answer will give you the number of higher cards that are held by the other three hands. Suppose partner has led the ♥6 and the heart suit lies as shown below.

You are sitting East and your ♥Q is won by declarer's ♥K. By applying the Rule of Eleven, you can tell that the North, East and South hands contain between them five cards higher than the ♥6. (You subtract 6 from 11, getting 5 as the answer.) You can see four of these cards in your own hand and the dummy (the queen, ten nine and seven of the suit). So the ♥K is the only high card that declarer holds in the suit. The defenders' hearts are ready to run. Such knowledge might enable you to rise immediately with an ace in a different suit, switching back to hearts.

Above: Rule of Eleven. By applying the Rule of Eleven to West's opening lead of the ♥6, East can determine the lie of the heart suit.

Let's see a complete deal featuring that heart suit. Take the East cards and plan your defence to this 3NT contract:

Right: Rule of Eleven. West leads the ♥6 to East's ♥Q and South's ♥K. East applies the Rule of Eleven to determine his future defence.

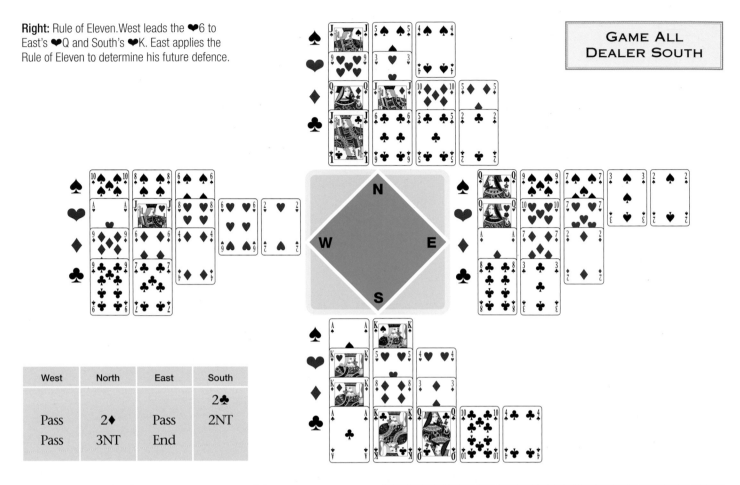

GAME ALL
DEALER SOUTH

West	North	East	South
			2♣
Pass	2♦	Pass	2NT
Pass	3NT	End	

West leads the ♥6 against South's 3NT contract and declarer wins your queen with the king. At Trick 2 he leads the ♦K and you must think carefully how to defend. If you consider the diamond suit in isolation, you might well decide to hold up the ♦A for a round or two, hoping to prevent declarer from enjoying dummy's diamond winners. Such a plan will not work well here, though. If declarer is allowed to make even one diamond trick, he will unveil seven more tricks in the black suits and make his contract.

To beat 3NT, you must win the very first diamond trick and return a heart. How can you be sure that this is the right thing to do? The Rule of Eleven tells you that declarer has no stopper remaining in hearts. There is also a good chance that your partner began with a five-card heart suit because he led the ♥6 and the five, four and two of the suit are missing. Unless declarer began with specifically ♥K–5–4–2, your partner started with at least five hearts and a heart switch will be successful. So, do not follow some

general rule about "holding up an ace to kill the dummy". Take the ♦A immediately and return the ♥10. Your partner will score four tricks in the suit to defeat the contract.

Sometimes the Rule of Eleven will tell you that partner's lead cannot be a fourth-best card, so he has led his second-best card from a weak suit. In that case it will usually pay you to abandon the suit that has been led and to seek tricks from elsewhere. A high-card lead is a warning that tricks are unavailable from that source.

Right: Diagnosing that the lead is from a weak suit. East calculates that the ♠7 lead must be from a weak suit and defends accordingly, switching to hearts.

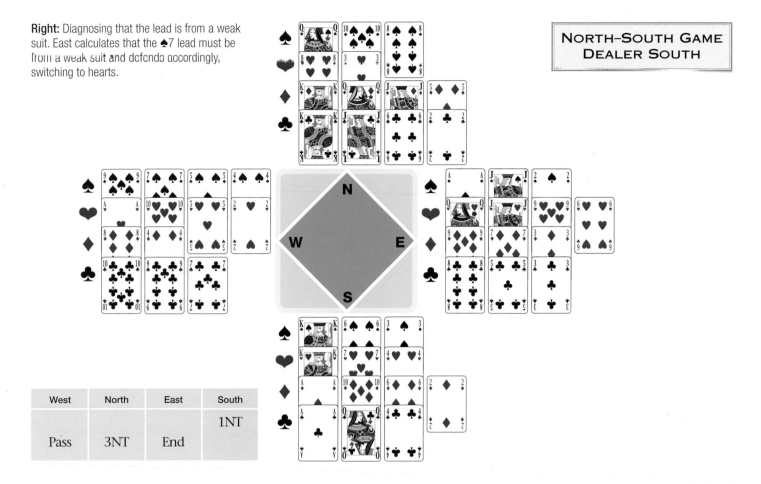

West	North	East	South
			1NT
Pass	3NT	End	

South opens a 15–17 point 1NT and is raised to game. West leads the ♠7 against this contract and the ♠10 is played from dummy. Sitting East, you must decide how to defend. Your first task is to read the lie of the spade suit. If West's spades are headed by the king, you will want to win the first trick with the ♠J and to continue with ace and another spade. You will then score at least four spade tricks, giving the defence a very good start.

Suppose you take the trouble to apply the Rule of Eleven before embarking on this line of defence. If the ♠7 is indeed a fourth-best card, the North, East and South hands will contain four cards in spades that are higher than the seven. In your own hand and the dummy, you can already see five such cards. You can therefore conclude that the ♠7 is not a fourth-best card at all. It must instead be a second-best card from weakness. West will hold either ♠9–7–x or ♠9–7–x–x.

Since there is no prospect for the defence in the spade suit, you should rise with the ♠A at Trick 1. The only chance of scoring several tricks for the defence now lies in the heart suit and you therefore switch to the ♥Q. When the cards lie as in the diagram, this smart defence will be rewarded. You and your partner will score four

heart tricks, putting the 3NT contract one down. If instead you were to play the ♠J on the first trick, declarer would win with the ♠K and quickly add four more tricks in each minor suit to make the contract.

Above: East can see five cards higher than the ♠7. He therefore knows that the lead cannot be fourth-best from strength.

CHOOSING BETWEEN ACTIVE AND PASSIVE DEFENCE

There are many positions where it will cost the defenders to make the first play in a suit. Suppose that, as declarer, you hold ◆J–8–3 in the dummy and ◆Q–6–5 in your hand. If you have to play the suit yourself, and the defenders hold one top honour each, you will probably make no trick at all from the suit. If instead the defenders make the first play in the suit, the defender in the third seat will have to rise with the ace or king. You will then be certain to score a trick with the queen or jack.

When to defend passively

The defenders often have to make an important decision. Do they need to play actively, attacking a new suit to score tricks there? Or will they perhaps do better to play passively, leaving declarer to play the new suit himself? To answer this question, the defenders must try to determine whether declarer, left to his own devices, will be able to discard his potential losers in the key suit. Look at this deal:

Sitting West, and defending the game in hearts, you lead the ♠Q, which declarer wins with the ♠K. He then leads a trump and you rise with the ♥A. The sort of defender who is always "trying another suit" might well switch to diamonds now. The effect is all too predictable. East would have to rise with the ◆A and declarer would then score a diamond trick, making the contract.

There is no need to play an active defence in this way because it is most unlikely that dummy's club suit can provide a discard of a diamond from the South hand. If declarer held three small diamonds and ♣A–Q doubleton, he would have taken a discard before playing trumps. Nor it is likely that he holds specifically ♣A–Q–J and can take a discard on the fourth round of clubs.

So, as West you do best to exit passively with a spade or a trump. Declarer will eventually have to play the diamond suit himself. He will lose three diamond tricks and go one down.

Right: A passive defence. If West defends too actively here, attacking the diamond suit, he will give away the contract.

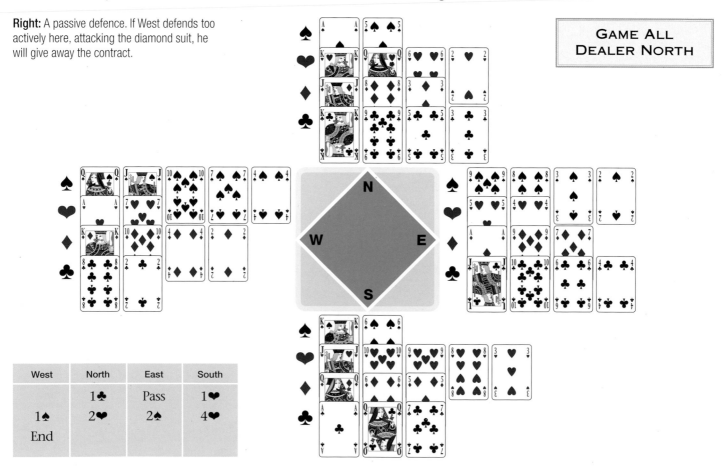

GAME ALL
DEALER NORTH

West	North	East	South
	1♣	Pass	1♥
1♠	2♥	2♠	4♥
End			

When to defend actively

To show the other side of the coin, here is a deal where the defenders do have to play actively. If they fail to do so, declarer will discard his potential losers.

West leads the ◆Q and, sitting East, you win with the ◆A. It is easy to predict what will happen if you exit passively with a trump or another diamond. Declarer will draw trumps and set up dummy's club suit, on which he can discard one or more heart losers.

You need to defend actively, attempting to set up some heart tricks before declarer can take discards on dummy's club suit. So, at Trick 2 you switch to the ♥4, South following with the ♥3. West plays the ♥10 and declarer is doomed to defeat, whether he wins the first or second round of hearts. When he eventually plays on clubs, you will win with the ♣A and cash a total of two hearts, one club and one diamond to beat the contract.

Right: An active defence. East must defend actively on this deal, attacking the heart suit to set up the defenders' winners in good time.

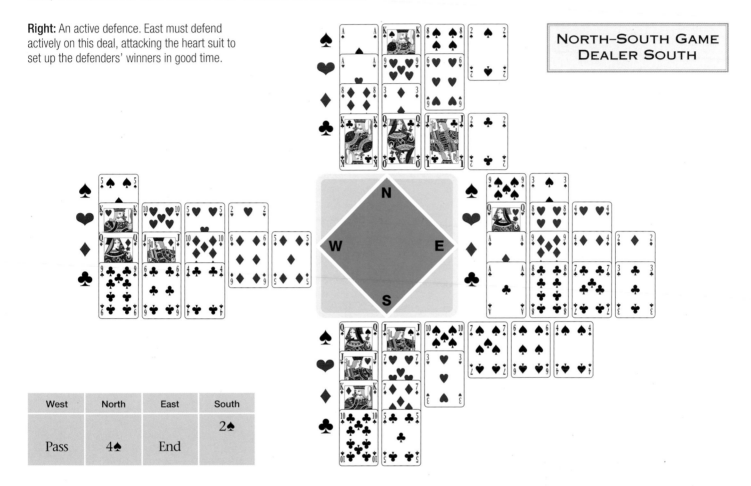

NORTH–SOUTH GAME
DEALER SOUTH

West	North	East	South
			2♠
Pass	4♠	End	

Right: Germany's Daniela von Arnim. In partnership with Sabine Auken-Zenkel, she won the women's world championship in 1995 and 2001.

WHEN TO COVER AN HONOUR WITH AN HONOUR

The advice sometimes given to beginners is "always cover an honour with an honour". In other words, if declarer plays an honour from one hand or the other the defender in second seat should cover with a higher honour. There are few hard-and-fast rules in bridge and, indeed, there are many exceptions to this one. Covering will often be a mistake.

Cover to promote a trick

Let us see first how a cover can prove effective. Look at this club position:

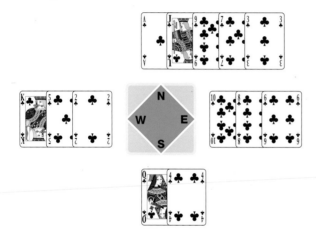

Declarer leads the ♣Q from his hand. If West fails to cover with the king, the queen will be run successfully. Declarer will finesse the ♣J on the next round and end with five club tricks. West should instead "cover an honour with an honour", playing his ♣K on the ♣Q. Dummy wins with the ♣A but East's ♣10 will now score a trick on the third round. The purpose of covering is clearly illustrated. You cover with the intention of promoting a lesser card, either in your own hand or in partner's.

The situation would be the same, of course, if the ♣Q and the ♣J were swapped. When South led the ♣J, West would cover in the hope of promoting the ♣10 with East. If South happened to hold ♣J–10 or ♣J–10–4, nothing would be lost. All five club tricks would be his, whatever the defence.

Suppose next that the ♣Q–4 were in the dummy, with declarer's club holding hidden from view. It would again be the correct defence to cover the ♣Q with the ♣K.

Do not cover when no promotion is possible

When there is no such prospect of promoting a trick, you should not cover. Suppose declarer is playing in 4♠ or 6♠ with this trump suit:

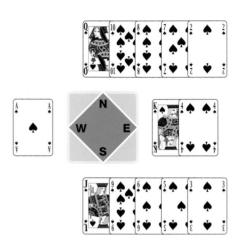

When the ♠Q is led from dummy East should not cover, because there is virtually no chance of promoting a trick by doing so. You can see what would happen if he did cover. West's ♠A would complete a heavily laden first round and declarer would lose only one trump trick. It is also possible that the spade suit lies like this:

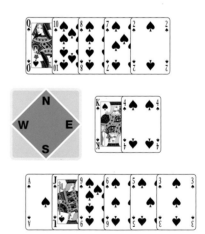

With only two cards missing, declarer has no intention of running the ♠Q. He has led it just in case you hold ♠K–4 in the East seat and are tempted to cover! Provided you follow smoothly with the ♠4, declarer will expect West to hold a singleton ♠K. He will rise with the ♠A and lose a trick in the suit when West shows out.

Do not cover the first of touching honours

When declarer leads one of touching honours, it is usually wrong to cover:

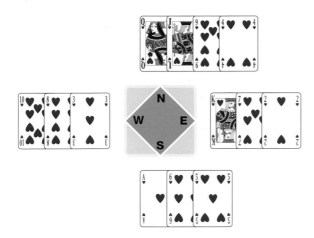

If East covers the ♥Q with the ♥K, declarer will win with the ace and subsequently finesse the ♥9 to score four heart tricks. East should not cover the first of touching honours. The queen is run successfully but declarer cannot then score more than three heart tricks. If he leads the ♥J on the second round, East will cover to promote his partner's ♥10.

It will also cost a trick to cover in this very common position:

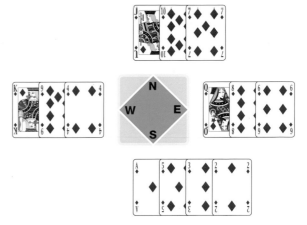

The ♦J is led from dummy. If East makes the mistake of covering with the ♦Q, declarer will win with the ace and lead back towards the ♦10. He will score three diamond tricks instead of the two that were his due. Again, East should not cover the first of touching honours. The ♦J is run to West's ♦K and declarer must now lose a second trick in the suit, however he continues.

JAMES BOND'S SLAM ON 6 POINTS
♠ ♥ ♦ ♣

Perhaps the most famous bridge hand in literature is a version of the Duke of Cumberland's hand, which was used by card cheats for decades. In Ian Fleming's novel, *Moonraker*, James Bond rigs the deck to give villain, Hugo Drax, the East hand shown below:

```
            ♠ 10 9 8 7
            ♥ 6 5 4 3
            ♦ —
            ♣ 7 6 5 3 2
♠ 6 5 4 3 2              ♠ A K Q J
♥ 10 9 8 7 2            ♥ A K Q J
♦ J 10 9               ♦ A K
♣ —                    ♣ K J 9
            ♠ —
            ♥ —
            ♦ Q 8 7 6 5 4 3 2
            ♣ A Q 10 8 4
```

Bond, who holds the South hand, is pretending to be drunk. He bids a grand slam in clubs. Drax doubles, scornfully, and Bond redoubles. A large side bet is agreed in addition and the grand slam cannot be defeated! Declarer can establish the diamond suit and pick up East's ♣K–J–9 with two finesses.

Above: With 31 points in his hand, East cannot believe that 7♣ will be made against him.

KEEPING THE RIGHT CARDS

One of the most important aspects of good defence is the ability to keep the right cards when you are forced to make some discards. One good guideline is that you should "match your length" with any length visible in the dummy. For example, if dummy contains ♠K–Q–8–2, you should not discard a spade from a holding such as ♠J–10–6–3. If declarer has the ♠A, your holding is necessary to guard the fourth round. Even if your partner holds the ♠A, you may still need all your spades to restrict declarer to the minimum number of tricks from the suit.

Matching the dummy's length

Let us see an example of "matching dummy's length" in the context of the complete deal shown below.

You are sitting East and your partner leads the ♥Q. Declarer allows this card to win, hoping to tighten the end position and cause discarding problems for the defenders later. He wins the next round of hearts with the ♥K and cashes four rounds of clubs, followed by dummy's ♥A. You must now find a discard from ♠10–9–6–2 ♦Q–10–7.

Right: Matching the length in dummy. There are four spades in dummy and East should therefore retain all four spades.

Dummy has four-card spade length and you must retain your four spades, matching dummy's length, to avoid giving a trick away when declarer holds the king and queen of the suit. You may be surprised to hear that your ♦Q–10–7 are virtually worthless. If declarer holds the ♦A–K–J sitting over them, he can finesse in the suit anyway. Otherwise your partner will hold the ♦J and can guard the diamond suit himself. So, throw a diamond and retain your important spade guard. The slam will then go down.

COUNT SIGNALS
♠ ♥ ♦ ♣

One of the important reasons for giving count signals (a high signal to show an even number of cards, a low signal to show an odd number) is to help your partner to decide which cards to retain. If your count signal implies that declarer holds three spades rather than four, for example, partner will not need to keep four spades.

LOVE ALL
DEALER SOUTH

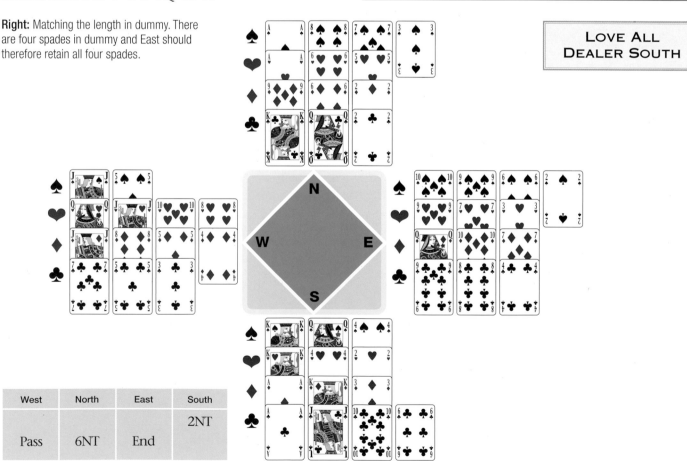

West	North	East	South
			2NT
Pass	6NT	End	

Making deductions from declarer's play

It is often possible to deduce declarer's length in a suit from the way that he has chosen to play the hand. Take the West cards on the deal shown below.

Sitting West, you lead the ♥Q against the spade slam. When this card wins the first trick, you play another heart, South ruffing. Declarer draws two rounds of trumps with the queen and jack. When you show out, throwing a diamond, he continues with three more rounds of trumps. You can safely throw all your hearts. On the last trump you must make one more discard from ♦Q–J–8 and ♣10–9–7–3. If declarer holds ♦A–K–10, you must keep your diamonds. If instead he holds ♣A–K–Q–x, you must keep your clubs. What would your decision be? If declarer did hold ♦A–K–10, he would have ruffed his diamond loser in dummy before drawing three rounds of trumps. So, you should throw a diamond and keep your potential guard in clubs. Declarer will then have no way to avoid a club loser and the slam will go down.

Right: Making a deduction from declarer's play. When declarer draws trumps without first taking a diamond ruff, West can deduce that South holds only two diamonds.

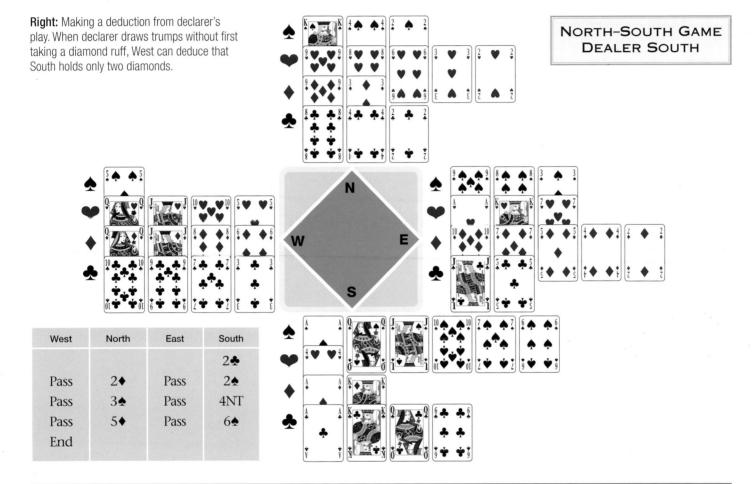

	NORTH–SOUTH GAME DEALER SOUTH		

West	North	East	South
			2♣
Pass	2♦	Pass	2♠
Pass	3♠	Pass	4NT
Pass	5♦	Pass	6♠
End			

BRIDGE BOOK COLLECTORS
♠ ♥ ♦ ♣

Since the year 1900 about 8,000 books and pamphlets in the English language have been published on bridge. The most prolific decade was the 1930s, with around 1,400 publications. The world's three biggest bridge-book collections in private hands are owned by Tim Bourke of Canberra, Australia, by Wolf Klewe of Winchester, England and by Gerard Hilte, of Leerdam in the Netherlands.

Right: Tim Bourke of Canberra, Australian bridge expert and owner of one of the world's largest collections of bridge books.

CHAPTER 10

ADVANCED BIDDING

This section looks at some of the most popular bidding conventions from the tournament bridge world. First you will see the Cappelletti defence to 1NT, one of several conventions that allow you to contest the bidding after the opponents have opened 1NT. Next there is a discussion on how you can use bids in the opponents' suit to indicate strong hands in various situations. An important aid to bidding slams is Roman Key-card Blackwood, where you can ask not only about aces but also about the king and queen of trumps. Puppet Stayman allows you to detect a five-card major in the hand of the 2NT (two no-trumps) opener. Splinter bids tell your partner where you hold a shortage, thereby allowing him to judge if the two hands will fit together well. The chapter ends with a discussion of lead-directing doubles, where you double an artificial bid made by an opponent to tell your partner what opening lead you would like against the eventual contract.

Right: Employing the Cappelletti convention, the player has bid 2♣ to show a long suit somewhere. Partner's 2♦ asks the overcaller to specify which suit it is.

CAPPELLETTI DEFENCE TO 1NT

The scoring table does not reward you very well when you defeat an opposing 1NT contract, particularly when the opponents are non-vulnerable. Whenever you take +50 or +100, defending 1NT, you will usually find that you could have scored at least +110 somewhere, playing the contract yourself. Apart from that, 1NT is a very difficult contract to defend. Declarer will often emerge with seven tricks when, with optimal defence, you could have set the contract. For these reasons, players are keen to contest the bidding when they hear an opposing 1NT bid. There are several conventions available and one of the most popular is the Cappelletti Defence.

Above: The Cappelletti Defence was invented by Michael Cappelletti, who is an expert at both bridge and poker.

The Cappelletti Defence

Both in the second and the fourth seats, these are the possible actions when playing Cappelletti:

Double	a penalty double
2♣	a single-suiter in an undisclosed suit (6–card suit)
2♦	both major suits (at least 5–4)
2♥	hearts and a minor suit (can be 4–5 or 5–4)
2♠	spades and a minor suit (can be 4–5 or 5–4)
2NT	both minor suits (at least 5–5).

Partner shows a single-suiter

When partner bids 2♣, you can pass if you hold six clubs or more, bid 2♦ to ask him to indicate his long suit, or respond in a major with a long holding there. This is a typical sequence:

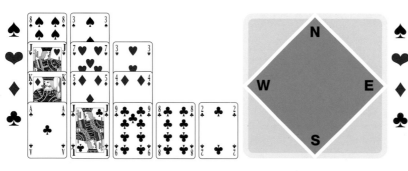

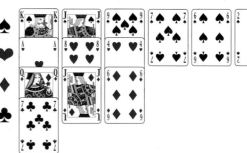

West's clubs are not long and strong enough to pass 2♣, particularly as he holds at least two-card support for whichever suit East may hold. As you can see, there is only a 5–1 fit in clubs, which will make nowhere near such a good trump suit as the 6–2 fit that exists in the spade suit.

To request partner's suit, West responds 2♦. East would pass this with long diamonds, but here he rebids 2♠ and this becomes the final contract.

West	North	East	South
	1NT	2♣	Pass
2♦	Pass	2♠	End

Partner shows both majors or both minors

When partner bids 2♦, showing both majors, you can pass with six diamonds and choose one of the major suits otherwise:

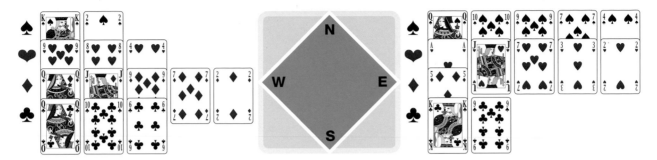

Sitting West, you give preference to hearts. This might sometimes be a 4–3 fit, yes, but that will not be your fault. You cannot always guarantee an 8-card fit somewhere.

West	North	East	South
	1NT	2♦	Pass
2♥	End		

Similarly, unless you hold a particularly strong hand, you will merely choose your better minor when partner overcalls 2NT.

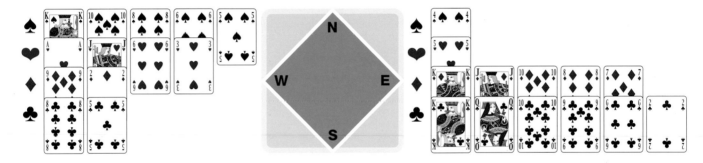

With two doubletons in the minors, there is some chance that you may be doubled. Bid 3♣ first, hoping that you escape a double. If you are doubled in 3♣, you will have to guess whether to try your luck in 3♦ instead.

West	North	East	South
	1NT	2NT	Pass
3♣	End		

Partner bids 2♥ or 2♠

When your partner bids 2♥ or 2♠, showing a major–minor two-suiter, you will often pass. If you wish to discover his minor suit, you respond 2NT:

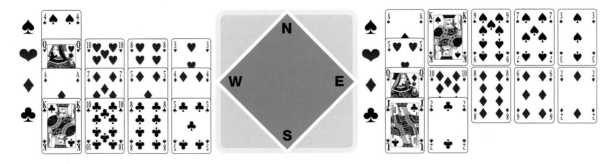

With a certain fit in one of the minors, West responds 2NT to ask East whether he holds diamonds or clubs as his second suit. East rebids 3♦, showing a two-suiter in spades and diamonds, and this bid ends the auction.

West	North	East	South
	1NT	2♠	Pass
2NT	Pass	3♦	End

CUE-BID RAISES

Less experienced players hardly ever make a bid in a suit that has already been bid by the opponents. Since there are only five denominations available (the four suits and no-trumps), this is a big opportunity wasted. Serious bridge players hate to waste any possible call and make very good use of a cue-bid in the opponents' suit. Such a bid will nearly always show a strong hand. When your partner has already bid a suit, a cue-bid shows a strong raise of that suit.

Above: With a sound raise of partner's 1♠ overcall, East cue-bids in the opponents' suit.

Cue-bid raise of an overcall

When partner has overcalled, as we saw earlier, any direct raise from you is pre-emptive. With a sound raise instead, you cue-bid the opener's suit. Let's see some typical sequences:

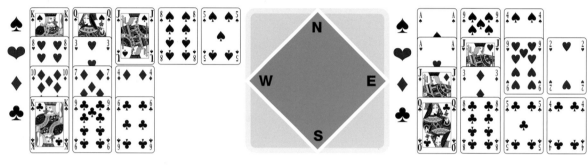

With 12 points and three-card spade support, East is interested in bidding a spade game. He shows his sound high-card raise with a cue-bid of 2♦. West has a minimum overcall and signs off in 2♠. East decides to bid no further, which is just as well because declarer could easily lose five tricks.

When the overcall was made in a minor suit, the purpose of a cue-bid raise will normally be to investigate a possible 3NT contract:

West	North	East	South
			1♦
1♠	Pass	2♦	Pass
2♠	End		

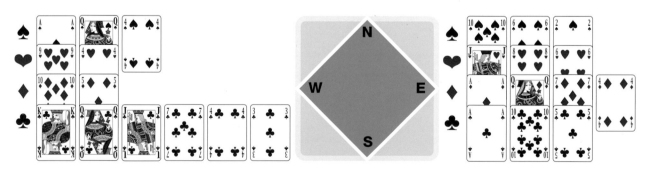

East makes a cue-bid in hearts, the opponents' suit, to show his sound raise in clubs. He hopes that West can rebid 2NT with a heart stopper. West has no reason to be ashamed of his overcall and shows his values in spades.

On some deals this would be enough for East to bid 3NT when he held a heart stopper himself. On this occasion neither player can stop the hearts and there is insufficient playing strength for a minor-suit game. Wisely, they stop in 3♣.

West	North	East	South
			1♥
2♣	Pass	2♥	Pass
2♠	Pass	3♣	End

Cue-bid raise of an opening bid

When your partner's one-bid has been overcalled, you have the opportunity to make use of a cue-bid response. Suppose the bidding has started like this:

West	North	East	South
1♠	2♦	?	

A raise to 2♠ would show three-card support and around 5–9 points. A raise to 3♠ would be pre-emptive, showing 4-card support and around 4–8 points. With a stronger hand including spade support, you would cue-bid 3♦. Suppose you held one of these hands as East:

1

With hand (1) you would raise to 2♠.

2

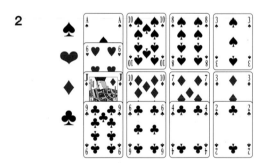

On (2) you would raise pre-emptively to 3♠, shutting out a possible heart fit for the opponents.

3

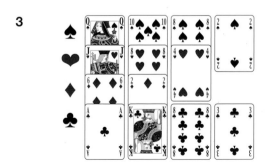

Hand (3) represents a genuine game-try hand in spades, with the values in high-card points. You would therefore cue-bid 3♦. Partner would then sign off in 3♠ when he held a minimum hand and would have passed the normal, uninterrupted sequence of 1♠ – 3♠.

A similar scheme is used when partner has opened 1♣ or 1♦. Suppose partner's 1♦ is overcalled with 1♥ and you hold one of these hands in the third seat:

1

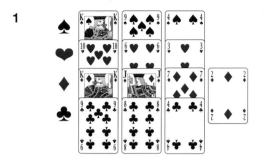

You would raise to 2♦ on (1).

2

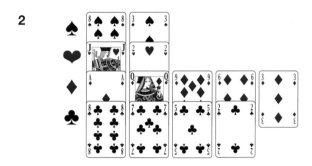

With hand (2) you would raise pre-emptively to 3♦, which might well shut out an opposing spade contract.

3

On (3) you cue-bid 2♥, showing a sound raise in diamonds with game ambitions.

ROTH-STONE BIDDING
♠ ♥ ♦ ♣

The Unusual No-trump convention, where 2NT shows a two-suited hand in the lowest unbid suits, was invented by the American Alvin Roth in the 1940s. It was subsequently developed by his partner for many years, Tobias Stone. In the Roth-Stone bidding system, strong opening bids were advocated in the first and second positions. Roth and Stone would often pass 12-point hands.

ROMAN KEY-CARD BLACKWOOD

In the original version of Blackwood, the responses stated only how many aces were held. When you are aiming for a slam in a suit, the king or queen of trumps can be just as important as an ace. A new version, known as Roman Key-card Blackwood, includes these two cards in the responses. It swept the tournament bridge world like wildfire and the time has come to take a look at it.

5♣	0 or 3 key cards
5♦	1 or 4 key cards
5♥	2 or 5 key cards and no queen of trumps
5♠	2 or 5 key cards and the queen of trumps.

Asking for key cards

When a trump suit has been agreed, either player may bid 4NT (Roman Key-card Blackwood, hereafter shortened to RKCB) to ask how many key cards partner holds. There are five key cards: the four aces and the king of trumps. The table shows the responses.

There is rarely any ambiguity as to whether 0 or 3 key cards are held (or 1 or 4). If the 4NT bidder is uncertain, he may sign off in the expectation that partner will bid again when he holds the more generous allocation. Here is a typical RKCB sequence:

West	East
1♥	1♠
2♠	4NT
5♠	6♠

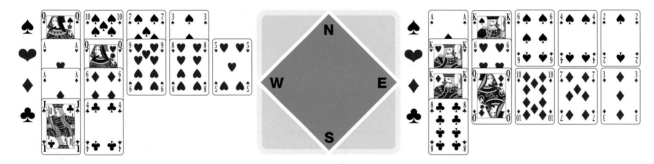

West's 5♠ response shows two key cards (two aces here) and the ♠Q. East is then prepared to bid a small slam.

Let's change West's hand, to give him a 5♣ response:

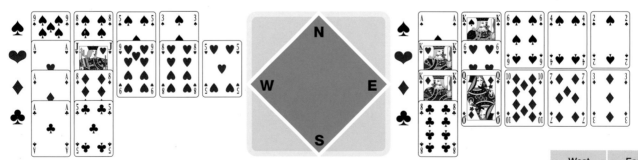

West	East
1♥	1♠
2♠	4NT
5♣	5♠
6♠	

EXCLUSION BLACKWOOD
♠ ♥ ♦ ♣

Exclusion Blackwood is a convention that allows you to ask for key cards even when you have a void in your hand. Instead of using 4NT as the enquiry bid, you jump to the five-level in the suit where you hold the void. In the auction 1♠ – 3♠ – 5♦, for example, the opener would be asking for key cards excluding the ♦A (a card of little value opposite a void).

When East hears the "0 or 3" response, it is possible if unlikely that West has no key cards. Playing safe, East signs off in 5♠. Since West holds three key cards rather than none, he advances to a slam anyway.

Asking for side-suit kings with 5NT

When you bid 4NT and hear how many key cards partner holds, you can continue with 5NT to ask how many side-suit kings he has. You should do this only when all the key cards are present, otherwise there is no chance of a grand slam anyway.

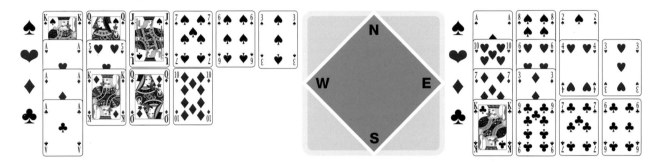

West bids 4NT and hears about the ace of trumps. He is willing to hope for the best in the diamond suit and therefore just needs to know whether a side-suit king is held. East admits to one king (5♣ = 0, 5♦ – 1, 5♥ – 2, 5♠ – 3) and the grand slam is bid.

West	East
2♣	2♦
2♠	3♠
4NT	5♦
5NT	6♦
7♠	

Asking for the trump queen

When your partner's RKCB response is 5♣ or 5♦, he has not told you whether he holds the queen of trumps. You can continue with the cheapest bid not in the trump suit to ask whether the trump queen is held. Responder will sign off without the trump queen. With the queen, he will cue-bid a side-suit king or bid 5NT.

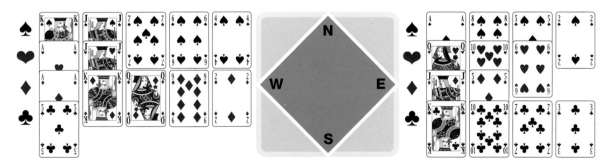

The 5♦ response tells West that an ace is missing. He is still willing to bid the slam, provided East holds the ♠Q. The sign-off in spades denies this card and West lets the bidding die at the five-level. Note that if East holds longer trumps than expected (five trumps rather than four in the present situation) he is entitled to pretend that he holds the trump queen. With ten spades between the two hands, there is a good chance that the defenders' ♠Q will fall on the first or second round. Even if a defender holds ♠Q–x–x, it may be possible to finesse the queen successfully.

West	East
1♠	3♠
4NT	5♦
5♥	5♠

TWO-SUITED OVERCALLS

Hands that contain two five-card suits are inappropriate for a take-out double, since partner is all too likely to respond in the short suit. It is therefore advisable to reserve certain bids to show specifically a two-suited hand. The most popular of these is the Unusual No-trump – a jump overcall of 2NT that shows the lowest two unbid suits. Almost as widely played is the Michaels cue-bid, which shows a two-suiter including any unbid major suit(s).

The Unusual No-trump

When an opponent has opened with one of a suit, a 2NT overcall in the second seat shows a two-suiter in the lowest two unbid suits. Although the point-count does not have to be as high as for an opening bid, the playing strength should be fairly sound because your partner will have to play at the three-level. Here is a typical example of the bid:

Above: With five cards in each minor suit, the player uses the Unusual No-trump convention.

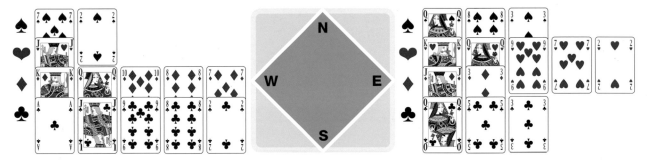

Although East has 10 points, he realizes that he is a long way from being able to suggest a game contract. He signs off at the three-level in his longer minor suit.

When the 2NT bidder has a very strong hand, he may indicate this by bidding again:

West	North	East	South
			1♠
2NT	Pass	3♣	End

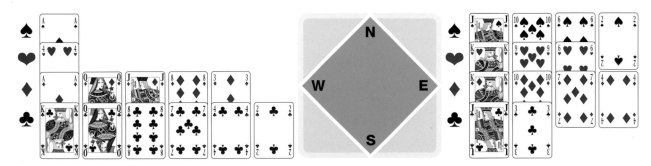

West raises to 4♦, announcing that he is very strong for a 2NT overcall. Although precision is not possible in such situations, East judges that his four-card trump support to the king entitles him to raise to game. This judgement proves sound and the game will probably be made unless the opponents score an immediate club ruff.

In the fourth seat (in an auction such as 1♠ – Pass – Pass – 2NT) the 2NT is normally played as natural, showing around 18–20 points.

West	North	East	South
			1♥
2NT	Pass	3♦	Pass
4♦	Pass	5♦	End

Michaels cue-bids

When an opponent has opened 1♣ or 1♦, a Michaels cue-bid in the same suit (2♣ or 2♦, respectively) shows both major suits. Over an opening of 1♥ or 1♠ a cue-bid in the same suit shows a two-suiter containing the other major and one of the minor suits. Here are some typical sequences:

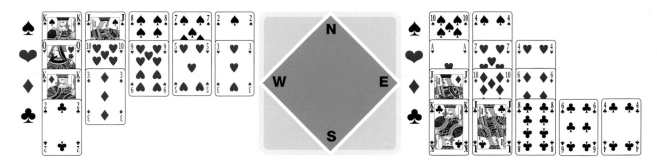

A Michaels cue-bid does not require as much playing strength as an Unusual No-trump bid, because the contract will usually be played one level lower, at the two-level. Here East responds at the minimum level in his better major. If West held 15 points or so, he might suggest a game by raising to 3♥.

West	North	East	South
			1♦
2♦	Pass	2♥	End

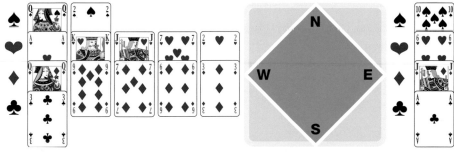

Opposite a major-suit Michael's bid, you may ask for a second suit by bidding 2NT. Here West shows diamonds and East is happy to pass out 3♦.

West	North	East	South
			1♠
2♠	Pass	2NT	Pass
3♦	End		

CONVENTION FORGOTTEN
♠ ♥ ♦ ♣

Even the top experts sometimes forget their conventions. At the 1957 European Championships, Terence Reese and Boris Schapiro were playing that a 4♥ response to 1NT was a transfer bid, showing spades. What is more, they had also agreed that anyone who forgot the method would have to pay a fine of 100 Austrian schillings. On one deal Schapiro did forget the convention, responding 4♥ on a hand with six hearts. When Reese rebid 4♠, Schapiro was nervous of bidding 5♥ in case this was taken as a slam try with spades agreed. Hoping to enlighten his partner, he bid 6♥. This was passed out and the contract was made when the Icelandic opponents failed to cash two aces. "Don't play the convention any more!" pleaded the rest of the British team. "No, no, we'll just increase the fine to 200 schillings," replied Reese.

MICHAELS CUE-BID
♠ ♥ ♦ ♣

In most situations you show a strong hand when you cue-bid the opponents' suit. The Michaels cue-bid is an exception to this general rule and your hand may be quite modest.

PUPPET STAYMAN

When you have a hand with 5–3–3–2 shape and 20–22 points, the only sensible opening bid is 2NT, even when the five-card suit is a major. In order to locate an eight-card fit when responder holds three cards in the suit, many tournament players use a modified form of Stayman opposite 2NT (and 2♣ – 2♦ – 2NT). It is known as Puppet Stayman and asks initially for a five-card major.

Bidding 3♣ to ask for a five-card major

The rebids by the opener after a start of 2NT – 3♣ are:

3♦	"I have at least one 4-card major but no 5-card major."
3♥	"I have five hearts."
3♠	"I have five spades."
3NT	"I have no 4-card or 5-card major."

Here are some typical sequences:

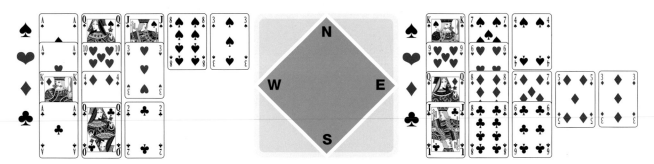

The 5–3 spade fit is discovered and 4♠ proves a better prospect than 3NT, which might fail on a heart lead. If West had bid 3♦ instead, showing at least one four-card major, East would have signed off in 3NT.

West	East
2NT	3♣
3♠	4♠

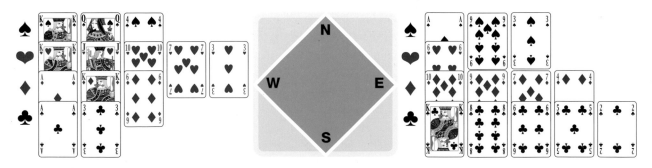

East would be happy to play in a 5–3 spade fit, in case the hearts are underprotected. When West shows five hearts, this fear vanishes and East bids the game in no-trumps. If West had rebid 3NT, denying even a four-card major, East would again play in 3NT since an 11-trick game in a minor suit is unattractive. Opposite a 3♦ rebid, East would have to seek a 4–3 spade fit or take his chances in 3NT.

West	East
2NT	3♣
3♥	3NT

Locating a 4–4 fit

When the bidding has started 2NT – 3♣ – 3♦, there is still enough bidding space to locate any 4–4 fit that may be present. A slightly complicated mechanism is used to ensure that the 2NT opener becomes the declarer. These are the continuations by responder:

3♥	"I have a four-card spade suit."
3♠	"I have a four-card heart suit."
4♦	"I have four hearts and four spades."

As you see, the responder bids three of the major suit that he does not hold. It may seem strange but the "puppet mechanism", as it is called, works very well. Here are some typical sequences:

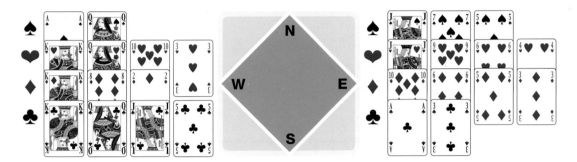

West	East
2NT	3♣
3♦	3♠
4♥	

When West rebids 3♦, saying that he holds at least one four-card major, East bids 3♠ to indicate a four-card heart suit. West duly bids the heart game and his ♦K is protected from the opening lead.

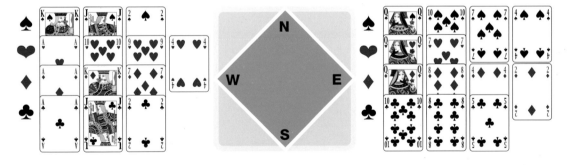

West	East
2NT	3♣
3♦	3♥
3NT	

East bids 3♥ to show a four-card spade suit. No 4–4 fit has come to light and West therefore bids 3NT, which ends the auction.

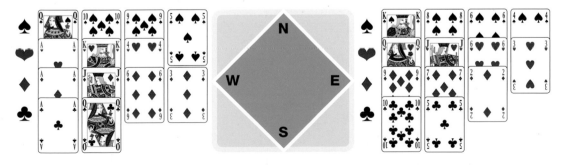

West	East
2NT	3♣
3♦	4♦
4♠	

East shows both four-card majors and West bids game in spades. The strong hand will be hidden from view.

SPLINTER BIDS

When two bridge hands fit well together, the trick-taking potential is greater than you might expect from the number of points held. One aspect of two hands fitting well is that little honour strength in one hand is wasted opposite a shortage. Suppose declarer holds ♦A–8–7–2 and the dummy holds ♦6. That represents an excellent fit. The ace will win the first round and the low cards can be ruffed. Suppose instead that declarer holds ♦K–Q–8–4 opposite a singleton. One point more in the suit, yes, but the fit is very poor. Not only will the first round now be lost, the king and queen may well be worth very little. They could have been ruffed anyway.

A "splinter bid" shows where you hold a side-suit singleton (or void). Your partner will then be able to assess whether the two hands fit well together. If they do, a slam may be possible. This is the scheme of splinter-bid responses after partner has opened bidding with 1♠:

Above: A splinter bid of 4♣ will allow the opener to judge how well the two hands fit.

4♣	shows a sound game raise with at most one club
4♦	shows a sound game raise with at most one diamond
4♥	shows a sound game raise with at most one heart.

A typical splinter bid by responder suggests around 10–14 points. Suppose partner has opened 1♠ and you hold one of these hands:

1
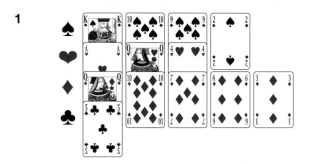

2
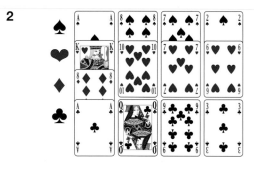

3

You would respond 4♣ on (1), showing a sound raise to game in spades and at most one club. Similarly, you would respond 4♦ on (2). The values in (3) are not quite sufficient for a game raise and you would respond just 3♠.

Over an opening bid of 1♥, the three splinter bids would be 3♠, 4♣ and 4♦. You may also agree to play splinter bids over an opening bid in a minor suit. Over 1♦, for example, the splinter bids would be 3♥, 3♠ and 4♣.

Let's see a couple of full auctions that involve a splinter bid by responder. In both cases the opener is able to judge whether the two hands fit together well.

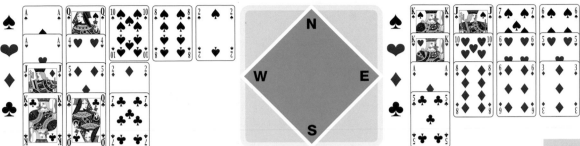

West	East
1♠	4♣
4♠	

West has a respectable opening bid but his ♣K–Q–7 represents a poor fit with partner's announced shortage in the suit. He therefore signs off in game.

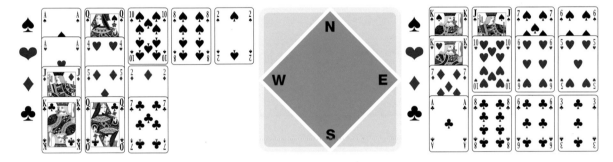

West	East
1♠	4♦
4NT	5♥
6♠	

When East's minor suits are switched, West has only one point wasted opposite the shortage and knows that the hands will fit very well. He bids Roman Key-card Blackwood, hearing of two key cards (the ♠K and the ♣A). He then advances to 6♠, in the reasonable expectation that there will be only one trick to be lost – in diamonds. This does indeed prove to be the case and an excellent slam is made on a combined total of just 27 points.

Splinter bid by the opener

The opener can make a splinter bid, when he has a good fit for responder's suit:

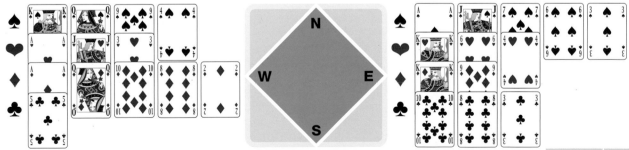

West	East
1♦	1♠
4♣	4NT
5♣	6♠

A rebid of 3♣ by West would have been natural and game-forcing. The higher bid of 4♣ is therefore available as a splinter bid. It shows a sound raise to 4♠ and at most one club. With three low cards in the splinter suit, East diagnoses a fine fit and heads for a small slam.

LEAD-DIRECTING DOUBLES

Even when you hold a poor hand, there are two good reasons to pay attention when the opponents are engaged on some lengthy auction. The first is that you may be able to use the information gained, when the time comes to defend their contract. Another reason is that you may have the chance to double a conventional bid, in order to suggest a good opening lead to your partner.

Doubling a transfer bid or Stayman

When the opponents are playing a strong 1NT, it is normal to play a double of a transfer bid or of a Stayman 2♣ as lead-directing:

West	North	East	South
	1NT	Pass	2♣
Dble			

West's double of the artificial 2♣ bid suggests a club opening lead. If South had responded 2♦ instead, a transfer bid to show long hearts, West would double when he held strong diamonds.

When North instead has opened with a weak 1NT, it is better to play that a double of Stayman or a transfer bid shows a hand that would have made a

---

TAKE-OUT DOUBLES FORBIDDEN

♠ ♥ ♦ ♣

In the early days of bridge, the staid and very conservative Portland Club (in London) decried the use of any conventional calls. Even the humble take-out double was not permitted in any bridge game that took place on their premises.

---

penalty double of 1NT. In other words, a double shows upwards of 15 points and says nothing whatsoever about your holding in the suit artificially bid.

Doubling a fourth-suit bid

When the opponents bid the fourth suit, you will have another chance to double. Do so when you hold strength in the suit and would like partner to lead it.

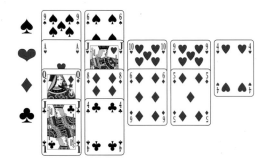

West	North	East	South
	1♦	Pass	1♠
Pass	2♣	Pass	2♥
Dble			

West has good hearts and doubles to suggest a lead of this suit.

Doubling a strength-showing cue-bid

When your partner has overcalled, the next player will sometimes cue-bid in the same suit to show a sound raise. When you would like partner to lead the suit he has bid, because you hold an honour there, you can double the cue-bid.

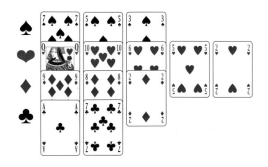

West	North	East	South
	1♠	2♣	3♣
Dble			

South shows a strong spade raise with his cue-bid in the suit that East has bid. Holding a doubleton ace in partner's suit, you would welcome a club lead. You announce this by doubling the cue-bid. Suppose instead that you had held two or three low cards in clubs. You would then have passed the cue-bid, letting partner know that you had no particular reason to welcome a club lead.

Doubling a Blackwood response or control-showing cue-bid

When an opponent responds to Blackwood, and your partner may be on lead against the eventual slam, you will again have a chance to double.

West	North	East	South
	1♠	Pass	3♠
Pass	4NT	Pass	5♦
Dble			

You double the 5♦ response to suggest a diamond lead. Similarly, you can double a control-showing cue-bid.

West	North	East	South
	1♥	Pass	4♥
Pass	4♠	Pass	5♣
Dble			

Since South is likely to hold the ♣A, you are willing to double the control-showing cue-bid when holding just the king, sitting over the ace. Such a double is only worthwhile because your partner will be on lead against the eventual heart contract.

If you failed to double 5♣, on the above sequence, partner would be entitled to draw the negative inference that you had no particular liking for a club lead.

Below: Holding the ♣K over South's likely ♣A, you double to suggest a club lead to partner.

CHAPTER 11

ADVANCED CARD PLAY

A skilled declarer looks everywhere for clues as to how he should play the hand. Here you will see how important clues can be drawn from the bidding. The next topics are how to create extra entries to the dummy, and how you can maintain control of the trump suit. You will see also how you can combine two different chances of making a contract, which is nearly always better than relying on just one chance. You will learn how to perform an elimination play, where you force a defender to make the first lead in a suit that you do not want to play yourself. Finally you will see the squeeze, the most famous card play technique in the game.

Right: The defenders have launched a forcing defence and declarer must be careful not to lose trump control.

CLUES FROM THE BIDDING

When you are declarer, one of your tasks is to build a picture of the defenders' hands. The opening lead is usually quite informative. Every time a player shows out of a suit, you move closer to obtaining a complete count on the hand. Another important source of information comes from any bids that the defenders made. In particular, when a defender has shown length in one suit (perhaps with a pre-emptive opening, or an overcall), he is likely to be shorter than his partner in any other suit.

Right: Length in one suit implies shortage elsewhere. East's pre-emptive opening shows long clubs and he will be correspondingly short in the other three suits.

Look at the deal below, where East has made a pre-emptive opening of 3♣, suggesting a weak hand and seven cards in the club suit.

West leads the ♣8 and you win East's ♣10 with the ♣A. Since there are at least three losers in the side suits, the first task is to pick up the trump suit without loss. With nine cards between the hands, you would normally play to drop a missing queen. This is only a 52 per cent chance, compared with 48 per cent for finessing one or other defender for the card.

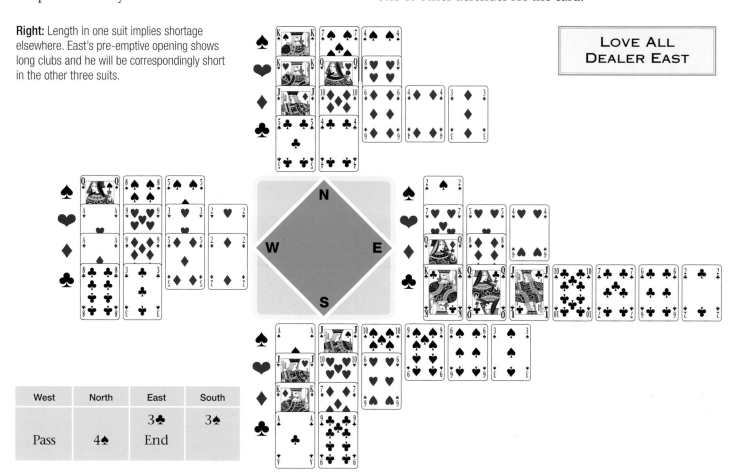

LOVE ALL
DEALER EAST

West	North	East	South
		3♣	3♠
Pass	4♠	End	

BEER CARD
♠ ♥ ♦ ♣

Among youth players, the seven of diamonds is known as the "beer card". When declarer makes his contract and scores the final trick with the seven of diamonds, his partner has to buy him a beer. Similarly, if a contract is defeated and a defender scores the last trick with the seven of diamonds, his partner too must buy him a beer. If the contract was doubled or redoubled, the drink order must reflect this.

Once a defender is known to be long in one of the side suits, the odds switch in favour of a finesse.

Here you expect East to hold seven clubs to West's two, so West is likely to hold longer spades than East. (You can see that, in fact, West is longer than East in all three of the suits outside clubs which predominates here.) You should therefore cash the ♠A and then run the ♠J.

This play proves successful and you draw West's last trump with dummy's ♠K. To make the contract, you now have to escape for just one diamond loser.

When the missing diamond honours are split between the two defenders, you will need to guess whether to run the ♦J or to lead towards the ♦K. Again the bidding will give you a big clue as to the lie of the diamond suit. If East held seven clubs to the K–Q–J and an ace, he would probably have rated his hand as too strong for a pre-emptive opening. It is therefore better to play him for the ♦Q. You run the ♦J and this does indeed force the ♦A from West. The contract is yours.

It can be just as important to bear in mind that a defender did not make a bid when he had the chance. On the deal shown below, for example, East did not find a response to his partner's opening bid. Since he would normally have done so when holding 6 points or more, it is reasonable for declarer to infer that he must hold fewer points than this.

Right: A deduction from the bidding. Declarer makes a valuable deduction from the fact that East did not respond to his partner's opening bid.

REMEMBER THE BIDDING
♠ ♥ ♦ ♣

At every stage of playing a contract, make sure that your card-reading for the defenders' hands agrees with any bids that they have made. It should also be consistent with any bids that they have declined to make. For example, suppose that a defender has shown up with 10 points outside hearts and he did not open the bidding. He is unlikely to hold the ♥Q in addition. You should therefore finesse the other defender for the missing queen. The same sort of inference can be drawn when a defender declined to overcall or to make a take-out double.

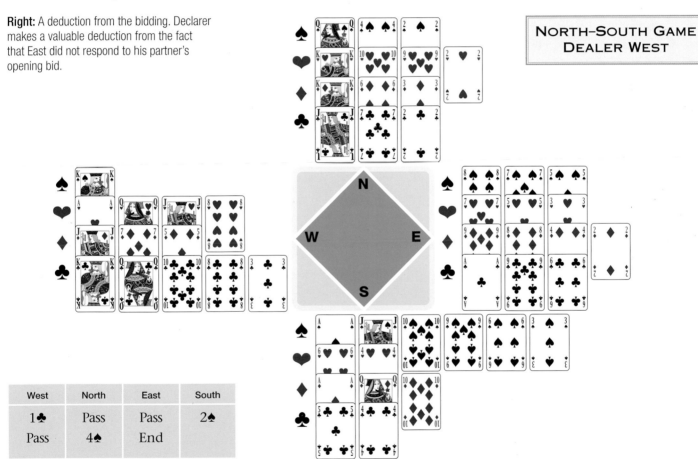

NORTH–SOUTH GAME
DEALER WEST

West	North	East	South
1♣	Pass	Pass	2♠
Pass	4♠	End	

An optimistic auction carries you to a game in spades and West leads the ♣K. East encourages with the ♣9 and West continues with the ♣Q and a third round of clubs to East's ace. You ruff in the South hand and see that you have three certain losers in the side suits. You will therefore need to pick up the trump suit without loss. Normally, with four cards missing, you would finesse East for the ♠K. Think back to the

bidding, though. If East held an ace and a king in his hand, he would have responded to West's opening bid. West must therefore hold the ♠K and the only chance of making the contract is that the card is singleton. You play the ♠A from your hand and, as if by magic, the ♠K does indeed fall from the West hand. You draw trumps in two more rounds and concede a trick to West's ♥A, making the game exactly.

CREATING EXTRA ENTRIES

When you are short of entries to the dummy (or to your hand), there are various techniques available to create an extra entry. Some of these involve conceding a trick in a suit that could otherwise have been cashed from the top. Here is an example:

Right: Sacrifice to gain an entry. By giving up a trump trick unnecessarily, declarer conjures an extra entry to dummy.

West leads the ♦J against your contract of 6♠ and you win with the ♦A. If you continue with the ace and king of trumps, there will be no way to avoid two subsequent heart losers. You will go one down. Instead you must seek a way to reach dummy's king and queen

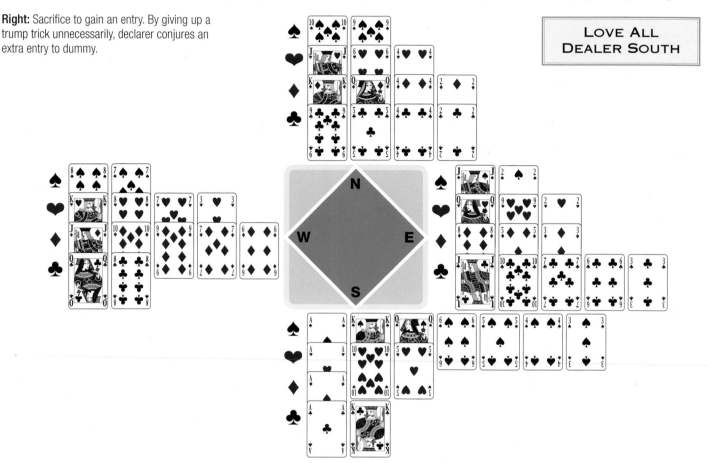

LOVE ALL
DEALER SOUTH

FOUR ACES MISSING
♠ ♥ ♦ ♣

In the 1971 world championship, the French pair of Roger Trézel and Jean-Louis Stoppa were playing against Brazil when they reached a grand slam (7♥) with no fewer than four aces missing! Trézel had asked for aces, by bidding 4NT, and the 5♣ response showed 0 or 4. He assumed that his partner held four aces, after a strong-sounding bid earlier in the auction, and bid the grand slam. The Brazilians doubled and the grand slam went three down (a void club prevented the cashing of the fourth ace). It was perhaps the most amazing bidding misunderstanding in the history of the world championship.

of diamonds. It is easily done in the trump suit. At Trick 2 you should lead a low trump from your hand. Dummy's ♠10 loses to the ♠J and East returns a heart. You rise with the ♥A, cross to the ♠9 and discard your two heart losers on the ♦K–Q. The slam is yours.

You would make the same play (a low trump from your hand) when dummy held only ♠10–2. You would then make the contract when West held the ♠J and dummy's ♠10 could therefore be set up as an entry. In both cases you would give away an unecessary trick in the trump suit but gain two diamond tricks in return.

(It is interesting to note that a trump lead would have beaten the contract, provided East is alert enough not to play his ♠J on the first trick! Declarer is then given the entry to dummy while the diamond suit is still blocked.)

Right: Overtaking to gain an entry. By overtaking the honour cards in clubs, declarer can create extra entries to the dummy.

EAST–WEST GAME
DEALER SOUTH

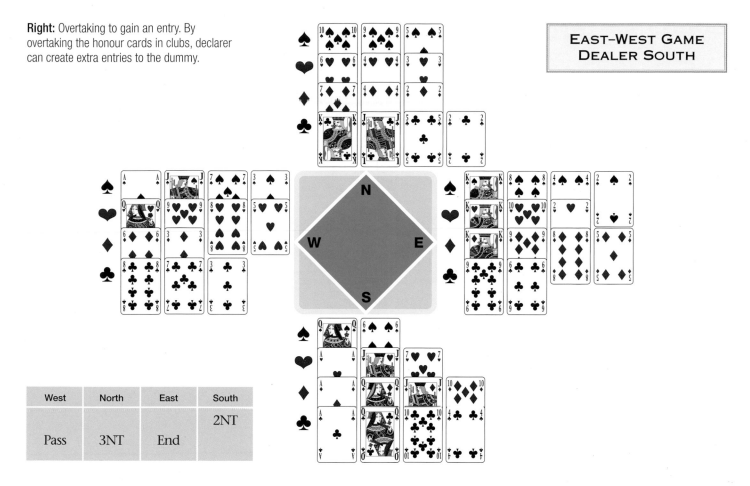

West	North	East	South
			2NT
Pass	3NT	End	

Extra entries may also be conjured by overtaking honour cards. On the deal shown above, you can create three entries to dummy by playing the club suit in clever fashion.

West leads the ♠3 against your no-trump game and the defenders take four spade tricks. You discard two hearts from the South hand and one heart from the dummy. The defenders switch to a heart, dislodging your ace, and you must now try to make four diamond tricks in addition to the four club tricks.

You need East to hold the ♦K, obviously. When he holds four cards to the king, you will need to reach dummy three times in order to take three diamond finesses. You begin by cashing the ♣A, following with dummy's ♣2. On the next round of clubs, you lead the ♣Q, overtaking with dummy's ♣K.

Both defenders follow suit, you are pleased to see, and you play a diamond to the queen, receiving further good news when the finesse wins. You next lead the ♣10, overtaking with dummy's ♣J. A finesse of the ♦J wins and you can now reach dummy for the third time by overtaking your ♣4 with dummy's ♣5.

Note that this play was possible only because you disposed of your queen and ten of clubs under dummy's king and jack. You take a third diamond finesse, playing low to the ♦10, and the contract is yours. Suppose you were to swap the North and South club holdings, moving the ♣A–Q–10–4 to the dummy. You would then be able to reach dummy no fewer than four times in the club suit (provided the defenders' cards broke 3–2). You could lead the ♣K to the ♣A on the first round, the ♣J to the ♣Q on the second round, the ♣5 to the ♣10 on the third round and finally the ♣2 to the ♣4!

KEEP THE LOWEST TRUMP
♠ ♥ ♦ ♣

Your lowest trump is often an important card that is worth preserving. Suppose your trump holding is ♠6–3–2 in the dummy and ♠A–K–Q–J–10–4 in your hand. If the defenders force you to ruff early in the play, it will often be right to take the ruff with a high trump. By preserving the ♠4, you would give yourself a possible route to the dummy. When the defenders' trumps broke 2–2, you would be able to cross to dummy on the third round of trumps, leading the ♠4 and overtaking with the ♠6.

KEEPING TRUMP CONTROL

When a defender holds four trumps, he will usually lead his strongest side suit. His aim is to force declarer to ruff, thereby eventually causing him to lose trump control. Declarer can sometimes repel this attack by using the short-trump holding, usually in dummy, to absorb the force. Here is an example of this technique:

Right: By using the short-trump holding in the dummy, declarer can avoid being forced in the long-trump holding.

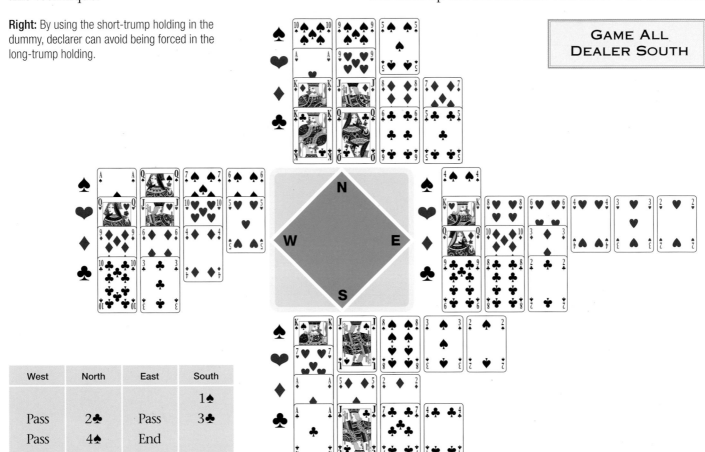

GAME ALL
DEALER SOUTH

West	North	East	South
			1♠
Pass	2♣	Pass	3♣
Pass	4♠	End	

With a chunky four-card trump holding, West embarks on a forcing defence by leading the ♥Q. You win with dummy's ♥A and run the ♠10, West winning with the ♠Q. When West continues with a second round of hearts, you must play carefully. Suppose you ruff in your hand. When you play another trump, West will hold up the ace and East will show out. There will then be no way to make the contract. If you play a third round of trumps, West will win with the ace and force your last trump with another heart. You will then lose three trump tricks and a diamond, going one down.

To survive this hostile attack on your five-card trump holding, you must call for assistance from the dummy's trumps. When West leads a second round of hearts, you should throw a diamond from your hand instead of ruffing. A third round of hearts will cause no problem, because you can ruff in the dummy, thereby preserving your own trump length. It will then be a simple matter to knock out the ace of trumps and ruff the heart continuation in the South hand. You will draw West's last two trumps and claim the remaining tricks.

On the next deal declarer's play in the trump suit is dictated by the need to use the short trumps in dummy to protect against a forcing defence.

Right: Declarer must give up a trump trick, while dummy's remaining trump will protect him against a continued force in hearts.

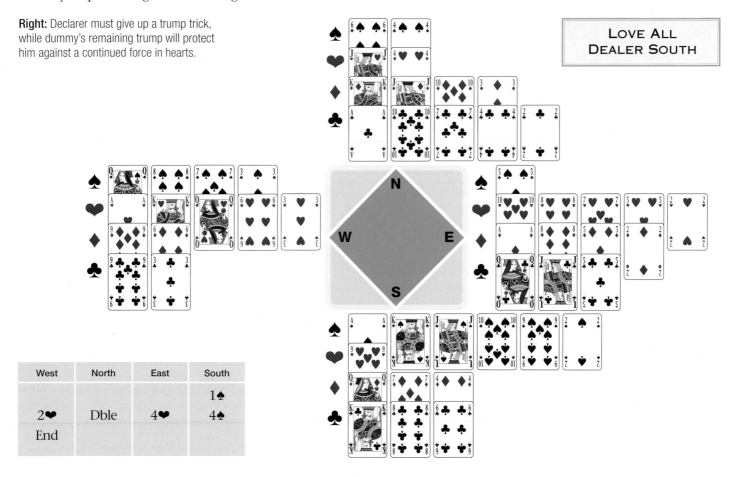

West	North	East	South
			1♠
2♥	Dble	4♥	4♠
End			

North makes a negative double on the first round, suggesting length in the minor suits. West leads the ♥A against the eventual spade game and continues with the ♥K (although a minor-suit switch would in fact work better). You ruff in the South hand and pause to consider your next move. If you play the ace of trumps, you will go down. When you continue with the king and jack of trumps, West will win with the ♠Q and force you with another heart. If you draw West's last trump then, you will have no protection against a heart continuation when you knock out the ♦A. If instead you play on diamonds without drawing the last trump, East will win and force your last trump with a heart, setting up a second trump for West.

To make the contract, you must lead the ♠J at Trick 3, giving up the trump trick that you can afford to lose at a moment that suits you. West wins with the ♠Q but cannot continue hearts effectively because you would be able to ruff in the dummy. When you regain the lead, you will be able to draw trumps and knock out the ♦A, making the contract easily.

Above: The defenders have launched a forcing defence and declarer must be careful not to lose trump control.

ELIMINATION PLAY

One of the most important, and frequently occurring, card play techniques is that of elimination play. You begin by eliminating one or more of the side suits (either by removing them from your own hand and the dummy, or by removing them from the defenders' hands). You then throw a defender on lead. He cannot play an eliminated suit, either because he has no cards left in that suit or because it will give you a ruff-and-discard. He will therefore be forced to make the first play in another suit, thereby giving you a trick. Here is a straightforward example of elimination play:

Right: A typical elimination play. Declarer does not want to play the diamond suit himself and uses elimination play to force the defenders to play diamonds.

Above: The Aces team that won the 1971 Bermuda Bowl for the USA, defeating France in the final.

LOVE ALL
DEALER SOUTH

West	North	East	South
			1♠
Pass	3♠	Pass	4♠
End			

West leads the ♥Q against your spade game. You have one loser in the heart suit and three more losers in diamonds, if you have to play the suit yourself. If the defenders had to make the first play in diamonds, however, you would be certain to score a diamond trick. By using elimination play, you can force them to do exactly that. Your plan will be to eliminate the black suits and then exit with a second round of hearts, forcing the defenders to win the trick.

TRUMPS IN BOTH HANDS
♠ ♥ ♦ ♣

An essential requirement for an elimination play end position is that you have at least one trump in both your own hand and the dummy. This means that the defenders cannot return an eliminated suit without giving a ruff-and-discard.

You win the heart lead and draw trumps with the ace and king. Your next task is to eliminate the club suit (so neither defender will be able to play a club when he is thrown in). You play the ace and king of clubs and ruff a club in your hand. You then cross to the ♠J and ruff dummy's last club. These cards remain to be played:

Right: Elimination ending. Declarer exits in hearts, forcing a defender to play a diamond (or give a ruff-and-discard).

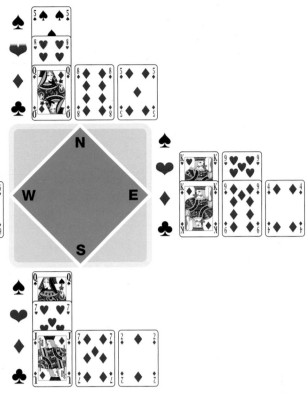

The preparation is complete and you now lead the ♥7. It makes no difference which defender wins the trick. A third round of hearts would give you a ruff-and-discard, allowing you to ruff in one hand and discard a diamond loser from the other. The defender who wins the trick will therefore have to play a diamond. You are certain to make a trick with the queen or jack and the game is yours.

Sometimes you can use elimination play to save you from having to guess in a suit. That is the situation here, where you have an apparent guess to make in the heart suit:

West	North	East	South
			1♠
Pass	2♠	Pass	4♠
End			

**GAME ALL
DEALER SOUTH**

Right: Elimination play to avoid a guess. Declarer uses elimination play to avoid having to guess which defender holds the ♥Q.

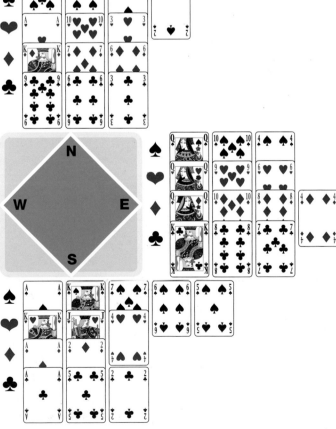

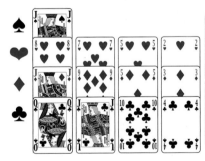

Sitting South, you win the ♣Q lead with the ace. When you play two rounds of trumps, you find that East has a trump trick. There are now three certain black-suit losers, so you will need to avoid a further loser in hearts. You could finesse either defender for the missing ♥Q. If you happened to guess wrongly, you would go down.

With the help of elimination play, you can avoid the need to guess in the heart suit. You play the ace and king of diamonds and ruff a diamond. Since diamonds are now eliminated from both your own hand and the dummy, neither defender will be able to play that suit without conceding a ruff-and-discard. These cards remain:

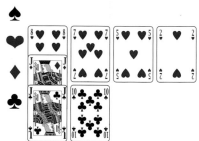

Right: Declarer exits in clubs, forcing a defender to play a heart (or give a ruff-and-discard).

You exit with a club. The defenders are welcome to cash two club tricks and the trump queen. Since you still have a trump left in each hand, the defender left on lead will have to play a heart (or concede a ruff-and-discard by leading a diamond). You will then be assured of three heart tricks and the contract.

Look back at the two deals we have seen. On the first deal, diamonds was your "problem suit" – the suit that you very much wanted the defenders to play for you. On the second deal, hearts was the problem suit. Sometimes you throw a defender on lead with the first round of the problem suit itself. Look at this deal:

EAST–WEST GAME
DEALER SOUTH

Right: Exiting in the problem suit itself. Declarer hopes to avoid a loser in clubs and performs the elimination play by exiting on the first round of clubs.

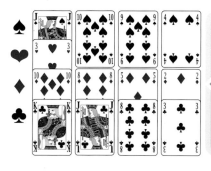

West	North	East	South
			2♣
Pass	2♦	Pass	2♥
Pass	3♥	Pass	4♥
Pass	6♥	End	

You win the ♠J lead in your hand and note that there are two potential losers in the club suit. If you had to play clubs yourself, you would first finesse the ♣9, forcing the king when East held both the jack and ten of the suit. If a finesse of the ♣9 lost to the jack or ten, you would win West's return in a different suit and then finesse the ♣Q. As you see, such a line of play would not succeed here. You would lose two club tricks and go down. To make the contract, you should eliminate spades and diamonds before playing a club to the nine. If West wins with the ten or jack, he will not be able to return a spade or a diamond without conceding a ruff-and-discard. He will be forced to play a club instead.

You draw trumps in three rounds, which still leaves you with at least one trump in both hands (an important requirement of elimination play, so that you could benefit from a ruff-and-discard). You then cash the king and ace of spades and ruff a spade, eliminating that suit from the battlefield. When you continue with three rounds of diamonds, ending in the dummy, the spades and diamonds have been eliminated. The lead is in dummy and these cards remain:

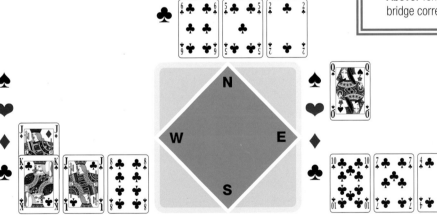

Left: By playing a club to the nine, declarer endplays West. He will have to return a club into the ace–queen tenace or give a ruff-and-discard.

All the preparation work is complete and you lead a club to the nine. West wins with the jack and has no safe return. A club will be into your ace-queen tenace and a diamond will give you a ruff-and-discard. It would do East no good to rise with the ♣10 on the first round of the suit. You would cover with the ♣Q and West would then have to lead into your ♣A–9 tenace when he won the trick.

COMBINING DIFFERENT CHANCES

It is almost always better to combine two chances of making the contract, rather than relying on just one. This may involve taking the second-best chance in one suit because this will allow you to retain the lead and take advantage of your chance in another suit. That is what happens on this deal:

Right: Declarer combines two chances. Declarer takes the second-best chance in the trump suit, so that he can combine the additional chance of discarding the diamond loser.

West leads the ◆K against your game in spades. You win with the ace and see four potential losers, one in trumps and three more in the red suits. Looking at the trump suit in isolation, the best chance of avoiding a loser is to cash the ♠K and then to finesse the ♠J. If you follow this line and the finesse loses,

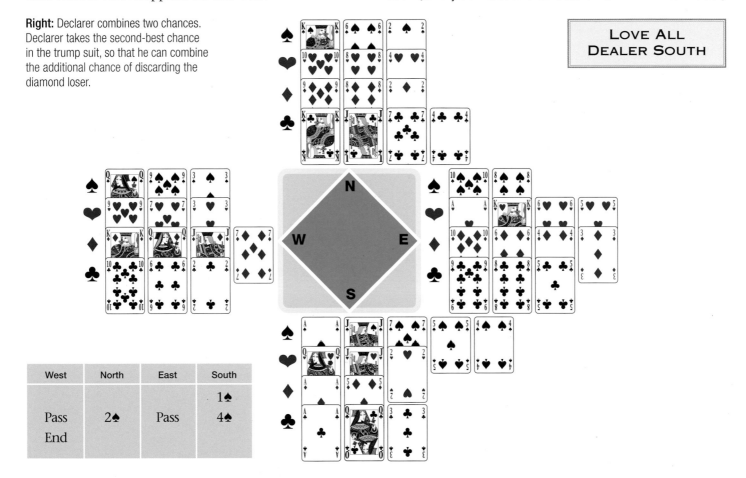

LOVE ALL
DEALER SOUTH

West	North	East	South
			1♠
Pass	2♠	Pass	4♠
End			

LUCK FACTOR REDUCED
♠ ♥ ◆ ♣

It was realized as long ago as 1857, in the days of whist, that the luck factor in card games could be reduced by playing each hand more than once and comparing results. Nowadays, nearly all competitive bridge (both for pairs and teams-of-four) employs this principle and is known as "duplicate bridge".

Right: Duplicate bridge. When the deal is over the cards will be returned to the board, ready to be played again at another table.

however, you will go down. When West wins with the ♠Q, the defenders will take one diamond trick and two hearts, beating the game.

A better idea is to begin with the second-best chance in trumps, playing the king and ace. If the ♠Q falls on the second round, which is quite a substantial chance, you will draw the last trump and make an overtrick. If the ♠Q does not fall, you will still be on lead. You will be able to take your second chance – discarding the diamond loser on the fourth round of clubs. With the cards lying as in the diagram you will be successful. West has to follow to three rounds of clubs and you throw the ♦5 on the fourth round of clubs, not caring whether West ruffs or not. You will lose just one trump and two hearts. By following the recommended line you make the contract when the ♠Q falls doubleton or when you can discard your diamond loser. That is a much better combined chance than relying solely on picking up the trump suit with a finesse.

It is sometimes important to combine your two chances in the right order. This is often the case when one chance will require you to lose an early trick in a suit. Look at the 6NT deal shown below, where you have prospects of an extra trick in both spades and hearts. You must seek to combine those chances.

West leads a safe ♦10 against 6NT. There are 11 tricks on top and two apparent chances of scoring a 12th trick. If East holds the ♠K, a finesse of the ♠Q will give you the slam. Another chance is that West holds the ♥Q. In that case a lead towards dummy's ♥J will yield the extra trick.

There is no need to choose between these chances. Provided you tackle the suits in the correct order, you can make the slam when either chance pays off. Suppose you win the diamond lead and finesse the ♠Q immediately. The finesse will lose and it will be too late to tackle the heart suit.

Since you will have to surrender a trick in hearts, even if the ♥Q is favourably placed, you should play that suit first. You win the diamond lead with the queen and lead a low heart towards dummy. Whether or not West chooses to rise with the ♥Q, you will score a third trick in hearts and make the slam. Suppose the cards had lain differently and the ♥J had lost to the ♥Q with East. You would still have been able to take your second chance in spades. That is because you would not need to lose the lead in order to take advantage of the ♠K lying with East. A finesse of the ♠Q would win and you could then cash the ♠A, scoring two tricks from the suit.

Right: Taking finesses in the right order. Declarer combines the chances in hearts and spades by taking the two finesses in the right order.

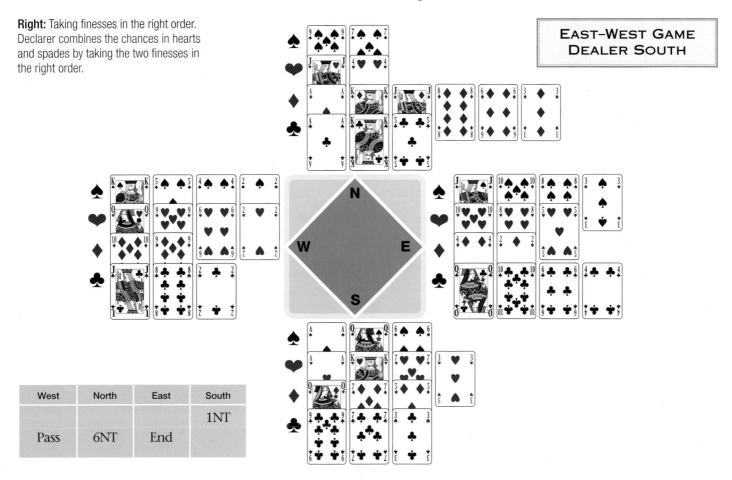

EAST–WEST GAME
DEALER SOUTH

West	North	East	South
			1NT
Pass	6NT	End	

THE THROW-IN

In an earlier section we looked at elimination play, where you threw a defender on lead at a time when both declarer's hand and the dummy still contained at least one trump. Because the defender could not afford to give a ruff-and-discard, he had to lead your problem suit, giving you a trick there. When one of the hands does not contain a trump, or the contract is being played in no-trumps, it is still possible to gain a trick by throwing a defender on lead. The play is then known, simply, as a throw-in. Here is an example:

Right: A typical throw-in play. Declarer makes 3NT by throwing East on lead in clubs when he has no safe return to make.

NORTH–SOUTH GAME
DEALER EAST

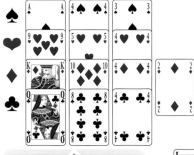

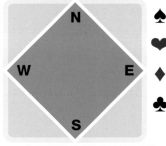

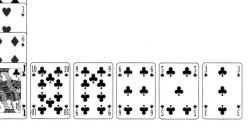

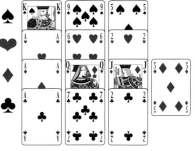

West	North	East	South
		3♣	3NT
End			

West leads the ♥K. You duck the first two rounds of hearts and win the third round, East throwing a club. You have eight top tricks and the only serious chance of a ninth trick is to throw East on lead with a club, forcing him to lead away from the ♣K.

To prepare for a throw-in, you must remove East's possible exit cards in the other suits. You must hope that East has no more than two cards in spades. You begin with four rounds of diamonds and continue with the ace and king of spades. When East follows twice in each suit, as he did in hearts, it is a near

certainty that his shape is 2–2–2–7. In that case he will have nothing but clubs left in his hand. You lead the ♣2 from your hand and West does indeed show out. You play the ♣4 from dummy and East wins the trick cheaply. Since all his remaining cards are clubs, he must lead a club from the king. You run this to dummy's ♣Q and nine tricks are yours.

On the next example too, an opening bid by East allows you to be fairly certain of the lie of the cards.

West leads the ♥7 against your no-trump game. East plays the ♥10 and you allow this to win.

Right: Reading the cards after an opening bid. Declarer is able to diagnose a throw-in play on East because of the values shown by his opening bid.

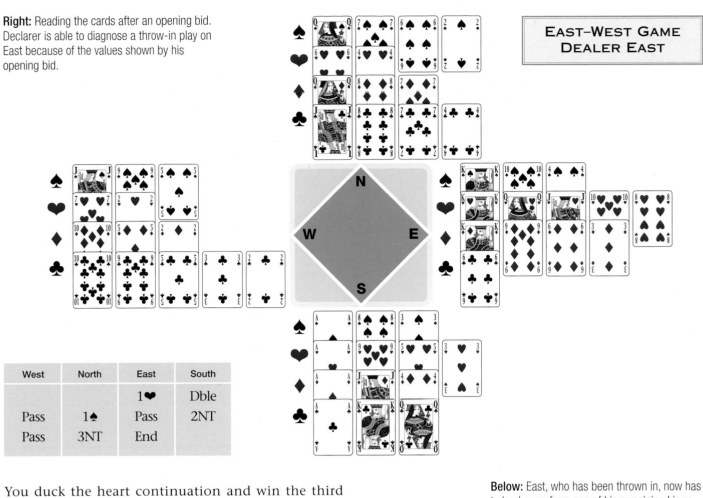

EAST–WEST GAME
DEALER EAST

West	North	East	South
		1♥	Dble
Pass	1♠	Pass	2NT
Pass	3NT	End	

You duck the heart continuation and win the third round of the suit, West discarding a club. You have only six tricks on top but the bidding marks East with the ♠K and the ◆K. He will therefore be in trouble when you throw him in.

You cash the ♣A–K–Q and throw East on lead with a heart. He cashes his last heart winner and you discard a spade from your hand. Meanwhile, you have thrown two spades and a diamond from the dummy. These cards remain:

Whichever card East plays next, you will have the remaining tricks. If he plays a low diamond, for example, you will win with the ◆Q and cash the ♣J to throw a spade. You can then finesse the ◆J and score the ◆A at Trick 13.

Below: East, who has been thrown in, now has to lead away from one of his remaining kings, giving declarer an extra trick and access to the ♣J in the dummy.

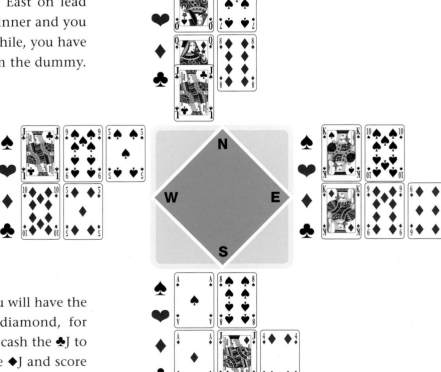

THE SIMPLE SQUEEZE

Perhaps the most famous play in bridge is the "squeeze". A defender who holds a guard on two of declarer's suits is forced to make a critical discard and has to release one of his guards. Here is a straightforward example:

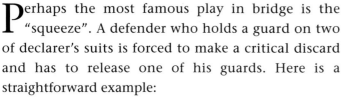

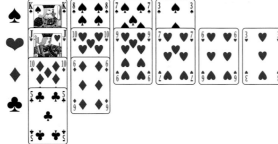

West	North	East	South
			1NT
Pass	6NT	End	

Above: A typical simple squeeze. East holds the guards in clubs and diamonds and will have to throw one of them away.

You win the heart lead with the queen, cross to the ♣A and run the ♠Q, losing to the king. You win the heart return and see that you have 11 tricks on top, 12 if the clubs break 3–2 or the diamonds break 3–3. Before testing your luck in the minor suits, you should cash your spade winners. This position will result:

Right: Squeeze ending. When the ♠10 is led, East has to throw away one of his guards.

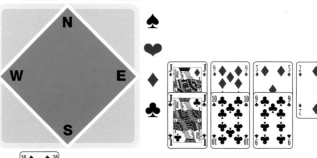

You cash the ♠10, throwing a club from dummy, and East is squeezed. He will have to throw a diamond or a club, releasing his guard in one of the suits. You will score your 12th trick from whichever suit he throws, making the slam.

216

An essential part of most squeezes is that you should lose at an early stage the tricks you can afford to lose. In other words, you should lose one trick in a small slam, four tricks in a 3NT contract. If you fail to do this, the defender with the two guards will have a spare card in his hand. He will not be squeezed when you play your last winner in the other suits. Look at this deal.

West leads the ♠10 against 6NT, East playing the ♠Q. Let's suppose first that you win immediately with the ♠A. You will not make the contract. West holds the

guards in both the red suits but he will not be squeezed. When you play four rounds of clubs, West will discard his three remaining cards in spades. You will score only 11 tricks.

Before playing to Trick 1, you should make a plan. You have 11 top tricks and can make a 12th when the diamond suit breaks 3–3, or when the same defender holds at least four diamonds and four hearts. In the latter case you will be able to squeeze the defender, but only if you lose one trick early in the play.

Right: Rectifying the count. Declarer gives up a trick at an early stage, so West will have no spare card to throw later in the play.

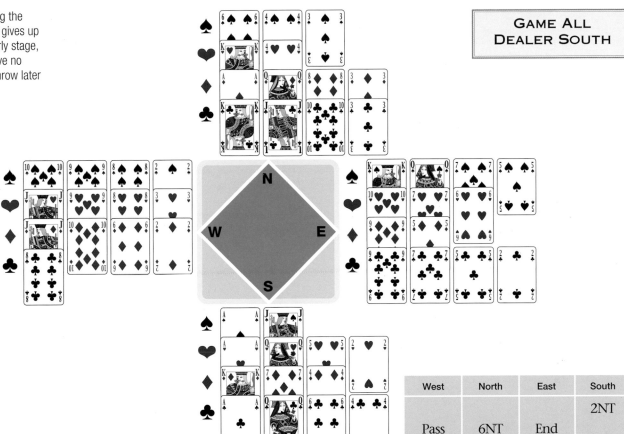

GAME ALL
DEALER SOUTH

West	North	East	South
			2NT
Pass	6NT	End	

BILL GATES
♠ ♥ ♦ ♣

Founder of Microsoft, Bill Gates, says: "Bridge is a game you can play at any age. If you take it up young, you will have fun playing it for the rest of your life. A lot of games don't have that depth. This one does." Gates competed in the 2002 world bridge championships in Toronto. In 2006 he partnered former world champion, Sharon Osberg, in the Verona world bridge championships. He told the press that programmers at Microsoft are working on sophisticated computer programs to play bridge.

Left: One of the world's richest men, Bill Gates is now a keen bridge player.

Now to see what happens if you duck the very first trick, allowing East to win with the ♠Q. You win the spade return and cash four rounds of clubs. The tableau to the right shows the position, where one club winner is still to be cashed. Because you ducked a round of spades at Trick 1, West has no card to spare when you lead the ♣Q:

Right: Squeeze ending. When the ♣Q is led, West has to abandon one of his red-suit guards.

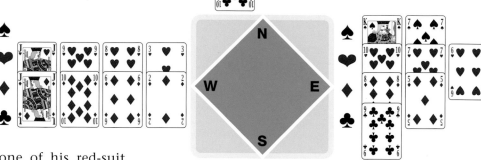

West will have to throw one of his red-suit guards and you will then score your 12th trick from the suit he has abandoned. The action of deliberately losing one or more tricks, to tighten the eventual end position, is known as "rectifying the count".

If we strip that end position down to the basics, we can visualize the elements of a simple squeeze. Let's suppose that you cash the king, ace and queen of hearts and the diamond ace and king, before playing the ♣Q. The minimal end position shown below would result:

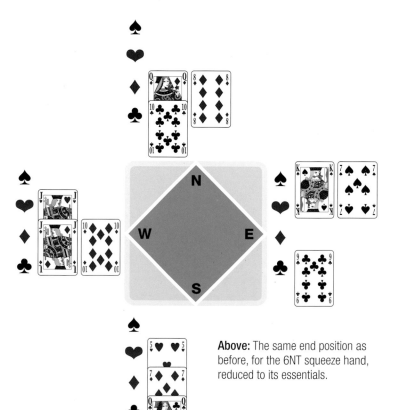

Above: The same end position as before, for the 6NT squeeze hand, reduced to its essentials.

Everything is now clearer. You have the three main elements of a simple squeeze:

- the "squeeze card" (♣Q), the card that you play to force a critical discard
- a "one-card threat" (♥5), guarded by West's ♥J
- a "threat with an entry" (♦Q–8) that lies opposite the squeeze card.

As before, West has no card to spare on the squeeze card (the ♣Q). If he throws a heart, the ♥5 in the South hand will become good. If instead West throws a diamond, you will score the last two tricks with dummy's ♦Q and ♦8.

CHARLES SCHULTZ
♠ ♥ ♦ ♣

The cartoonist Charles Schultz was a keen bridge player and featured bridge in several of his Peanuts cartoons. His Snoopy character is the only "honorary lifemaster" of the American Contract Bridge League.

So, every time you plan a simple squeeze, you must look for a squeeze card, a one-card threat and a threat with an entry. It is all rather daunting on first acquaintance but after a while you will find it becomes easier. Opportunities for simple squeezes are very frequent and will give you many a tricky contract. Let's see one more example:

Right: The Vienna Coup. Declarer prepares for a heart–club squeeze by playing the ♥A, thereby freeing the ♥Q to act as a threat card against either defender.

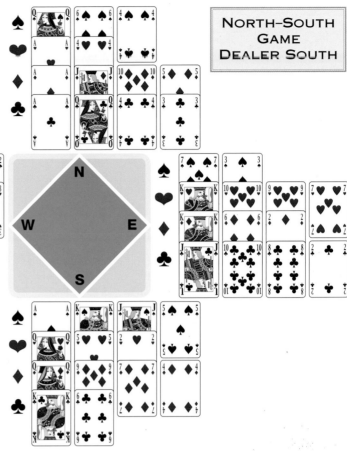

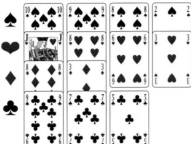

NORTH–SOUTH
GAME
DEALER SOUTH

West	North	East	South
			1NT
Pass	6NT	End	

You win the spade lead and run the ♦Q to East's ♦K, winning the diamond return. You have 11 top tricks and can score a 12th if the same defender holds the ♥K and the club guard. Try to visualize the components of the squeeze. The one-card threat will be the ♥Q. The "threat with an entry" will be dummy's club suit. The squeeze card will be the last spade. After playing dummy's top diamonds, you cash the ♥A to free your ♥Q as a one-card threat. You then play the remaining spades, arriving at the position shown in this tableau:

Below: Squeeze ending. When the ♠J is led, East has to throw one of his guards.

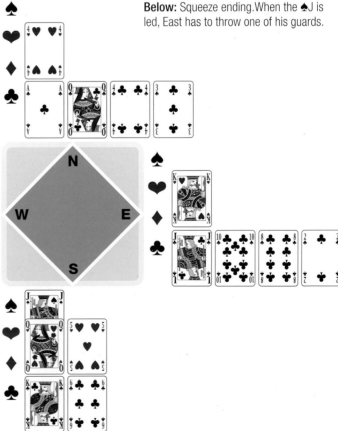

You play the squeeze card (the ♠J), throwing the ♥4 from dummy. East is squeezed and must discard one of his guards. If he throws a club, you will make four club tricks with the king, ace, queen and four of the suit. If instead he throws the ♥K, you will score a trick with the ♥Q.

Chapter 12

Advanced defence

Much good play at bridge involves counting. This is particularly true in defence, where you can count declarer's points to allow you to calculate which cards your fellow defender may hold. You will see why it is important to hold up high cards in defence and how to conduct a forcing defence, where you attack declarer's trump holding. When you hold a doubleton honour in defence, it is often right to throw the high card away, rather than risk being end-played with it later. Another important topic is how you can break declarer's communications, in particular by attacking an entry to dummy. Finally the two main ways in which the defenders can promote extra trump tricks for themselves are discussed – the straightforward trump promotion, where a defender is threatening to overruff, and the more spectacular "uppercut".

Right: East unblocks the ♠K on his partner's ♠Q lead. If he fails to do so, he will win the second round and be unable to continue the suit.

COUNTING DECLARER'S POINTS

Counting is an important part of the game, for the defenders as well as for declarer. By counting declarer's points and comparing this total with the points indicated in the bidding, the defenders can often tell which line of defence has the best chance.

Ruling out a defence by counting points

Take the East cards on this deal and see how you fare.

Right: Counting points to determine the right defence. East diagnoses the winning defence by counting declarer's points and ruling out a continuation of partner's suit.

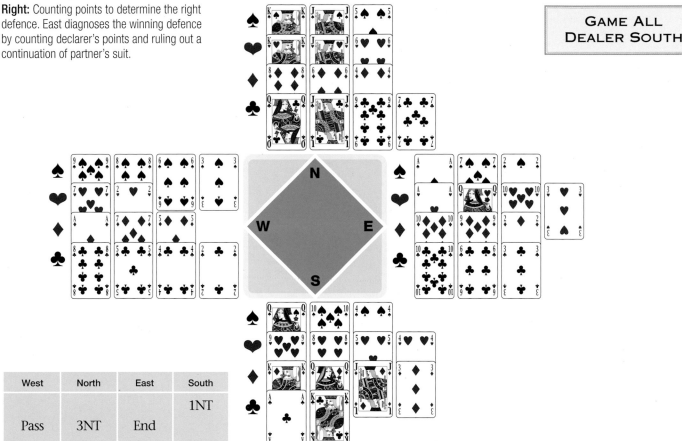

GAME ALL
DEALER SOUTH

West	North	East	South
			1NT
Pass	3NT	End	

South opens with a 15–17 point 1NT and is raised to game. Your partner, West, leads the ♠8 and declarer plays low from dummy. Sitting East, you pause to make a plan for the defence. Your partner would not have led the ♠8 from ♠Q–10–9–8, so the opening lead must be his second-best spade from a weak suit. Declarer is therefore marked with the queen and ten of spades. You win with the ♠A and must decide what to do next.

If you follow the general guideline to "lead up to weakness in the dummy", switching to the ♦10, declarer will easily make the contract. Before making such a play, you should count the points that are out.

You hold 10 points and there are 11 in the dummy. This leaves only 19 points for the two closed hands, of which South must hold at least 15. So, your partner can hold at most one high card in diamonds. What is more, declarer will have to play on diamonds himself, to stand any chance of scoring nine tricks.

Having worked this out, you should switch to a low heart – into the teeth of dummy's ♥K–J–6. It may seem strange to lead into strength in this way, but see the effect of it. When declarer wins the heart switch and plays a diamond, your partner wins with the ace and plays back a second round of hearts. You score three heart tricks and the game is defeated.

Calculating which useful card partner may hold

By counting declarer's points, you can deduce how many points are left for your partner. Only a good player in the East seat would defeat this 3NT game:

Right: Calculating which useful card partner holds. By counting declarer's points, East determines which useful card it is possible for West to hold.

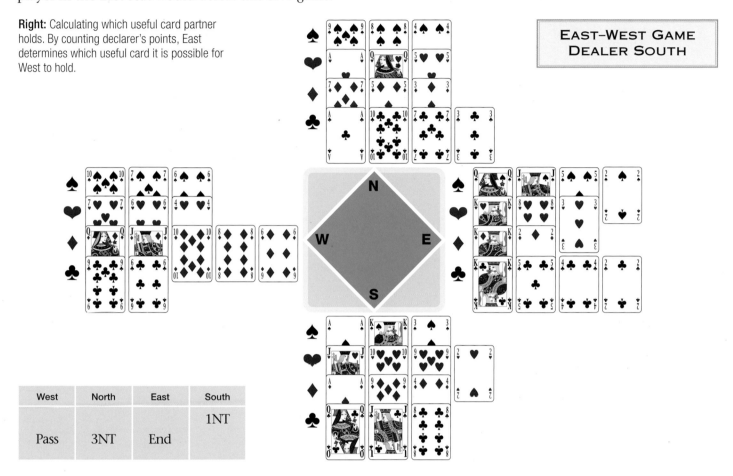

EAST-WEST GAME
DEALER SOUTH

West	North	East	South
			1NT
Pass	3NT	End	

South opens a 15–17 point 1NT and is raised to game. Take the East cards now. West, your partner, leads the ◆Q and you must plan your defence. The first move is clear – you must overtake with the ◆K. Otherwise you risk blocking the suit. Declarer could then win the first trick and run the ♣Q to you, making the contract easily.

Declarer allows ◆K to win, breaking your link with partner's hand in diamonds. Many East players would now return their remaining diamond. It is not a strong defence. You can see 22 points between your hand and the dummy. Declarer is marked with at least 15 points for his 1NT opening, so your partner can hold no honour card outside his ◆Q–J. If you set up his diamonds, he will have no possible card of entry.

Once you have deduced that a diamond return cannot be successful, it is obvious that you should switch to a low spade. If partner holds ♠10–x–x, you will be able to set up two tricks in the suit before your remaining two kings are dislodged. Declarer wins the ♠2 switch with the

♠A and runs the jack of hearts to your king. You clear the spade suit and cash the setting tricks in spades when declarer takes a losing club finesse. If you returned a diamond instead, declarer would win with the ◆A and finesse in clubs. When you won with the ♣K, it would be too late to attack the spade suit. Declarer would win your spade switch and finesse in hearts, setting up enough tricks for the contract while he still held a spade stopper.

CHINESE FINESSE
♠ ♥ ◆ ♣

Suppose you need to avoid a loser with a side suit of ◆Q–9–8–3 opposite ◆A–5. If there is no possibility of an end-play of some sort, you may try the desperate manoeuvre of leading the ◆Q. When the player in the second seat holds something like ◆K–7–2, he may place you with ◆Q–J–10–x and thus decline to cover with the king. This deceptive play is known as a "Chinese Finesse".

DEFENSIVE HOLD-UPS IN A SUIT CONTRACT

It is a familiar technique for the defenders to hold up an ace (or even a king), when defending in no-trumps. The same sort of move can work well against a suit contract too. The purpose, as always, will be to interfere with declarer's communications.

Holding up to prevent declarer taking a discard

Take East cards on this deal and see how you get on.

Right: A hold-up to prevent a discard. East holds up the ♦A, to prevent declarer from obtaining a discard on the suit.

GAME ALL
DEALER SOUTH

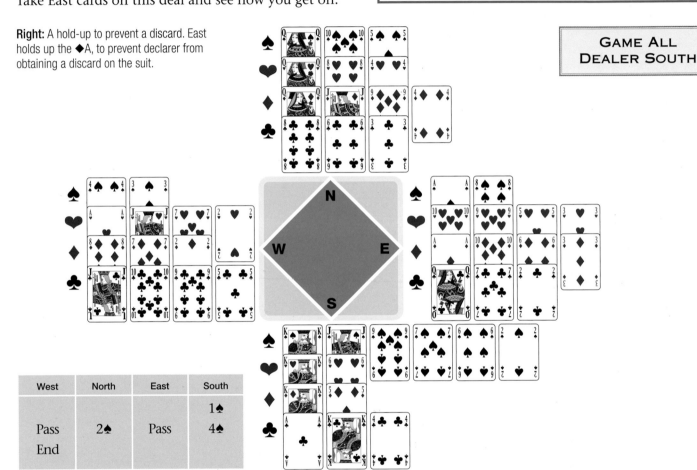

West	North	East	South
			1♠
Pass	2♠	Pass	4♠
End			

West leads the ♣J. South wins with the ♣A and plays the ♦K from his hand. Sitting East, you must decide whether to win with the ♦A or to hold up the card. Suppose first that you do win the ace immediately, returning a club. This will be very much to declarer's liking. He will win the club return with the king and cross to dummy with the ♦Q. He can then throw his club loser on the ♦J. He will make the game, losing tricks only to the three aces.

When the ♦K is led, West will give a "count signal". A high diamond will indicate an even number of cards in the suit; a low diamond will show an odd number.

Here he will play the ♦2. Sitting East, you can then place West with three diamonds and declarer with two. On that basis you should hold up the ♦A on the first round. You win the second diamond and clear the club suit. Declarer has no quick entry to dummy, to take a discard on the ♦J, and will now go down. When he plays a trump to the queen, you will win with the ace and cash a club winner, followed by a heart to West's ace.

Suppose instead that West held ♦8–7–5–2. He would signal his count with the ♦7 (second highest from four cards). East would then take his ♦A immediately, preventing declarer from scoring the singleton ♦K.

Holding up to prevent declarer taking a finesse

Sometimes a hold-up will keep declarer out of dummy, preventing him from taking a finesse through your hand.

Right: A hold-up to prevent a trump finesse. East holds up the ♦A to prevent declarer from entering dummy with the ♦Q to finesse in trumps.

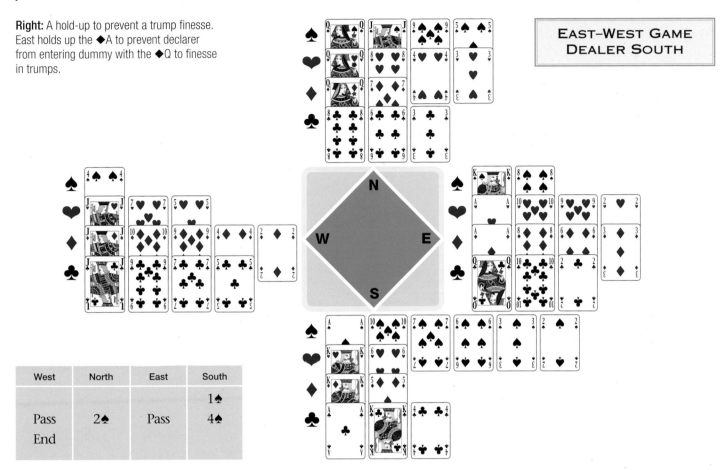

EAST–WEST GAME
DEALER SOUTH

West	North	East	South
			1♠
Pass	2♠	Pass	4♠
End			

West leads the ♦J and declarer plays low from dummy. You must consider your defence from the East seat. If you rise with the ♦A, declarer will unblock the ♦K from his hand and subsequently enter dummy with the ♦Q to finesse against your king of trumps. You should therefore play low at Trick 1. Another reason to play low is that you do not want declarer to score two diamond tricks (throwing a club from dummy on the third round of the suit) if he began with ♦K–x–x.

Declarer wins the first trick with ♦K and immediately leads the ♥K. Your partner follows with the ♥5, his lowest card in the suit showing an odd number of cards in the suit. You must hold up the ♥A, to prevent declarer from crossing to the ♥Q to take a trump finesse. After this bright start to the defence, declarer cannot reach dummy and will not be able to finesse against your ♠K. He will have to cash the ♠A from his hand. He cannot avoid a loser in every suit, as the cards lie, and will go one down.

RULE OF FIFTEEN
♠ ♥ ♦ ♣

When you are short in spades, it is somewhat risky to make a light opening bid in the fourth seat. The defenders may then discover a spade fit and end in a successful part score (or even a game) in that suit, when you could have passed the deal out. Some players use the "Rule of Fifteen" to decide whether to open: *When the sum of your high-card points and the number of spades in your hand is 15 or more, you should open the bidding.* Suppose, after three passes, your hand is :

♠3 ♥A–J–9–8–4 ♦K–Q–8–4 ♣Q–10–5.

You have 12 points and only 1 spade. According to the Rule of Fifteen, you should pass rather than opening 1♥. In any of the first three seats this hand would be worth an opening bid. The Rule of Fifteen applies only in the fourth seat.

THE FORCING DEFENCE

W hen you hold four trumps in defence, it is often best to lead your strongest side suit. Your aim is to force declarer to ruff, thereby weakening his trump holding. If you can end with more trumps than declarer, he will have lost trump control and may well go down.

Playing a forcing defence

West holds four trumps, defending this spade game, and therefore leads from his powerful heart side suit. His ♥K wins the first trick, and he continues with a low heart to East's ♥10.

Right: A typical forcing defence. By continually leading hearts, West forces declarer to lose control of the trump suit.

<table>
<tr><td colspan="2" align="center">**MULTIPLE MEANING**
♠ ♥ ♦ ♣</td></tr>
</table>

Many bridge words, such as "forcing" here, have more than one meaning within the game. A "forcing bid" is one that partner is not allowed to pass. A "forcing defence" describes the situation where the defenders force declarer to ruff, in order to weaken his trump holding. Also a defender might play a king, "forcing out dummy's ace".

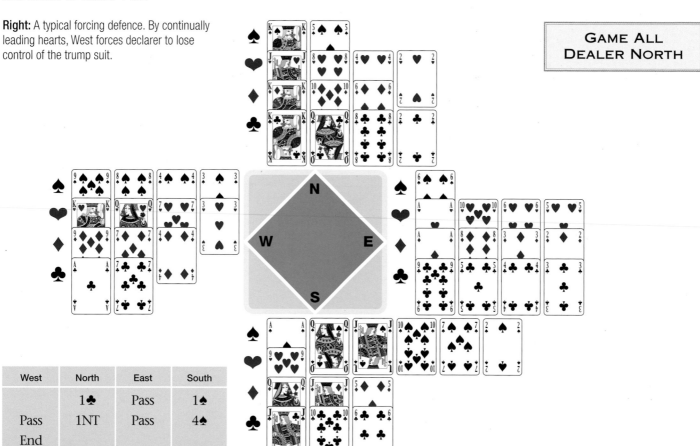

**GAME ALL
DEALER NORTH**

West	North	East	South
	1♣	Pass	1♠
Pass	1NT	Pass	4♠
End			

Declarer ruffs and now holds five trumps to West's four. He plays two rounds of trumps and discovers the 4–1 break. Suppose he draws West's last two trumps and then plays on clubs. West will win with the ♣A and force declarer's last trump with a third round of hearts. Declarer can score three club tricks, but this will bring his total only to nine tricks. When he eventually plays on diamonds, East will win and the defenders will score a heart trick to beat the contract. The outcome will be exactly the same if declarer plays on clubs before drawing West's last two trumps. Another heart will reduce him to just two trump winners and he will not be able to set up and enjoy a diamond trick.

Even though South began with six trumps to West's four, the force was successful. That is because declarer needed to dislodge two high cards and the defenders would have two more chances to force him.

Holding up the trump ace to maintain the force

Suppose you are conducting a forcing defence and you hold four trumps headed by the ace. You will often have to hold up the ace until the trumps in declarer's shorter holding (usually the dummy's trumps) are exhausted. You can then persist with your force on the longer trump holding. The deal below is an example of this technique:

Right: Taking the trump ace at the right moment. By holding up the ace of trumps, West is able to continue his forcing defence.

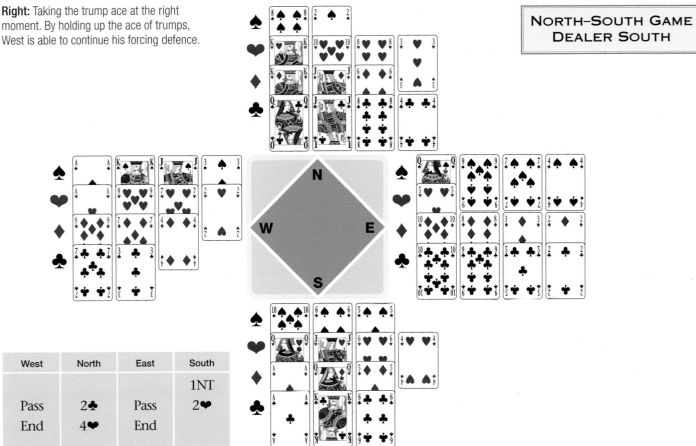

West	North	East	South
			1NT
Pass	2♣	Pass	2♥
End	4♥	End	

West leads the ♠A against South's heart game and the defenders play two more rounds of spades, forcing the dummy to ruff. When declarer leads the king of trumps from dummy, the key moment of the hand has been reached. If West makes the mistake of winning this round of trumps, he will not be able to persist with his forcing defence. That's because a fourth round of spades could be ruffed in dummy, in what has now become the shorter trump holding. Instead West should duck not only the first round of trumps but also the second round.

If declarer continues with a third round of trumps, dummy will have no trumps left. West will be able to win with the ♥A and force declarer's last trump with another spade, setting up his ♥9 as the setting trick. Declarer's only alternative is to abandon trumps after two rounds and to turn to the side suits. West will then ruff the third round of clubs, again scoring two trump tricks to beat the game. In the common situation where declarer has four trumps in each hand, you need to attack the trump length in both hands. The idea is to reduce the trump length in one hand, hold up the ace of trumps until that hand has no trumps remaining and then attack the trump length in the other hand.

Above: Dummy's trumps have been forced once already. West now holds up the ace of trumps twice, planning to win the third round and force out declarer's last trump with another spade.

UNBLOCKING HONOURS IN DEFENCE

Any time that you have a doubleton honour in a side suit, you must consider playing the honour on the first round. Failure to do this can cost you in various ways. You may block your partner's long suit, for example. You may also leave yourself open to an end-play by the declarer.

Unblocking an honour in partner's suit

When you hold a doubleton honour in the suit that partner has led against no-trumps, it is generally right to play it on the first round, even if this is not necessary in an attempt to win the trick. Take the East cards here:

Right: Unblocking in the suit led. West leads the ♠Q against 3NT and East must play the ♠K to avoid the suit becoming blocked.

Above: East unblocks the ♠K on his partner's ♠Q lead. If he fails to do so, he will win the second round and be unable to continue the suit.

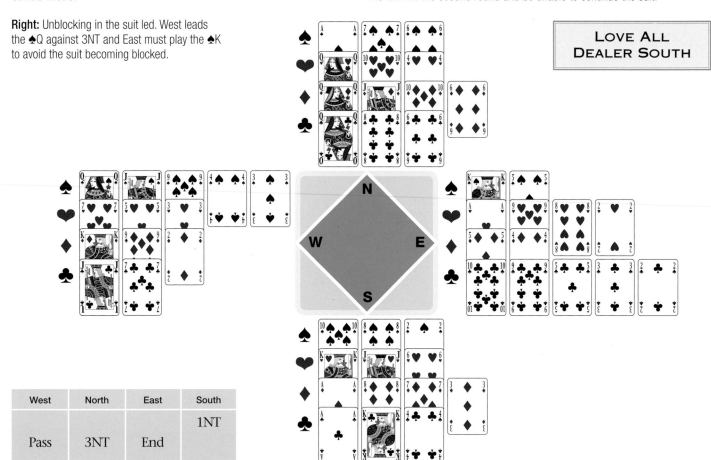

LOVE ALL
DEALER SOUTH

West	North	East	South
			1NT
Pass	3NT	End	

Your partner leads the ♠Q and declarer plays low from the dummy. It is essential you unblock your ♠K on the first round. You then return the ♠5, clearing the suit whether your partner has led from ♠Q–J–10–x–x or ♠Q–J–9–x–x. Declarer must take a diamond finesse at some stage. Your partner will win with the king and cash his spade winners. Four spades, the king of diamonds and the ace of hearts puts the contract two down.

Suppose instead that you fail to unblock, following with the ♠5. Declarer will duck the second round of spades and you will have to win with the bare ♠K. With his spade stopper intact, declarer will easily make the contract.

You would make the same unblocking play of the king if declarer played the ♠A from dummy at Trick 1, or if dummy had held ♠7–6–2.

Unblocking to avoid an end-play

When declarer holds plenty of trumps in both hands, you must be particularly careful not to leave yourself with a bare honour in a side suit. If you do, you may be thrown in with the card and forced to give declarer a ruff-and-discard. Take the West cards here:

Right: Unblocking to avoid an end-play. When declarer plays the ◆A, West must unblock the ◆K to avoid being end-played later.

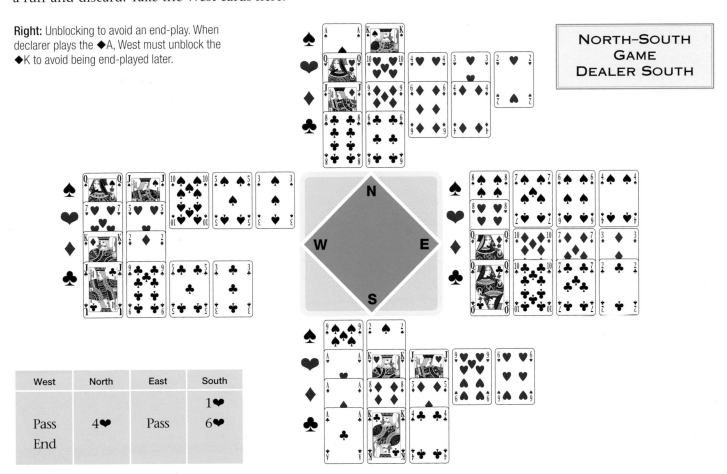

NORTH–SOUTH
GAME
DEALER SOUTH

West	North	East	South
			1♥
Pass	4♥	Pass	6♥
End			

Above: World Grand Master Catherine D'Ovidio, shown on the extreme right of the French national team, has ranked World's top female player.

Sitting West, you lead the ♠Q against the slam. Declarer wins in the dummy, draws trumps in two rounds and cashes the ◆A. Suppose you see no need for special action and follow with the ◆2. Declarer will cash dummy's other spade winner, followed by the two high clubs in his hand and a club ruff. With the black suits eliminated, he will then play a second round of diamonds. You will have to win with the bare ◆K and return a black suit, conceding a ruff-and-discard. Declarer will ruff in the dummy, throwing the last diamond loser from his hand. Sadly for you and your partner, 12 tricks will then be his.

Difficult as it may seem, you must play your ◆K under South's ◆A. Your partner will then be able to win two diamond tricks. If declarer held the ◆Q or the ◆10, he would doubtless have finessed in the suit, rather than cashing the diamond ace.

BREAKING DECLARER'S COMMUNICATIONS

Attractive as it may be for the defenders to set up extra tricks for themselves, sometimes this has to take second place behind the need to disrupt declarer's communications. Before you automatically "return partner's suit", you should take a look around and see if you can destroy an important entry to the dummy.

Killing an entry to dummy

Take the East cards here and see how you would defend this 3NT contract. Your partner leads the ♠2 and you win with the ace.

Right: Killing the entry to dummy. East wins the spade lead against 3NT and must switch to hearts to kill the entry to dummy's diamonds.

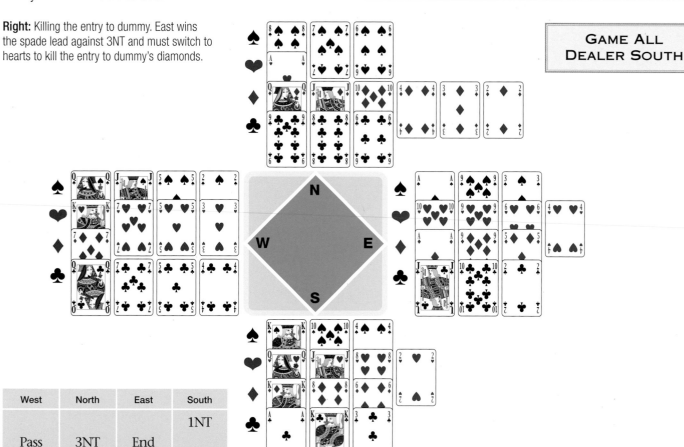

GAME ALL
DEALER SOUTH

West	North	East	South
			1NT
Pass	3NT	End	

Suppose you follow your natural instincts and return the ♠9. Declarer will win with the king and lead the ♦K. It will not do you any good to hold up the diamond ace for a couple of rounds because the ace of hearts is still intact as an entry to dummy. The defenders can score three spades and a diamond but declarer will then score five diamonds and the four top winners in the other three suits, making the no-trump game.

At Trick 2 your top priority, sitting East, is to kill declarer's source of tricks in dummy's diamond suit by removing the heart entry to dummy. You should switch to a heart, won by dummy's ace. The job of cutting declarer off from his diamond winners is only half done. When he plays on diamonds, you must hold up the ace until the third round. Declarer will then make two diamond tricks, rather than five, and will go two down.

The Merrimac Coup

As we have just seen, it is easy enough to dislodge a bare ace from dummy. When the ace is guarded, something more spectacular may be required. Take the East cards here:

Right: A spectacular sacrifice. East notes that dummy's diamonds are threatening and sacrifices his ♠K to remove the ♠A entry to the dummy.

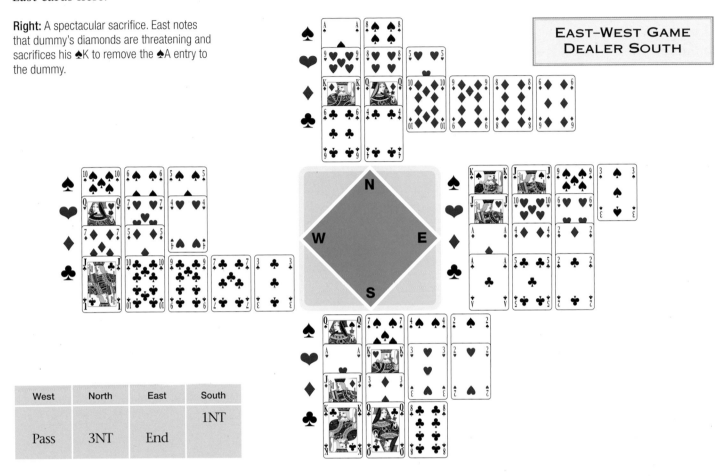

EAST–WEST GAME
DEALER SOUTH

West	North	East	South
			1NT
Pass	3NT	End	

West leads the ♣J and you must plan the defence from the East seat. There are only 18 points missing from the West and South hands. West has already shown the ♣J, so declarer is marked with the ♣K as well as the ♣Q.

If you play low at Trick 1, declarer will win and clear the diamond suit while the ♠A is intact as an entry. He will make the contract with an overtrick, however you defend thereafter. Instead you must rise smartly with the club ace and attack the spade entry to dummy. Switching to a low spade will not be good enough, as the cards lie, because declarer will be able to win with the spade queen. The only winning defence is to switch to the ♠K! Declarer has no answer to this. If he wins with dummy's ace, you will subsequently hold up your ♦A to cut him off from the diamond suit. If instead declarer allows your ♠K to win, you will continue with a low spade, removing dummy's side entry. Either way, the contract will go at least one down.

Above: The Merrimac Coup, a sacrificial play, is named after the deliberate scuttling of the American coal-carrying ship, *Merrimac*, in Santiago Harbour in 1898. The aim was to bottle up the Spanish fleet.

PROMOTING TRUMP TRICKS IN DEFENCE

Few things are more enjoyable in defence than promoting extra trump tricks. You can do this in two different ways. The first is to lead a suit where declarer (or the dummy) is now void and your partner is in a position to overruff. If declarer chooses to ruff low, your partner will indeed overruff. If instead declarer ruffs high, this may promote a trump trick for one or other of the defenders. The second promotion technique is known as the "uppercut". A defender ruffs with a high trump, aiming to force declarer to overruff with a higher trump. The intention is to promote some lesser trump in the other defender's hand.

The trump promotion

The deal below shows an example of the basic form of trump promotion where one defender is in a position to overruff the declarer.

East opens with a weak two-bid in spades and South arrives in 4♥. West leads the ♠9 and East wins with the ♠J. He cashes the ♠A and then leads a third round of spades in the hope that this will achieve a trump promotion. If declarer ruffs with the ♥9, West will overruff with the ♥10 and the trump ace will give the defenders a fourth trick for one down. Since declarer knows from the bidding that the spades are breaking 6–2, he may well ruff with the ♥K instead.

All will now depend on West's reaction. If he succumbs to the temptation to overruff with the ♥A, the contract will survive. When declarer regains the lead, he will draw West's remaining two trumps with the queen and jack. West should decline to overruff, discarding a diamond instead. His ♥A–10–4 will then be worth two tricks, sitting over South's ♥Q–J–9–7–2. The third round of spades will have promoted an extra trump trick in the West hand. West will score both the ace and the ten of the suit.

Suppose West had held ♥A–9–4 instead of ♥A–10–4. Again it would be right to decline to overruff. By defending in this way, he would promote a second trump trick when his partner held the ♥10.

Right: A typical trump promotion. West leads the ♠9 against the heart game and East plays three rounds of the suit for a trump promotion.

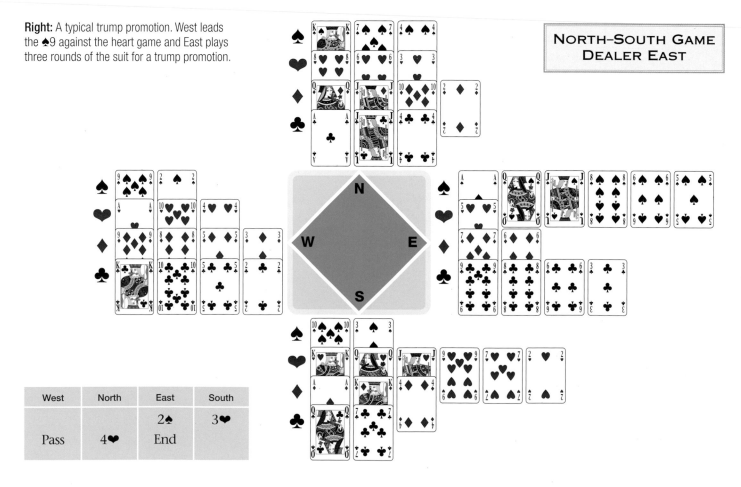

NORTH–SOUTH GAME
DEALER EAST

West	North	East	South
		2♠	3♥
Pass	4♥	End	

The uppercut

You can also promote a trump trick by ruffing high when you expect to be overruffed:

Right: An uppercut. East defeats the spade game by administering an uppercut, ruffing with the ♠Q on the fourth round of hearts.

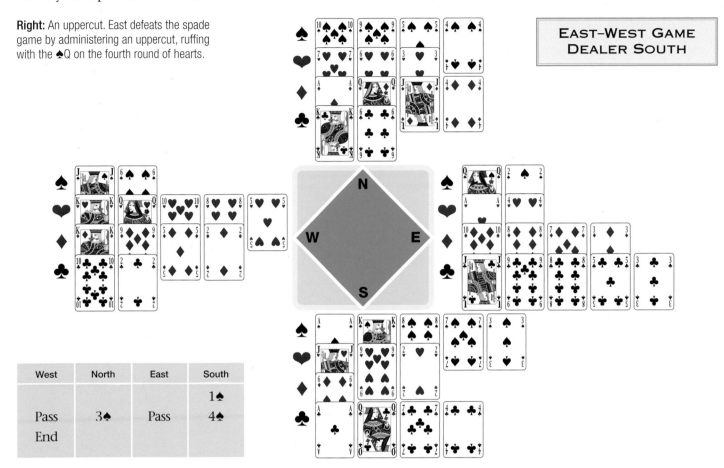

| | | EAST–WEST GAME DEALER SOUTH | |

West	North	East	South
			1♠
Pass	3♠	Pass	4♠
End			

West leads the ♥K. If East follows with the ♥4, an overtrick will be made. He will have to win the next heart with the bare ace and that is the last trick that the defenders will take.

Instead, East overtakes with the ♥A and returns the ♥4. West scores the ten and queen of the suit, giving the defenders the first three tricks. On the third round of hearts East discards the ♣3, showing no interest in that suit. With his ♦K sitting under the dummy's ♦A–Q–J, West can see no prospect of a minor-suit trick for the defence. The only chance is to promote a trump trick. West continues with a fourth round of hearts and East ruffs with the ♠Q (a play known as an uppercut). Declarer overruffs with the king or ace and now has to lose a trick to West's ♠J. The game goes one down. The same defence would have been successful if East had started with a singleton ♠Q, or a singleton or doubleton ♠K.

MOST PROLIFIC BRIDGE WRITERS
♠ ♥ ♦ ♣

The world's top bridge writers (in terms of the number of books written) are:

1. Terence Reese (England)
2. David Bird (England)
3. Ron Klinger (Australia)
4. Hugh Kelsey (Scotland)
5. Brian Senior (England)
6. Ely Culbertson (USA)
7. Victor Mollo (England)
8. Eddie Kantar (USA)
9. Charles Goren (USA)
10. Danny Kleinman (USA)

Above: David Bird and Terence Reese, who have written the greatest number of books about bridge.

CHAPTER 13

FAMOUS PLAYERS

Every game or sport has its larger than life characters, who catch the public eye and are remembered for decades. Bridge is no exception. It is largely a game for extroverts and this section pays homage to some of the outstanding figures who have spent their lives gracing the bridge table. Film star Omar Sharif is perhaps the most well-known bridge player in the world. Robert Hamman and Jeff Meckstroth of the USA, Gabriel Chagas of Brazil and Zia Mahmood of Pakistan (now of the USA) are all currently playing at the top level. Maestro Benito Garozzo, star of the fabulous Italian Blue Team, still plays bridge on the Internet. The other three players described in this section are no longer alive – the great player and writer, Terence Reese of England, and two of the finest women players of all time: USA's Helen Sobel and Rixi Markus of Austria (later of England).

Right: Omar Sharif plays a tense game of bridge with some of the world's best players as part of a televised competition in Mayfair, London, in 1970. The opponent to his right is Jonathan Cansino of England.

GABRIEL CHAGAS (BRAZIL)

Gabriel Chagas is by far the most successful bridge player to emerge from South America. Since 1968, he has won the South American championship 22 times and the Brazilian championship 24 times. He has also represented Brazil in more than 40 world championship events. He is one of only eight players ever to have won bridge's Triple Crown: the Olympiad, the Bermuda Bowl and the World Pairs. A company director living in Rio de Janeiro, Chagas speaks eight languages fluently and can communicate well in several others. He is also proficient at tennis, sings and plays the piano.

Here is a brilliant deceptive defence of his, from the 1995 Rio Teams Championship. Chagas was East on the deal shown below. North had promised a four-card major, by using the Stayman convention, and his subsequent 3NT denied four cards in the heart suit. Deducing that there was a 4-4 spade fit, South bid 4♠ over his partner's 3NT.

Following the scheme popular in the USA, West led the ♣2 from his holding of three small cards. Chagas could see 25 points between his own hand and the dummy. South's 1NT bid had promised 15–17 points, so Chagas knew every honour card in declarer's hand. Suppose East wins with the ♣J and switches to a diamond at Trick 2. Declarer will have no alternative but to finesse the ♦J. This will succeed and he will make the game easily. He will draw trumps, play the ♦A and lead a club to the 10. After scoring two club tricks, East would be end-played, forced to lead a heart into dummy's tenace or to concede a ruff-and-discard.

Chagas decided to put up a smoke screen. Pretending that he held ♣A–J doubleton, he cashed the club ace at Trick 2. He then switched to the ♦9. How could declarer possibly take the finesse now? If it lost, West would surely give his partner a club ruff and beat the contract. Barbosa duly rose with the ♦A, drew trumps and took what he assumed was the guaranteed finesse of the ♣10, to set up a discard for his diamond loser. We can only imagine his reaction when the club finesse lost to the ♣Q and Chagas proceeded to cash the ♦K.

Right: A brilliant deceptive defence. Chagas disguises his club holding to persuade declarer not to finesse in diamonds.

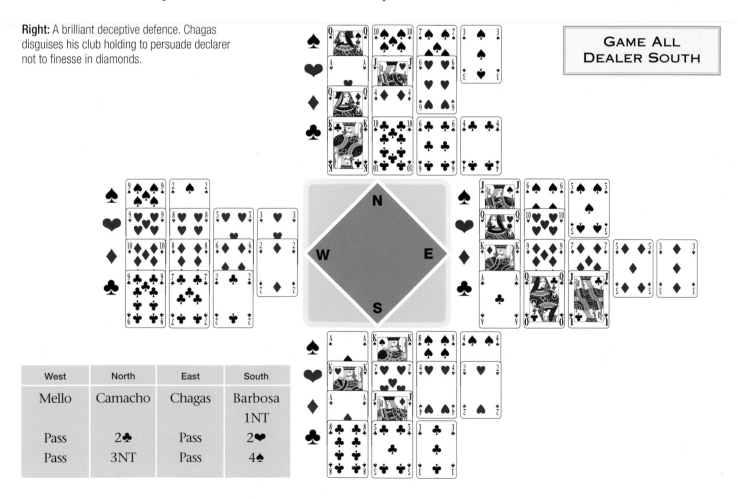

GAME ALL
DEALER SOUTH

West	North	East	South
Mello	Camacho	Chagas	Barbosa
			1NT
Pass	2♣	Pass	2♥
Pass	3NT	Pass	4♠

BENITO GAROZZO (ITALY)

Benito Garozzo was born in Naples in 1927. He learnt to play bridge with some friends during World War II (1939–45). Amazingly he attributes his early fascination with card combinations to Autobridge. (Autobridge was a teaching aid, containing hands set by Culbertson. The player had to slide open small windows in a plastic box to reveal the cards.) By 1954 Garozzo was playing with the top players in Italy and he eventually became a leading light in what was perhaps the greatest bridge team ever – the Italian Blue Team. His list of partners includes many of Italy's finest players. From 1961–72 he played with Pietro Forquet. Then, from 1972 for three years he joined forces with the fiery Giorgio Belladonna. Arturo Franco and Lorenzo Lauria were his next partners, each for a two-year period, and from 1982–5 he rejoined Belladonna. Throughout these years the Blue Team was almost unbeatable. Garozzo won the Bermuda Bowl ten times and the World Teams Olympiad three times. From the time of his first

Above: Garozzo considers his next move.

Bermuda Bowl win in 1961, he never played in a losing team in international competition until 1976, an incomparable record of excellence.

Garozzo rates as his finest performance the closing stages of the 1975 Bermuda Bowl in Bermuda. The Italian team had been forced to withdraw one of their three pairs, after an allegation of passing signals via foot-tapping. The remaining two pairs therefore had to play throughout, which was exhausting. At one stage in the final they were 70 IMPs behind a very strong American team. Amazingly they fought their way back to win.

Here is a fine deceptive play, made by Garozzo during the 1975 Italian Open Teams.

Right: An imaginative deceptive play. By ducking a trick that he could have won, Garozzo misleads the defender and makes an "impossible" game.

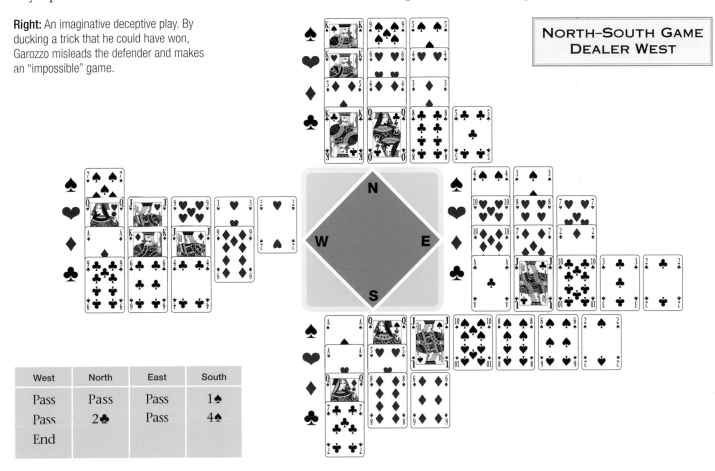

NORTH–SOUTH GAME DEALER WEST

West	North	East	South
Pass	Pass	Pass	1♠
Pass	2♣	Pass	4♠
End			

Most players would open on the West cards nowadays and a surprising number would open on the North cards too. As it was, Garozzo opened 1♠ in the fourth seat and leapt to game in spades when Belladonna responded at the two-level.

West led the ♦K and received a discouraging signal from his partner. He then switched to the ♥Q. Garozzo had a fair idea how the cards must lie. West had indicated the ♦A–K with his opening lead and had also shown at least two points in hearts. If he held the ♣A in addition he would have 13 points, enough to open the bidding. It was therefore certain that East held the ♣A. If declarer played in straightforward fashion, drawing trumps and trying to establish a diamond discard on dummy's clubs, East would win the first round of clubs and sink the contract by switching back to diamonds.

Rather than accept defeat, Garozzo made the brilliant deceptive play of allowing the ♥Q to win! A club switch, followed by a return to diamonds, would now have put the game two down. West naturally

assumed that his partner held the ♥A, however. He continued with a second round of hearts and the contract was home. Garozzo unmasked his deception, winning with the ♥A, and then drew trumps in two rounds, ending in the dummy. He discarded his singleton club on the ♥K and led the ♣K for a ruffing finesse. When East covered with the ace, he ruffed in the South hand and returned to dummy with a trump to discard one of his diamonds on the established ♣Q. He had made the seemingly impossible game.

In these days of full-time professional players, it is an interesting reminder of times gone by that Garozzo had another professional "day job" throughout his great bridge career – he owned a jewellery store in Naples, Italy. He now lives in California, USA, where he plays bridge frequently on the Internet, and is also found at the table with Lea DuPont. In both cases you can be sure that an army of admirers will be following his every move.

ROBERT HAMMAN (USA)

Robert Hamman became the world's top-ranked player in 1985 and retained that status for an amazing 20 years. He has won an unparalleled number of North American titles, the 1988 Olympiad, and the Bermuda Bowl an almost unbelievable nine times (1970, 1971, 1977, 1983, 1985, 1987, 1995, 1999 and 2003). He also won the World Open Pairs championship with Bobby Wolff in 1974. Unlike most of the USA's top players, Hamman achieved all this success while performing an important job outside the game – he was president of SCA Promotions, a prize promotion company.

Hamman joined Ira Corn's Dallas Aces team in 1969, initially partnering Eddie Kantar. He went on to partner Mike Lawrence, Paul Soloway, Billy Eisenberg and Don Krauss, before forming a 25-year-long partnership with Bobby Wolff. His wife, Petra, won the Venice Cup in 2000.

Here is a fine play by Hamman, from USA's win in the final of the 1970 Bermuda Bowl. The Chinese West led the ♠K and Hamman allowed this card to win.

Above: Robert Hamman, playing in the 1973 World Bridge Championship at the Casa Grande Hotel in Guaruja, Brazil. The USA team reached the final but were defeated by Italy.

He took the next round of spades and now had to set up a diamond discard on the club suit. It was not just a question of finding clubs 3–3 with the ace onside, because the defenders might be able to establish their diamond trick before declarer could enjoy his discard.

At Trick 2 Hamman led the ♣7 from his hand. Suppose West were to rise with the ♣A now and switch to a diamond. East's ♦10 would force the ♦A, yes, but declarer could then run the ♦9 to establish a discard for his remaining club loser. West in fact played low on the first round of clubs and Hamman played accurately by passing the trick to East's ♣10. East, who could not attack diamonds successfully from his side of the table, returned another spade. Hamman ruffed and drew trumps with the king and queen. He could then lead a second round of clubs towards the king, setting up the discard that he needed whether West took his ♣A now or on the second round. (If trumps had broken 3–1, the ♥A would have served as an entry to the long clubs.)

As the cards lay, West could have defeated the game with the amazing play of the ♣J on the first round! If declarer wins with dummy's ♣K, West can win the second round of clubs with the ♣A and clear a

Above: The USA win the 1983 Bermuda Bowl in Stockholm. Hamman is shown with team-mates Ron Rubin, Bobby Wolff and Peter Weichsel.

diamond trick. If instead declarer ducks in the dummy, West can switch to a diamond then, with two club tricks guaranteed.

Right: Clever play justifies a bold bid. By ducking the first round of clubs, Hamman avoids a damaging diamond switch.

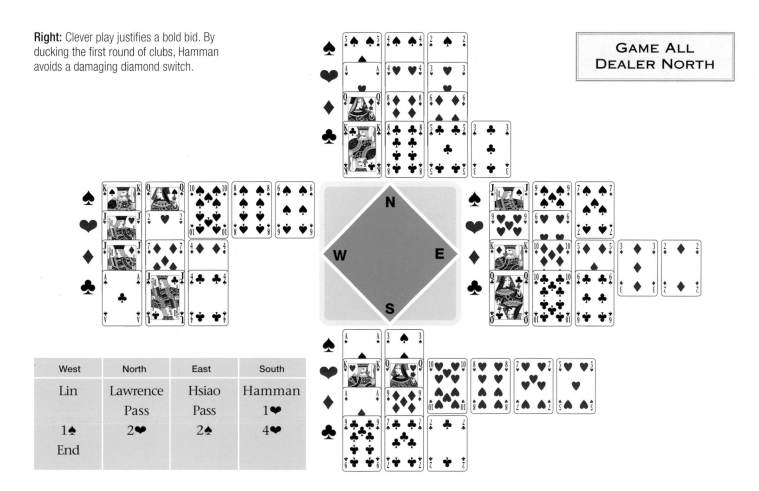

GAME ALL
DEALER NORTH

West	North	East	South
Lin	Lawrence	Hsiao	Hamman
	Pass	Pass	1♥
1♠	2♥	2♠	4♥
End			

ZIA MAHMOOD (PAKISTAN/USA)

Zia is one of the most colourful and skilful players in the game today. If you enter the playing area of a tournament where he is competing, you can easily find his table. It will be the one with the greatest number of spectators (a large proportion of them female). Born into a wealthy family in Pakistan, he represented his home country with great distinction. The highlight was in 1981 when Pakistan exceeded all expectation by reaching the final of the Bermuda Bowl, eventually losing to the USA.

Zia did not learn bridge until he was 25. At that time a beautiful woman invited him to play with her that evening at the local club. "You do know how to play, don't you?" she said. "Of course," Zia replied. He spent the afternoon studying *Five Weeks to Winning Bridge* by Alfred Sheinwold, but was nevertheless exposed as a completely hopeless player in the evening bridge session. Zia soon lost interest in the woman but became addicted to the game of bridge and could not learn quickly enough.

Nowadays Zia has homes in London and New York and represents the USA at bridge. On his first major appearance for an American team he persuaded his team-mates to wear Pakistani costume, to quell any guilt he might have had on switching allegiance. Zia's regular partner is Michael Rosenberg, formerly of Scotland but now also representing the USA. Zia and Rosenberg finished 2nd in the 2002 World Open Pairs in Montreal.

In 1990, in Atlantic City, Zia won the Omar Sharif World Individual Championship, where players are required to partner every other player for one round and a fixed bidding system is played. The event carried a $40,000 first prize. By winning the 2004 World Transnational Teams Championship in Istanbul, Zia acquired the coveted rank of World Grandmaster.

Shown below is a big deal from the semi-final of the 1981 Bermuda Bowl – contested in Port Chester, New York – with Pakistan sitting in the North–South seats and facing Argentina:

GAME ALL
DEALER SOUTH

Below: A fine grand slam in the 1981 Bermuda Bowl. Zia establishes the heart suit to dispose of his diamond losers.

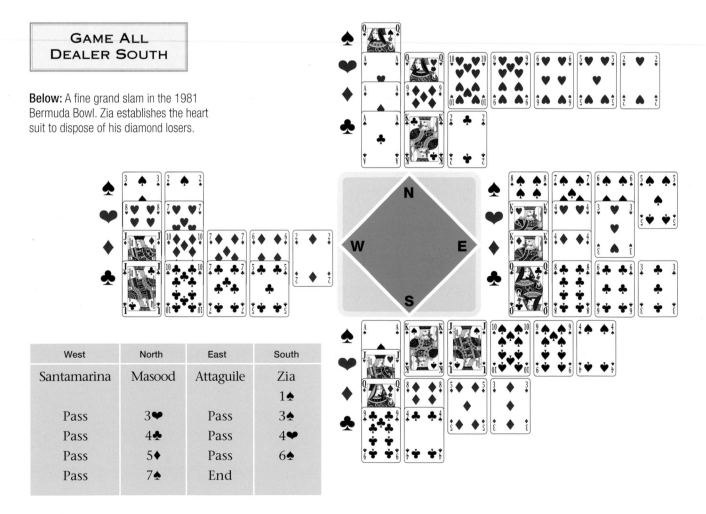

West	North	East	South
Santamarina	Masood	Attaguile	Zia
			1♠
Pass	3♥	Pass	3♠
Pass	4♣	Pass	4♥
Pass	5♦	Pass	6♠
Pass	7♠	End	

led the ♠Q to Trick 2, overtaking in his hand. After drawing trumps in four rounds, he led the ♥J to dummy's ♥A and ruffed a heart. When hearts broke 3–2, he was able to cross to dummy with a club and establish the heart suit with a further ruff. He could then return to the remaining club honour and enjoy the rest of the heart suit, claiming his grand slam. Pakistan went on to defeat Argentina, eventually losing to the USA in the final.

Above: Zia Mahmood is a great advocate of natural bidding, rather than artificial bidding – another reason why he is a favourite with kibitzers.

Zia's leap to 6♠ on the fourth round persuaded Masood that the trump suit would be solid. Trusting that the heart suit could be brought in, he raised to the grand slam. (At the other table, after the same first six bids, the Argentinian South bid only 5♠ and passed his partner's raise to 6♠.)

Zia went on to win the diamond lead with dummy's ace. He knew that to play on hearts immediately, ruffing the second round high, would lead to trouble if the trumps broke 5–1. Zia therefore

Above: Zia lent his strong support to the building of a school, to be known as the World Bridge School, in an earthquake-stricken part of Pakistan.

RIXI MARKUS (AUSTRIA/ ENGLAND)

Rixi Markus was born in Austria and represented that country as they won the 1935 and 1936 European women's teams championships, followed by a win in the women's world championship in 1937 in Budapest. Driven to England in the war years, she formed a fearsome partnership with Fritzi Gordon, another émigré Austrian. At the time they were rated by many as the top women's pair in the world. Rixi won another seven European Championships, now representing Great Britain. In 1962 she and Fritzi won both the World Women's Pairs and the World Mixed Teams, followed in 1964 by a win in the Women's Olympiad in New York. In 1974 the pair again won the World Women's Pairs, by a record margin. Rixi became the first female World Grandmaster. For her services to the game of bridge she was honoured by the Queen with the MBE.

A tiger at the bridge table, Rixi was charming socially and had countless friends around the world. Her bidding was undisciplined and she entered the auction in situations that would terrify a lesser personality. It was in the card play that she excelled.

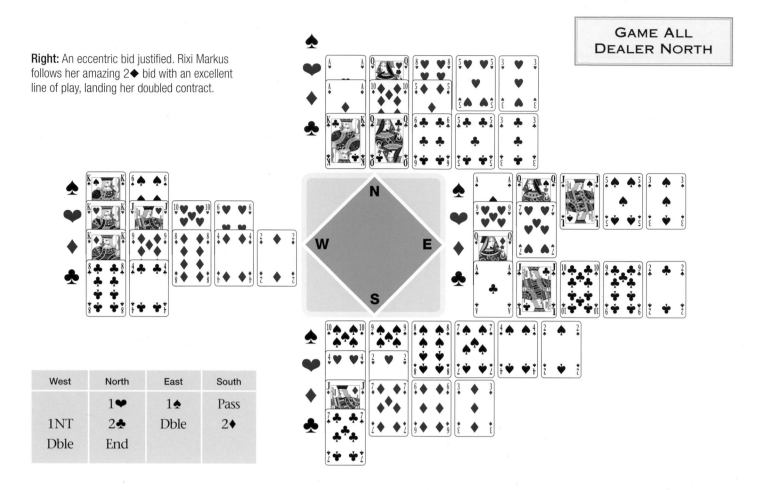

Right: An eccentric bid justified. Rixi Markus follows her amazing 2◆ bid with an excellent line of play, landing her doubled contract.

GAME ALL
DEALER NORTH

West	North	East	South
	1♥	1♠	Pass
1NT	2♣	Dble	2◆
Dble	End		

Above is a typical piece of Rixi action, taken from a rubber bridge game.

Expecting her partner to be void in spades, after the opponents' bidding, Rixi tried her luck in 2◆. West was happy to double this. He led the ♠K, which Rixi ruffed in the dummy. When she continued with the ♣K, East won with the ace and returned the ◆Q to dummy's ace. Some players now might cash the ♣Q, throwing a heart, and then score as many tricks as possible by ruffing hearts in hand and spades on the table.

Rixi realized that this line would bring her only seven tricks. Abandoning her established club trick, she ruffed a low club in her hand. She was then able to take the heart finesse, which was a near certainty on the bidding and the play so far. She then cashed the ♥A, ruffed a heart, ruffed a spade, ruffed a heart and ruffed another spade. In this way she scored two hearts and six trump tricks. She made the doubled contract exactly, without ever scoring her established second trick in clubs.

Right: Fritzi Gordon, long-time partner of Rixi Markus. She won the World Women's Teams in 1964, the World Women's Pairs in 1962 and 1974 and the World Mixed Teams in 1962.

JEFF MECKSTROTH (USA)

Ask any top bridge player nowadays who they rate as the toughest opposition in the world and the likely answer is Jeff Meckstroth and Eric Rodwell of the USA. Meckstroth was a scratch golfer as a teenager. He learnt bridge before going to college, met Rodwell in 1974 and formed a partnership with him the following year. Together they have won almost everything worth winning in bridge – several Reisingers, Vanderbilts and Spingolds (the premier championships in the USA), the Macallan Invitational Pairs in 1995 and 1996, the World Team Olympiad in 1988 and the Bermuda Bowl in 1995, 1999 and 2003.

Meckstroth and Rodwell play a very scientific version of the Precision Club system, one that involves light opening bids. The printed description of their bidding system runs to two or three hundred pages. They are noted for their supreme temperament at the table, despite fiery reputations from their younger days. In 1992 they joined Robert Hamman and Robert Wolff to represent the Scientists against the Naturals in a £50,000 challenge match in London, winning by 70 IMPs.

The deal below features a supremely inventive piece of declarer play by Meckstroth, when facing the world class Norwegians, Geir Helgemo and Tor Helness.

South's 3♣ was a weak response, as the Americans play it. Rodwell rebid 3NT, the contract bid and made at the other table, but Meckstroth took another bid and ended in the apparently doomed club game.

Helness led a diamond and Meckstroth saw that there was little prospect in trying to set up the hearts for a spade discard. When he knocked out the first heart, the defenders would surely switch to spades, establishing a third trick for themselves there. To make life more difficult for his opponents, Meckstroth made the amazing play of the ♦10 from dummy! Helgemo won with the ♦Q and could see no pressing need to switch to hearts. He returned another diamond, on which Meckstroth discarded one of his hearts. The defenders could no longer beat the contract. A heart was played to the queen and ace and a spade switch would not now help the defenders. Declarer was subsequently able to take a ruffing finesse through East's ♥A, setting up a discard for his spade loser.

<table>
<tr><td>GAME ALL
DEALER NORTH</td></tr>
</table>

Below: A brilliantly inventive deceptive play. Jeff Meckstroth surrenders an unnecessary diamond trick, causing the world-class defenders to go wrong.

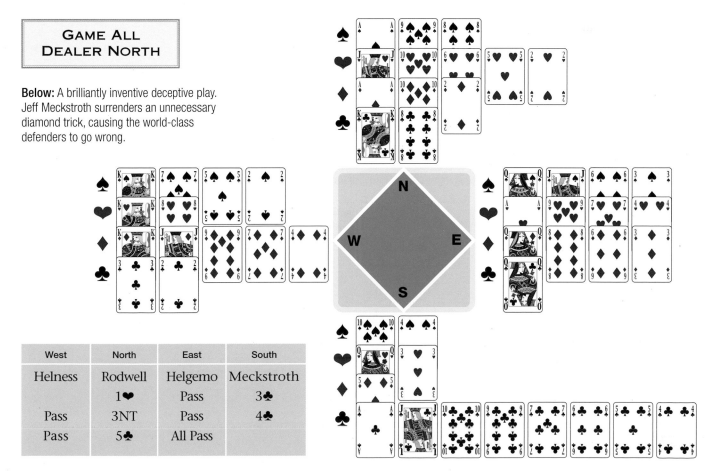

West	North	East	South
Helness	Rodwell	Helgemo	Meckstroth
	1♥	Pass	3♣
Pass	3NT	Pass	4♣
Pass	5♣	All Pass	

TERENCE REESE (ENGLAND)

There can be little doubt that Terence Reese is the greatest bridge writer there has ever been. He wrote 107 titles, which included several genuine masterpieces that were years ahead of their time: *The Expert Game*, *Reese on Play* and *Play Bridge with Reese*. He named various expert techniques, including the Crocodile Coup, the Dentist's Coup, the Vice Squeeze and the Winkle Squeeze. He also wrote eruditely on the Principle of Restricted Choice, which mystifies many players even today.

At his peak, Reese was rated by many as the best bridge player in the world. He formed an outstanding partnership with Boris Schapiro and won four European Championships, the 1955 Bermuda Bowl, the 1962 World Pairs championship and the 1961 World Pair championship (where very difficult hands are set for the players). On the domestic front, he won Britain's Gold Cup eight times and the Master Pairs seven times.

Reese's parents met when they were "First Gentleman" and "First Lady" at a whist drive. He learned to play cards before he could read and learnt Auction Bridge at the age of seven. He recounts in his autobiography *Bridge at the Top* how he had to dismount from his chair to sort his cards behind a cushion, 13 being somewhat of a handful.

Reese's career as a player was severely dented by a cheating allegation at the 1965 Bermuda Bowl in Buenos Aires. It was claimed that he and his partner Boris Schapiro had been using finger signals during the bidding, to inform their partner how many hearts they held. The pair was convicted by the World Bridge Federation but later acquitted by a special inquiry set up by the British Bridge League. Although photographs had been taken that showed unusual finger positions by the pair, there was remarkably little evidence from the records of the play of any advantage having been taken of the knowledge supposedly gained. To this day, players will dispute whether any cheating did in fact take place. Be that as it may, the partnership never played again in any international event.

Below: Press photographers await Reese and Schapiro on their return from Buenos Aires. The allegation of finger signalling was news across the world.

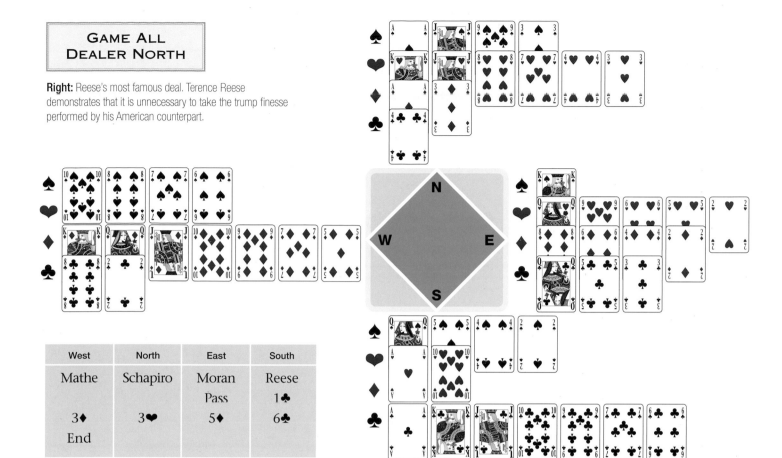

GAME ALL
DEALER NORTH

Right: Reese's most famous deal. Terence Reese demonstrates that it is unnecessary to take the trump finesse performed by his American counterpart.

West	North	East	South
Mathe	Schapiro	Moran	Reese
		Pass	1♣
3♦	3♥	5♦	6♣
End			

The slam shown above is perhaps the most famous contract that Reese ever played.

A brief auction carried Reese to a small slam in clubs. West led the ♦9, rather than the normal top honour from a sequence, in the hope that East might win with the ♦A and deliver a heart ruff. Reese ruffed the opening lead and spurned the trump finesse, cashing the ace and king. When the ♣Q did not fall, he needed to set up dummy's heart suit to avoid losing a spade trick.

Reese played the ♥A, West showing out, and continued with a heart to the king and the ♥7, covered and ruffed. He then threw East on lead with the queen of trumps. Whatever card East played next, Reese would have enough entries to dummy to take a ruffing finesse in hearts and eventually enjoy the winners in the suit. He would be able to throw all his potential losers in spades.

At the other table, Rosen (for the USA) reached the same contract. He won the diamond lead with dummy's ace and took a successful trump finesse, making the slam easily. A flat board, yes, but he would have gone down if the trump finesse had lost to a doubleton queen with West. The superior line taken by Reese would be remembered for decades.

PERFECT COMBINATION
♠ ♥ ♦ ♣

Many of the world's top bridge partnerships have consisted of one steady, technical player combined with a more flamboyant partner. A classic example of this was the long-standing partnership of Terence Reese and Boris Schapiro. Reese was a scholarly card-player but a somewhat cautious bidder. Schapiro was less accurate in the play and far more ambitious in the bidding. The pair won many championships, including a record number of Gold Cups.

Above: Boris Schapiro (left) was never afraid of displaying his emotions at the bridge table. His partnership with Terence Reese (right) lasted some 25 years.

OMAR SHARIF (EGYPT)

Omar Sharif, the film actor who first came to public attention playing the role of Ali Ibn Kharish in *Lawrence of Arabia* (1962), has had a life-long fascination with the game of bridge. He captained the team representing the United Arab Republic in the 1964 Bridge Olympiad and by 1968 had formed an attachment with some of the best players in the world. A team known as the Omar Sharif Bridge Circus was formed, containing Delmouly and Yallouze of France, the incomparable Belladonna and Garozzo of Italy and Omar himself. They played a match in London, against England's Flint and Cansino, for the huge stakes (then) of £100 a 100. Sharif's team won handsomely but were generally thought to have had the better of the cards.

In 1975 Sharif's team toured the USA, playing 60-board matches against the champion teams of each region. They were sponsored by Lancia cars and any team that could beat them would win a red Lancia sports car each! The team's PR man, the famous tennis player Nicola Pietrangeli, did not enjoy phoning the sponsors in Rome no fewer than three times, to tell them that they should arrange the shipment of another set of cars.

In his book *Omar Sharif Talks Bridge*, Omar tells this story:

Playing bridge and acting have one thing in common. When you are performing, your heart beats very much faster than normal. When I first started to play with members of the Italian Blue Team, they tended to frown every time I put down the dummy. This put a great strain on my heart. As often as not, all would turn out well in the end and the contract would be made. Meanwhile I had been suffering a thousand deaths, thinking that I made some big mistake in the auction.

After a while I explained gently to them that a man has only one heart. I asked them to take pity on me and not to frown so much. We even arranged a code by which they could let me know how good the final contract was. Members of our team often switched from one language to another during a session and my idea was that if the contract was cold my partner should say *"Merci"* when I put down the dummy. If the contract was touch-and-go and might require some luck or good play, my partner would say *"Thank you."* Finally, if the contract was hopeless, the response to dummy's appearance would be *"Grazie."*

In a tournament in Deauville, I was partnering Pietro Forquet. After a very long auction, he arrived in a club grand slam. A trump was led and I put down the dummy.

"Grazie," said Forquet.

"With a splendid dummy like that?" I cried. "How can it be *Grazie?*"

BUSINESS BEFORE PLEASURE

When asked whether acting or bridge was more important to him, Omar Sharif replied "Acting is my business – bridge is my passion."

Left: Omar Sharif shows his hand during the Sunday Times International Bridge Pairs Championships, at the Hyde Park Hotel, London in 1980.

Right: A fine play by Omar Sharif at trick one. By ducking the first round of diamonds, Sharif ensures that his diamond entry cannot be removed.

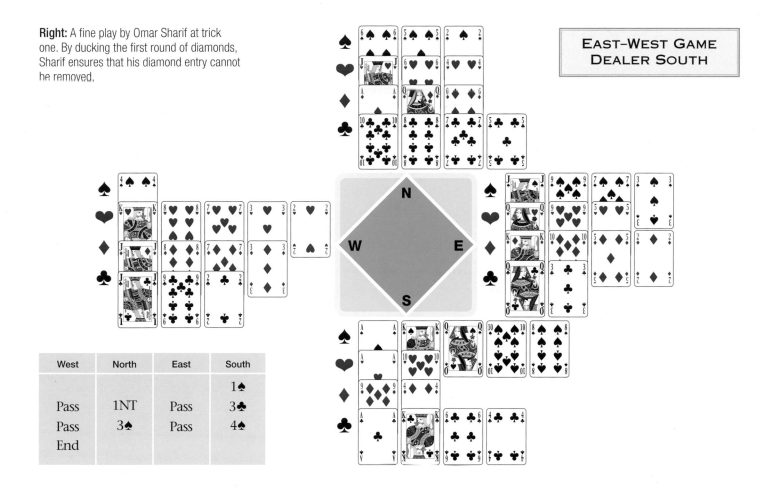

EAST–WEST GAME
DEALER SOUTH

West	North	East	South
			1♠
Pass	1NT	Pass	3♣
Pass	3♠	Pass	4♠
End			

Here is a deal that Omar played well, partnering Paul Chemla in a big tournament in the Deauville casino in France.

West led the ♦3 and Sharif made the excellent play of the ♦6 from dummy. East won but could not continue diamonds into dummy's tenace. He switched to a heart and Sharif won with the ace. When he played the ace and king of trumps, the position in that suit became clear. He crossed to the ♦A and took the marked finesse in trumps. When the clubs came in for only one loser, the game was his. Suppose West had turned up with four trumps to the jack and it was therefore necessary to dispose of the heart loser. Nothing would have been lost by the diamond play at Trick 1. Declarer could finesse the ♦Q on the second round of the suit!

You can see what would happen if declarer was tempted to play the ♦Q on the first trick. East would win with the ♦K and return the suit. When the two top trumps revealed the position in that suit, there would be no entry left to dummy to take a trump finesse.

Several years ago, Sharif underwent a heart triple bypass operation. He gave up playing top-level bridge and now lives a somewhat reclusive life in a Paris hotel. Still, suppose you step into a busy street in London or New York and ask the first passer-by who is the world's most famous bridge player. What answer are you likely to get? "Omar Sharif, isn't it?"

Above: Actor Omar Sharif at the start of the Macallan International Bridge Pairs Championship in 1997. Sharif joined a line-up of 32 top-class players competing for the trophy, a bottle of The Macallan whisky worth $19,500.

HELEN SOBEL (USA)

There are several claimants for the title "greatest woman player ever" and the USA's Helen Sobel is certainly among them, having won 33 national championships. She won the McKenney Trophy, for most master points won in a calendar year, on three occasions. Between 1948 and 1964 she was the leading woman in the American Contract Bridge League's all-time master point rankings.

No one meeting a 16-year-old chorus girl in the Marx Brothers' show, *The Coconuts*, would have guessed that they were in the presence of a future great bridge champion. Chico Marx was, in fact, one of the best bridge players in show business. It was from a fellow chorus girl, however, that Sobel learnt the rudiments of bridge. After her first visit to a bridge club, she remarked to a friend, "You get to know something about trumps, playing pinochle, so I found bridge easy to pick up."

Sobel herself admitted that in her first couple of years of tournament play, she gained an advantage over any smug male opponents who might have taken her for a dumb blonde and expected soft pickings.

The word soon passed around that the "tiny blonde who looks like Gertrude Lawrence" played a very tough game indeed.

Her first marriage, at the age of 17, ended in divorce after just three years. It was a second marriage, to bridge expert Al Sobel, that was to change her life. Soon afterwards Ely Culbertson installed her as hostess at the Crockford's Club in New York, while her husband took over the editorship of the magazine *Bridge World*.

In 1937 Sobel was asked by Culbertson to join his team in a world championship event organized by the International Bridge League in Budapest. This was recognition indeed that both she and Josephine Culbertson were rated as the equal of any male player of the day.

Helen Sobel is probably most well known, however, for her enduring partnership with the great Charles Goren. Together they made an incredible team, and represented the USA in the 1957 Bermuda Bowl and the 1960 Olympiad.

Sobel's 33 national titles include the Spingold five times, the Chicago (now the Reisinger) four times and the Vanderbilt twice.

Below: Helen Sobel at the table. Edgar Kaplan, editor of *Bridge World*, said of her "In my lifetime, she is the only woman bridge player who was considered the best player in the world."

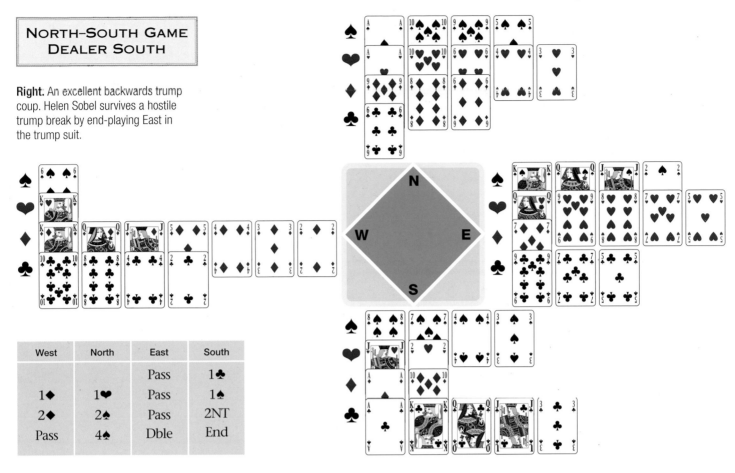

NORTH-SOUTH GAME
DEALER SOUTH

Right. An excellent backwards trump coup. Helen Sobel survives a hostile trump break by end-playing East in the trump suit.

West	North	East	South
		Pass	1♣
1♦	1♥	Pass	1♠
2♦	2♠	Pass	2NT
Pass	4♠	Dble	End

It's time for us to see an example of Sobel's dazzling card play, also her bravery in the bidding. The deal above shows her sitting South during the 1944 Summer Nationals.

Many players of the day would have refused to bid a spade suit of four cards to the eight. Helen Sobel not only bid the spades but continued to 2NT, over a single raise, on a hand that was not much more than a minimum. With a stack of trumps in his hand, East somewhat unwisely doubled the eventual spade game.

Sobel won the ♦K lead with the ♦A and played three rounds of clubs, discarding dummy's two diamond losers. She then led a heart, West's king appearing, and won with the ace in dummy. A second round of hearts was won by East's queen, West discarding a diamond. At this stage the defenders had one trick in the bag and it seemed likely that East would score three more with his ♠K–Q–J–2 poised over dummy's ♠A–10–9–5. See how the play developed, though.

East returned a heart and Sobel ruffed carefully with the ♠7, preventing an overruff from West's ♠6. She continued with a trump to the six, nine and jack. Declarer won the heart return in dummy, throwing the ♣3. She then led another heart, ruffing with the

♠4 in her hand. Trick 11 had been reached and East's last three cards were the ♠K–Q–2. Sobel ran the ♠8 to East's ♠Q and he was forced to lead a trump into dummy's ♠A–10 tenace at Trick 12. It was a splendid example of the technique known as a backward trump coup. If East's double had not alerted declarer to the bad trump break, it is unlikely that the winning line of play would have been found.

It was a source of minor aggravation to Sobel that the question most frequently asked of her, by worshippers of Charles Goren, was: "What is it like partnering a great player?" Her standard reply was: "Ask Charlie!"

MAN'S WORLD
♠ ♥ ♦ ♣

In an age where it was almost unheard of for women to compete at world level in open events, Helen Sobel was part of the USA open team that finished second in the World Team Championships in New York, 1957. She also finished fourth representing the USA open team at the 1960 World Team Olympiad, contested in Turin.

GLOSSARY

balanced A balanced hand is one containing no singleton or void, usually 4-3-3-3, 4-4-3-2 or 5-3-3-2 shape.

bid An undertaking to take a specific number of tricks, with a chosen trump suit or at no-trumps. A bid of 2♠ (two spades) means you think you can score eight tricks with spades as trumps.

Blackwood A conventional bid of 4NT, asking partner how many aces he holds.

call A term covering any bid, pass, double or redouble.

clear To clear a suit is to drive out all the winners held by the opponents.

combination finesse A finesse where two adjacent cards are missing, such as in A-J-10.

communication The ability to go from hand to hand.

contract The final call determines the contract in which the hand is played – for example, 4♠ doubled.

control A holding that will prevent the opponents from scoring two quick tricks in a suit (ace, king, singleton or void).

convention An agreement between partners to use a bid in an artificial sense.

cross To move from one hand to another.

cue-bid (a) A bid in an opponent's suit, usually to show strength. (b) A bid that shows a control, such as an ace, rather than a suit.

declarer The player who must attempt to make the contract, playing the dummy's cards as well as his own.

defenders The two players who attempt to stop declarer from making his contract.

denomination The chosen trump suit, or no-trumps.

discard The play of a card (not a trump) which does not belong to the suit led.

distribution The pattern of suit lengths in a player's hand (for example, 5-4-3-1).

double A call that increases the penalties if a contract is not made, also the bonuses if it is made.

double finesse A finesse that seeks to entrap two cards, as when you lead to the 10 in an A-Q-10 combination.

double raise A raise that covers two steps – raising 1♥ to 3♥, for example.

doubleton A holding of two cards in a suit.

drop To cause an opposing high card to fall by playing higher cards.

dummy (a) The partner of the declarer. (b) The hand exposed opposite the declarer.

duck To play low, making no attempt to win a trick.

entry A card used to cross from one hand to the other.

establish To set up winners in a suit by removing the opponents' high cards.

finesse An attempt to win a trick with a lesser card in a tenace. You hope that the outstanding higher card lies to the left.

forcing bid A bid that requires your partner to bid again.

forcing defence A style of defence where you attack declarer's trumps by forcing him to ruff.

forcing to game A bid that requires both partners to continue bidding until game is reached.

game To make a game, you must score 100 points below the line.

grand slam A contract to win all 13 tricks.

guard A high card that prevents the opponents from running a suit.

hold up To refuse to part with a high card.

honour card Ace, king, queen, jack or 10.

insult A bonus awarded to the side that makes a doubled contract.

intervening bid A bid by the side that did not open the bidding.

jump A bid, rebid, raise or response made one or more levels higher than necessary.

key cards The four aces and the king of the agreed trump suit.

knock out Remove a defender's high card.

lead To play the first card to a trick.

limit bid A bid which defines the strength of your hand within narrow limits.

major suit Spades or hearts. A contract of 4♠ or 4♥ will give you a game.

minor suit Diamonds or clubs. A contract of 5♦ or 5♣ will give you a game.

negative double A double of an overcall (for example, 1♣ – 1♠ – Dble) that is intended for take-out.

no bid Call that denotes a pass. (In the USA the word "Pass" is used.)

no-trumps Denomination with no trump suit.